THE GUV'NOR

LENNY MCLEAN

WITH

PETER GERRARD

BLAKE

Published by Blake Publishing Ltd,
3 Bramber Court, 2 Bramber Road, London W14 9PB, England

First published in hardback in Great Britain 1998

ISBN 1 85782 335 4

British Library Cataloguing-in-Production Data:
A catalogue record for this book is available
from the British Library.

Typeset by BCP

Printed and bound in Great Britain by
Creative Print and Design (Wales) Ebbw Vale, Gwent

20

INTRODUCTION

Lenny and I first met when Reg Kray asked me to speak to him concerning a project we were involved in. I knew of his fearsome reputation and had witnessed on television his ferocity in dealing with the opposition. You can imagine it was with some trepidation that I knocked on his door.

The sheer size of the man overwhelmed me for a moment, as did the warmth and friendliness of his greeting. We discussed our business, one thing led to another, and we began working on this book together. It meant being with Lenny for a number of weeks, either sitting in his front room, plied endlessly with tea from his wife, Val, or out and about meeting acquaintances.

I was struck by the old-world courtesy within his circle, where mutual respect is held above all else. A lack of respect towards myself created an incident, which allowed me to glimpse a side of Lenny that I had begun to think was a myth outside the ring.

We had gone to the gym to meet someone who could give me some background information. We were introduced and Len disappeared to take a sauna. I was given a drink, then the man I was interviewing left me for a few minutes to talk to someone else on the other side of the gym. Suddenly, Len was back in the room, beside himself with rage. He seemed to have doubled in size as he ran over to the two men. The hair on the back of my neck stood up as I watched him verbally assault the two blokes.

The controlled threat of violence was awesome as he ordered one of them out of the club. His outburst was due to the fact that I was being ignored while my interviewee was passing the time of day with a 'no-account grass' referred to later in the book.

This incident gave me an insight into Lenny that I could not have gained in a hundred interviews. Control is the keyword, for he is by no means the 'lunatic' he likes to call himself or be called by others.

I speak as I find and no coercion is needed for me to say that I found Lenny to be a very caring person, a shrewd judge of character and highly intelligent. He told me, 'Nobody can pretend with me. I just have to look in their eyes and I can tell just what they are thinking.'

He is an extrovert — a showman. His personality matches his physical appearance, and he can be an over-whelming presence wherever he goes.

I have spoken to many people about Len and I include quotes from some of them as an example of the respect and esteem he has earned and been given.

Peter Gerrard, 1998

Reg Kray
(Currently serving his thirty-year sentence)
'Though he is not of the age group, he is one of the old school in principle. Also, he is definitely a positive thinker, yet without it becoming a task in life. He always keeps his word and values his friends. He chooses his company carefully so that he only has good people around him. He also has the unusual combination of brains as well as brawn. My friend Lenny does not give up easily. He is a legend in his own lifetime and he has become a legend on his own merit. Above all, he is a man.'

Ron Kray
(Deceased)
'Lenny is one of the best people I have ever met. He is a gentleman and one of the best fighters I have ever seen. God bless.'

Charlie Kray
(HM prison)
'Lenny and myself have been friends for a long time. While I have the greatest respect for him as a fighter, I have an even greater respect for him as a man. He told me that he intends to break into the acting game. Well, all I can say is, "Move over, all you screen heroes, there's another Victor McGlagen on the way up."'

Charlie Richardson
(Businessman)

'I heard of Lenny's fearsome reputation many years ago while I was serving my own sentence in prison. Through mutual friends we met and after that he would visit regularly and bring in videos of his fights, which were well received by the other inmates. What strikes me most about him? His integrity and honesty. In my life I have dealt with all kinds of businesspeople, bankers, lawyers and government ministers. These people, pillars of society and supposedly above reproach, will, given the opportunity, rip the coat off your back. Lenny has made a living with his fists, and in younger days on the other side of the fence, but give me his kind of honesty any day. His values are a hundred per cent and he can be totally relied on. When my kids spend a night out in the clubs minded by Lenny, I can rest easy knowing they are in the safest hands.'

Joe Pyle
(Promoter and businessman)

'I used to manage and promote the original Guv'nor, Roy Shaw. At the time, Roy was unbeaten and unbeatable. He was taking on challenges and the first thing I would ask was: "Can you sell at least £6,000 worth of tickets?" If they couldn't, they didn't get the fight. Roy was riding a crest, then along came a young fellow from Hoxton. His name was Lenny McLean. I had never heard of him. Roy had never heard of him. We took up Lenny McLean's challenge. After two fights and a win each, a return was arranged and Roy walked straight into a right-hander. Lenny became the Guv'nor. Since that time we have become friends. Lenny is a great guy with a lot of respect. One look at Len's pugilistic features and one can see what he has come through. He has been a good pal to me and I know both sides of him, as a fighter and a gentleman. Funny — he reminds me of the character in the book *Of Mice and Men* ... his name was Lenny, too.'

Ronnie Knight
(HM Prison Send)

'Before I knew of Len's reputation, I went to a fight at the Rainbow where he was on the card. I put my money on the other man and lost every penny. After that, my money was on the "Big Fella" and still is. He's a very tough guy, but he's also got a big, big heart. No one could wish for a more loyal friend when the chips are down.'

GLOSSARY

boat	face
busies	police
chokey	solitary
clock	notice
cozzers	police (constables)
derby	belly
exes	expenses
face	somebody of note — usually a villain
gaff	home
GBH	grievous bodily harm
gee	compliment
grass	informer
khyber	arse
knock-off	stolen
KO	knockout
leery	arrogant git
lifted	arrested
monkey	£500
niagras	balls
nonce/nonce cases	sex/child molester
Old Bill	police
on the knock	credit
pikey	gypsy
pony	£50
QT	quickly
ricket	balls-up
to rump	to stitch up
slag	no-good bastard
slaughter	hide-away
SP	starting price
sprauncing	lying, fibbing
strides	trousers
tooled up	armed
tug	pulled over by police

FOREWORD

I'm known as the Guv'nor — I am the Guv'nor. But what does that mean? For a start, it ain't like picking up some boxing title over 12 rounds. I don't want to take anything away from anybody who comes out on top, whether it's the boys' area championships or a world title. But that's where it ends for them — in the ring. Between the winning bout and the next all they've got to do is keep fit, look after themselves and keep ready to defend the title in six months' time. Outside the ropes, life goes on as normal, working, if you're an amateur, doing the celebrity rounds if you're a pro. But being the Guv'nor takes over your whole life — 24 hours a day.

So how did I get there? I'll tell you — by having something deep inside me that wouldn't let me break down or turn away from any trouble or aggravation, no matter how bad or how dangerous. If you're the Guv'nor, you can't pick and choose. Whatever comes up or is thrown at you has got to be faced. People on the outside looking in could say I'm a bit cocky or an arrogant bastard. Not to my face though. And perhaps that's how they saw me. They said the same about Muhammad Ali, but he always delivered what he said he would, same as me, although, unlike him, I never went round saying I was the greatest. I knew I was, but I kept my mouth shut and just got on with whatever I had to do.

Remember, I wasn't looking for a name — it was just something that crept up. I did the business, other people put a name to my reputation.

Becoming the Guv'nor doesn't just come from bashing people; there's more to it than that, otherwise every titleholder in the boxing world would have the name. Prince Naseem, Chris Eubank, Frank

Bruno — are they the Guv'nors? Not bloody likely! They're great fighters, but that's where it stops because they haven't got that bit extra that I have. Get a bit of aggro and stick their names up — who's going to worry? You wouldn't want a slap from any of them. But, come on, they're boxers; everything stops at the ropes. Lenny McLean? That's different. He's a mean bastard and, if pushed, a raving lunatic.

I might be retired now, but only six months ago a fella by the name of Eric Forbes got in touch because he was having a load of trouble at Taffy Bradys, a pub he runs. Some punters were running wild, fighting and smashing the place up — it was costing Eric a fortune. Anyway, he asked if he could put the word out that the pub was under my wing. Of course he could, as long as I was well looked after. Simple. Overnight you could have taken your old mum there for a quiet drink. And I never even showed my face. That's what being the Guv'nor means.

Some time after that, Eric got a double result for his money. He sold a few motors so I slipped down his car lot to pick up my share. As I stepped out of my car, I could see Eric arguing with two big blokes. As I walked towards them, one of the geezers turned and spat at Tracey, Eric's wife, who was with me at the time, and was standing well back. Well, nobody spits at a lady in front of me. Eric looked up, they looked round and I cracked their foreheads together like two coconuts. Down they went. I gave them both a slap to bring them round, then told them to piss off. It turned out they were pressuring Eric for another car after wrecking the one they'd bought from him months before. He tells me he's never seen or heard from them since.

I mentioned that I never pick and choose. I'm the Guv'nor — if I'm asked, it's done.

Somebody put my name up and I got a visit from four faces looking for a minder. They told me they had a bit of business going down with a North London firm and they wanted me on the meet in case of trouble. They told me that it was a good money deal, but that it might be a bit heavy. I agreed to look after them and we arranged a meet at Highbury tube station.

I came out of the station and they were waiting for me in a black cab. 'Don't worry about the driver,' one of them said, 'he's family.'

'Right,' I said, 'fill me in on what you want me to do.'

'You don't have to do nothing. Bloke like you just has to stand there while we're talking. You look the business so they ain't going to try anything.'

I said, 'If they make one move to get out of the pram, I'll put the lot of them down.'

'OK, Len, but we've told you, you don't have to do nothing, we're well covered.'

With that they all opened their coats and there were guns everywhere. Fucking hell! I came prepared with a pair of fingerless leather gloves, and this lot are all hiding behind about a dozen shooters. If the other mob are kitted out with the same hardware, I can't help thinking that if anything goes wrong, they'll probably go for the big fella first. Still, I'm aboard now, so I might as well go along with it.

The firm turned up — mean-looking bastards and everyone an Irishman. As we walked into a local club and straight into a back room, my nut was doing overtime. I gave one of our blokes a tug and asked him if these people were who I thought they were. He didn't really have to say 'IRA' — it was written all over them.

The only furniture in the room was a card table in the middle and about 50 fold-up chairs. The main face on my team pulled up a chair opposite the Irish leader. The other six blokes sat behind their respective bosses and I stood between all of them. Two briefcases were thrown on the table and the meet began. The deal was over £2 million worth of bearer bonds for cash and both blokes were doing their best to rump the other. These two argued, swore and threatened for what seemed like hours. This was mid-August; the sweat was running down my legs and I was dying for a lemonade. I was just wondering why I need to be there at all, when my bloke screams out, 'You bog Irish c**t.' He stood up, kicked his chair back and pulled two pistols from his belt. These people are all professionals and in the blink of an eye all the chairs were over and enough guns to start a war were clicking out of belts. I grabbed the gun hand of the Irishman nearest me, pulled him towards me, got hold of his face and swung him across the room, smashing him up against the wall, shouting, 'Anybody moves and I'll rip his fucking face off.' It was a stand-off. I don't think any of them wanted to fire those guns because we were right next door to a busy club. I held the Irishman for about 30 seconds and then slowly let him go.

Nobody moved, so I said, 'Just do the business and let's get the fuck out of here.'

The two main men disappeared into a walk-in store room, leaving us all staring at each other. Five minutes later, they returned. Briefcases were exchanged and it was all over.

I didn't get a handshake or a kiss my arse from any of the Irishmen. Just a lairy look from the one with the thumbhole in his cheek and the four red marks on his face. Bollocks to 'em. I just wanted my wages and to get home.

Back home, I gave my Val the money and she said, 'Been busy?'

It's just another day, so what can I say? 'Not too much, babe, not too much.'

I had only been in for about five minutes when the phone went. It was Asil Nadir's nephew, and he wanted a favour.

It turned out to be a nice little earner and I didn't have to lift a finger — that suits me nicely these days. All he wanted me to do was to give some young kids a bit of support when they came up in court on a murder charge.

Apparently, these boys had suffered abuse and violence from their father for years, until one day they couldn't take it any longer. They got together, and ended up stabbing him. I've got to say I understood the way they felt.

I went down to the court and had just arrived when their brief came steaming over.

'Mr McLean,' he said, 'I know the boys will appreciate you being here, but I am trying to get them acquitted. One look at you and I am afraid the judge might think that the company they appear to keep qualifies them for a custodial sentence.'

'No problem, pal, I'll go and sit in the car.'

I reclined the seat, stuck a Pasty Cline tape on, and started having a nice smoke. Patsy and I are just harmonising nicely on 'Crazy' when Old Bill surround me. The usual — get out of the motor slowly, hands on the roof, the works. I noticed that a couple of them were tooled up, but if they gave me too much hassle and I lost my temper, it wouldn't stop me chinning a few of them. It didn't come to that, though, and we sorted it with no aggro. It turned out that they had a terrorist in one of the other courts, and when somebody clocked me outside, they thought I was getting ready to spring him. Now do I look like a villain or what?

Asil's nephew bunged me a grand for my trouble and if he's got a fraction of the money his uncle's got, he must have felt like he was parting with tuppence ha'penny.

What I'm doing is giving you an idea of what it means to be the Guv'nor. If somebody's got trouble, they think of Lenny, because they know that once I've taken their problems on board, it isn't a problem for them any more. Sometimes, all I have to do is growl over the phone, or perhaps not even get involved, just let my name be put up. But every now and then I have to stare death or serious injury in the face without ever backing off. Would you want my life? Would you want my title?

If you wonder why a man would choose to be involved in violence every day of his life, perhaps by the time you've read my story you'll understand.

CHAPTER ONE

I've never been one for looking back — I never saw the point. It didn't matter how much I might have wanted to change my past, it just couldn't be done, so I never really tried. I was always looking forward, that was me — to that deal round the corner or the clever move round the next; on my toes all the time. As far as I was concerned, anyone rambling on about their past was a mug without a future.

So when me and my pal Peter got settled in the front room to make a start on this book, I thought, as long as my Val keeps the tea coming, no problem. Was I in for a surprise! Not only was it hard work thinking back over nearly 50 years, but many childhood memories that I'd buried away were very painful to bring to the surface and I'm not ashamed to say that, more than once, they brought a lump to my throat.

I was born in my Nan Campion's bed on 9 April 1949. My mum Rose and dad Lenny lived with her at 61 Gopsall Street, Hoxton, which I and most people put slap bang in the East End of London. But Mr Know-All writer sitting opposite me, who's got my Val running up and down making tea, reckons that after looking at the map, the part I was born in really lies in a corner of Islington in North London. Still, it doesn't matter where they stick it on the map, up until the Sixties it was the roughest and toughest corner of London. Hoxton has always been well known for its market, and even today it brings the tourists and punters in from miles around, but back then it was better known as a place to keep away from if you didn't belong. The people who lived there were a breed apart and had a worse reputation than those who lived in Bethnal Green, and that's saying something. I expect some college professor could explain why that little area turned out more villains to the square inch than anywhere else. And I don't just mean toe-rags, Jack the Lads or plastic gangsters. I mean men like the Krays who ruled London's underworld. I don't know the answer to that, I just know it's a fact.

In the old days, the whole of London was a collection of villages. They were all joined together but every one of them had its own identity. You were known by where you came from, and everyone was very suspicious of outsiders, and would fight to protect anybody from their own community, even killing for them, if it came to it.

Hoxton was one of those villages. It was a close-knit community where everyone talked, knew each other's business and shared what little they had with each other. Everyone was in the same boat, with nothing to prove, so there was a friendly atmosphere. You could go into this house or that and no one ever worried about the street doors being open all day or even all night — you just walked in. What little unskilled work there was was badly paid. Everybody was hungry and everywhere people were just trying to get by — it was a very, very hard life.

For working-class people to get a living in those days, you had to be involved in some sort of villainy or be 'at it', so everyone was breaking the law and the black economy flourished. The police were the enemy, because there was no money about. Outside the ghettos it was only people with anything worth having who relied on the police, because they worried about their property or their own skin. Then the police became their friends. People like us knew the police were no good, so they didn't have any time for them. If the streets needed looking after, they did their own policing. Step out of line in those days and the guv'nors of the manor would put the word out and then you'd be in for a bloody good hiding. If that didn't do the trick, you'd get a striping across the face or the cheeks of your arse. You didn't get a third warning.

Today, things are different. Society has changed and lots of the old values have gone out of the window. Old families have moved away, loyalties have become weaker, and in the gap that's left a new breed of villains have sprung up. I don't think most of them deserve the name 'villain', because that word makes you think of tough men trying to survive, but at the same time having respect for each other and the law. No, what we've got today is a lawless society, full of no-value toe-rags, druggies and nonce cases, and that's why we all need the police minding our backs, because the violence and senseless murders have gone beyond being controlled by the local guv'nor. So remember, when I'm slagging off Old Bill, I'm going back years to what I think were better times.

With the war over, changes were taking place all over London. Bomb damage was still being put to rights and the councils were taking the opportunity of clearing away the areas they classed as slum housing. Perhaps they weren't up to today's standards, but they had stood for decades and, with hindsight, it seems wicked that close communities were ripped apart and families shunted into anonymous blocks of jerry-built flats, many of which have now been demolished. Still, as I said, that's with hindsight. At the time, if you got the offer of one of the new flats, you thought that you were the business.

We were the first family to move into Godwin House. It wasn't until then, when we crossed the boundary of Kingsland Road over to Godwin House in Kent Street, Bethnal Green, that we were in the East End proper. It might have been well over 40 years ago, but I can still feel the sense of excitement as we climbed down from the open lorry and stood looking at our new home. It seemed colourful and shining, like something out of one of my picture books. Bright-red brickwork, white concrete and fresh paint everywhere. You could take a shiny, clean lift or use the concrete stairs with their iron handrail to reach the flat. It had three bedrooms, kitchen, bathroom, and sitting-room. One of the bedrooms was used as a storeroom so all of us kids slept in the one room.

I went back there a few months ago, the first time for over 30 years, and afterwards I wished I hadn't. It's a dump now. A shabby, depressing piss-hole. I stood on the pavement in front of the flats on the spot where we'd jumped down from the lorry all those years ago, and just let the memories flood back. Some of the feelings were nice, but mostly they were bad and those bad ones hit me right in the stomach. And I've got to say, they hurt worse than any punch that's been thrown at me over the years.

That first day, though, I couldn't imagine anything ever being bad. It's funny, but I can picture that little family standing there. It's like looking at a cracked and faded old photograph. I know it's me I can see, but looking at that baby in my head, all smiling and clutching his dad's hand, I can feel choked knowing what that poor little sod had got to go through.

I expect that Mum and Dad were feeling pretty chuffed with life then. They had four healthy kids: Linda, six; me, five; Barry, four; and Lorraine, three. Mum was pregnant with Raymond. Dad was grafting well and they had this lovely new home. Being a kid, I was only aware of what concerned me, so as far as I could see everything was perfect. My strongest memory is of feeling warm, loved and happy. I know Mum had her hands full but she always seemed to be laughing and singing. Dad used to sing as well. He'd wait until she was washing up then he'd grab her and start singing 'Yellow Rose of Texas', and she'd be flicking him with soapy water telling him to get off.

They were always messing about like that, or kissing and cuddling. I remember one day he caught a mouse. He put his fingers to his lips for us to be quiet, then opened the kitchen door. 'Present for you, Rosie,' I heard him shout, then he pulled the door shut quick. Bloody hell, you never heard anything like it. I bet the Hayes upstairs thought Mum was being murdered. When he came in that night, he had his hands behind his back. 'Got another present for you, Rosie.' Of course, she starts squealing straight off and the look on her face made us nearly wet ourselves. But this time it wasn't a mouse, it was a box of Black Magic chocolates. He was like that, a lovely man.

As far as I'm aware, he was a good money-getter in those days. To tell you the truth, and I'm not ashamed to say it, he was 'at it', which meant he earned his living however he could. He'd do a bit of running for bookies at the races, a bit of thieving, flogging knock-off gear, anything that would turn a shilling. But he was best at conning people. He never conned his own, but he'd go up West and talk some greedy mug into buying a lorryload of iffy figs. When they had unloaded them, they'd find most of the boxes full of newspaper. By then, though, he was on his toes. Another time, I remember our sitting-room was nearly full up with boxes of Liquorice Allsorts. He told us he was looking after them for a bloke who had a shop. He let us have some, but we couldn't take them outside. It was only a long time after that I realised why.

As I said, he was a lovely man, and unlike a lot of dads, he seemed to make time for us. I was watching him dry himself in the bath one day and I noticed a great big scar that went right round his chest and back. When I asked him what it was, he laughed and said the Germans had done it, but he got his own back because he killed them all and that's how we won the war. I looked at this great, tall man and thought, 'My dad's Superman.'

He had served in the Marines, but the truth of the scar was a major heart operation about a year before. I learnt later that he'd picked up a germ in India which affected a valve. After the operation, he was told he probably only had two years to live — and he died two years later to the day. At the time, I didn't realise his health wasn't good. If I'd known, it would have explained why every now and then I'd walk into the room and Dad would be sitting in the armchair and Mum would be beside him holding his hand and crying. That used to frighten me, but when I put my arms round her shoulders and asked what was the matter, she'd just smile through the tears and say, 'Don't worry, son, I've just got a little headache.'

To me, that man was a giant, and when he carried me down to the Bethnal Green Road market on his shoulders I felt like a giant as well. Other times, I'd walk behind him with my hands behind my back, copying him and taking great strides to keep up. I'd clomp around in his boots and he'd stick his trilby on my head and we'd fall about laughing. He loved us all, but looking back I like to think I was his special favourite because I was his first son and took after him in name and looks.

Then one day this lovely, laughing handsome man was gone. It's all a blur now. All I can remember is him being there one day, then we never saw him again. Perhaps he'd been taken into hospital first, I don't know.

The only people in the block who had a television at that time were the Hayes, who lived in the flat above us, so every chance we got we were up there. In those days, people used to watch telly in the dark, so there was me, Barry, Lorraine and the Hayes' kids, all sitting on this big dining table watching *The Flowerpot Men* — it was a puppet show where the sets wobbled and you could see the strings, or every now and then a big old microphone dangling down. Simple stuff, but we loved it. Mr and Mrs Hayes had bundles of kids, some about my age and others a lot older. And if I sit and scratch my head for five minutes I can put a name to every one even now, 40 years later — Alfie, Patsy, Timmy, Billy, Johnny, Hilda, June, Robert, Fred, Rose and Pauline.

It's funny how little things stick in your mind, but Barry was being a right pain, squeaking, 'Weed, Weed,' in my earhole like the puppet on the telly. The next thing I knew, Mrs Hayes came in and said, 'Your mum's here, you've got to go.' I couldn't see her face in the dark but I think she was crying. We jumped down and ran out, and there was Mum holding Raymond, who was only tiny, and she was crying as well. She took us down the stairs and we were all crying by now, but we didn't know why.

She wrapped her arms around us and cuddled us all at once in a tight little bundle, and said, 'Your dad's gone to heaven. He's gone to be an angel.' I couldn't take it in. I gave her a kiss on the cheek, which was all wet, and I said, 'Don't cry, Mum, he'll come back tomorrow.' To me, it was like he'd gone to do a job or something.

It's as though my mind blanked out what I didn't want to know. You'd think I would remember every detail, because I loved that man so much, but all I can recall of that time is the funeral, or a bit of it. We were in a great big church about a mile long and there were hundreds of people, all crying, and next we're standing by a hole in the ground and they're putting the coffin down it. Everything after that is blank.

Then that night, and many nights after, I'd be in bed with my brothers and sisters, with Mum in the other room, and I'd hear her crying out, 'Oh, God ... Oh, God ... why, why, why? Oh, Lenny, I want you.' I thought she was calling me at first, so I'd creep through and get into bed with her and we'd have a cuddle until eventually she'd fall asleep, but still sobbing his name. It brings a lump to my throat even now to remember that time. She was 24 years old, had five kids to look after and the light had gone out of her life.

Some years later, my cousin, Tony McLean, and I were on the hop from school. I must have been about 12. Don't ask me why, but with nothing better to do, I suddenly thought I'd like to go and see where my father was buried. We had a few bob from some thieving or other, so we got a bus to Stamford Hill, then walked up the hill to Albany Park Cemetery.

As we approached, we could see these great stone archways over the entrance, and I said to Tony, 'Cor, this looks just like a place where they bury kings and queens.' Once we got through the gates we followed the paths which wound through trees, just like being in the woods. We ran up and down reading the names on black marble headstones, carved angels and gold-leafed crosses. No luck. Then

Tony said, 'Ask the old bloke in the shed — he'll know where your dad is.'

It took this bloke about 20 minutes, then without even looking up, he said, 'Oh, yeah, follow the path straight up, then turn right,' adding, 'it's number four.' That didn't mean anything to us so off we went. Finding nothing with McLean on it, we went back to the shed. 'Ere, mister,' I said, 'somebody nicked me dad's headstone.' You know what, that bastard laughed.

'Look, son,' he said, 'I told you it was number four. It's a pauper's grave, they don't have headstones. Anyway, there's probably 20 people down there keeping him company.'

Heartless git. I felt my eyes filling up, I was only 12 but I knew what pauper meant. I was gutted. I know money was tight in those days, but Dad had come from a big, loving family. Surely they could have all put a few quid in for a proper grave?

Thirty-two years later I went back to Albany Park Cemetery, this time with Peter, my co-writer. The church where we had Dad's funeral is derelict now and seems to have shrunk a lot from what I remember when I was five. Anyway, Pete and I searched for hours, up and down, this way, that way, then we found the little cross that marked my dad's grave. It was half buried in brambles, nettles and broken bits of stone. It was a pathetic reminder of the man who's a great part of me. I promised then that I would see a decent headstone erected for that lovely man and it'll be done. When Lenny makes a promise you can depend on it.

Dad's death obviously had a great effect on all of us, but being young kids we soon got on with our lives. Mum seemed to get older and didn't seem to want to do anything any more, but gradually she must have come to terms with it because she started to dress nicely and put make-up on, so after a year or so she was our beautiful mum again.

What we didn't realise was that she had a reason to look nice — she'd met another bloke. One day I was sitting in the front room when Mum came in with this great big man, taller and wider than my dad had been. When she went to make a cup of tea, I followed her into the kitchen and asked who the geezer was. She said, 'He's your Uncle Jim and he's going to look after us.'

Suddenly, I got this horrible feeling. 'But, Mum, we've already got a nice Uncle Fred,' I said, a bit put out.

'I know, luv, but Uncle Fred has got to look after your Nan, and anyway Jim is going to love us all just like your dad used to.'

So that was that.

For a few weeks, this bloke was a regular visitor. He'd bring little toys for us and his pockets would be stuffed with sweets. He'd bounce Raymond on his knee, cuddle the others, and ruffle my hair — any old bollocks to worm his way in. The next minute he'd parked himself in full time and our lives were never the same again.

Up until he married our mum it wasn't too bad. I suppose he was playing it softly softly. But as soon as the knot was tied I suppose he thought he could drop the pretence of loving us kids. Looking back from an adult point of view, I was probably a pain in the arse. Moody, resentful and definitely jealous of him taking over my dad's place so soon. But if he'd been any sort of man at all he would have understood and not treated defenceless kids the way he did.

The first time I came up against him was when he told me to pass him a cup of tea from the table. I slopped most of it in the saucer and some down the chair. He let me put the cup down then, without a word, he slapped me in the face. The pain and shock was so great that for a moment I couldn't breathe. Then, when I could draw breath, I couldn't stop shaking, but I didn't cry. I was six years old and I just looked at him until he looked away, saying to me, 'Get that look off your face — you asked for it.' That was the first time in my life I'd been hit with such violence. I'd had the occasional clip on the arse from Mum, that's something a kid expects, it shows she loves you or something, but Dad had never laid a hand on us. Now this. He was a crafty bastard. And Mum never seemed to be around when he hit us — not at first, anyway.

When Mum came in she must have noticed my swollen face but she didn't say anything. Nor did I — it's like you feel guilty in some way, so ignore it and then it never happened.

If I thought that was a one off I was to get a rude awakening. The word 'Guv'nor' has always meant the top person. Every village or manor had its Guv'nor, the toughest person, the boss, and over the years I earned that title of respect myself. But when you're a little kid there is only one Guv'nor and that's where me and Jim Irwin disagreed.

Mum had taken the others out shopping or visiting somebody, and I was indoors with my stepfather. I was running some little cars up and down the breadboard pretending it was a hill when he must have told me to keep quiet. Knowing how I resented him, I probably mumbled something under my breath, though it was probably not quite discreet enough. He flew at me, grabbed me by the collar of my jersey and the seat of my trousers, and swung me right above his head. He shook the bollocks out of me and shouted, 'Who's the Guv'nor? Who's the fucking Guv'nor?' I was so scared I couldn't open my mouth. 'Answer me, you little bastard.'

'It's me mum,' I muttered. The next thing I know, I'm flying through the air. I hit the table and a chair on the way down and ended up against the wall. Then he towered over me, shouting, 'Wrong, you little shit. *I'm* the Guv'nor now and don't forget it.' Forget it? — I wasn't likely to. That animal had broken my leg and my kneecap.

It's no good you reading this and thinking something like that couldn't happen, because it did all the time. You've got to understand this was the early Fifties, not the Nineties. Today, if your child falls over, the social workers or the law come running, but back then there was no such thing as child abuse. We all know there was, but nobody saw it, nobody heard it and nobody spoke about it, so it couldn't be happening, could it? In those days, neither the hospital nor the law could give a toss about some scruffy little East End kid with a few bruises or fractures. Patch him up and send him back quick to the slums where he belongs and make room for clean, decent kids.

So where was our mum? I'll tell you — stuck right in the middle of a situation she couldn't and didn't know how to change. It goes without saying that she knew what a terrible mistake she'd made bringing that pig into our home. But batter us or not, he was paying the rent and putting bread on the table. She might have been blonde and beautiful, but women with five kids don't stand much chance of getting a man to look after them. So what did she do? She blanked out what he was doing to us all.

Was he an actor or what? I couldn't believe the rubbish he was telling everybody, and that included Mum.

'I feel terrible ... wicked thing to happen ... but it's that temper of his that done it ... threw himself right out of my arms when I'm giving him a little telling off,' he said by way of explanation. And while he was spouting on, with tears in his eyes, he shot me looks that said,

'Get out of that, you little shit, and keep it shut.'

And me? I must have been mad, because I didn't contradict him. See what I mean about being made to feel guilty? I think Mum knew the truth, though. When I was in hospital, she'd sit by my bed with her eyes full of tears, saying, 'I'm sorry, son. I'm sorry.' She never actually came out with what she was sorry about, but we both knew.

Once I got back home, Jim Irwin carried on where he'd left off as though nothing had happened. Whenever he thought we were due for another belting, he'd come out with 'spare the rod, spoil the child', like it was a good excuse for giving us a good seeing to. I used to dread hearing that old chestnut, because it always meant one or all of us was in serious trouble.

His sick mind dreamt up a points system for punishment. He'd give us a point for being too noisy, another one for wetting the bed, perhaps two for breaking something. Then at the end of the day, we'd all have to stand in line and get a belt for every point. Even then the bastard would pull a fast one. If you were due four belts, you'd get five or more — he just had to get the extras in. When I say 'belt' I don't mean a blow with a belt-strap across the arse. He gave us the business. Punches in the face, in the stomach, and if you scrunched up to protect yourself you'd get his shoe in your ribs. We used to go to school black and blue. The teachers would say, 'Been fighting again, McLean?' Yeah, I had; bit one-sided, though.

If he was at home, we'd be in bed by half-past five. Imagine, we're all laying in bed, the sun's still shining outside, and we couldn't talk. We had to lie there listening to the distant voices of happy kids playing football or riding their bikes up and down. We'd be hungry as well. He might have been the breadwinner, but it was mostly for his own greedy self. No wonder he was a big fat bastard. He called it 'his food'.

I remember one night we'd been sent to bed with no tea. We heard him go out, then about ten minutes later Mum came in with a plate of bread and jam. 'Ooh, thanks, Mum, smashing.' Then we're just going to tuck in when the door burst open. He's come back, hasn't he? He went crazy, punching our mum on to the bed, grabbing the plate and flinging it straight through the window. There was glass everywhere.

We all yelled with fright and he shouted, 'I don't work my bollocks off for you lot to thieve my grub.' Then he made a dive for us. Mum threw herself right across all of us and took every punch he threw in the back. Lying underneath her we could feel every blow. He was like a wild man — face red, spit dribbling down his chin. Then he was gone, leaving us all screaming and crying.

Mrs Hayes from upstairs came down, she'd heard the set-to and she wanted to call the law, but Mum wouldn't have it. She just slumped in the chair coughing. Every now and then, she'd wipe blood away from her mouth. It turned out that bastard — and I want to kill him stone dead right now just thinking about it — that beast had broken five of her ribs.

That night we all slept upstairs with the Hayes, and I remember one of their boys, my mate Alfie, saying, 'Why don't you kill him, Lenny?' That must have planted a seed in my nut because from then on I used to plan how I'd do it. I think my favourite was to stab him with a knife when he was asleep. It never happened, but the thought gave me strength.

There was a time, though, when he came very close to getting it, and it wasn't from a little kid either. I came home from school one day. It must have been winter because it was dark and freezing cold. As I came up the last flight of stairs my little brother Kruger was huddled on the floor by the door. This was Raymond, but we all called him Kruger because when he was a baby he looked just like an old German man who lived downstairs. Anyway, he's crying, his nose is running, and he's wet himself. I put my arm round him and I asked, 'What's up, mate, did you think we'd all left you?' He sort of nodded and said, 'There's no one in.' I knew that or he wouldn't have been sitting there. Then we both jumped as the lift door opened right beside us and there was Jim Irwin, who had appeared like a fucking genie from a lamp.

'What's up with you, cry-baby?' he said to Kruger.

'I think I've wet meself,' he said and I felt my stomach turn over. That was definitely the wrong thing to say.

Irwin flung the door open, grabbed him by the collar, and dragged him inside the flat. He stripped him naked and started slapping his bare backside with his open hand. That wasn't enough, so he took his belt off and used that. I could see the buckle cutting into Kruger's skinny little body so I tried to grab the belt. It earned me such a punch in the head I went cross-eyed for a minute. But I had another go and Jim kicked me twice without releasing his hold on my brother. I wasn't counting but he must have hit him about 30 times, and then he threw him on to the bed.

While he was being beaten Kruger was screaming, but now he was all scrunched up on the bed, lying so quietly I thought he must be dead. When Mum came in, Irwin told her not to go near him. 'Rose, luv, I've had to give him a bit of a smack for wetting himself, so leave him to think about it in bed until the morning.'

When we all went to bed at about six, I looked under the covers and his body and bottom were all covered in bloody welts. He just lay there, white faced and shivering. Four years old and beaten worse than a dog. I got into bed and cuddled him, and do you know what that brave little lad said?

'I'm sorry I wet meself, Lenny,' he said. He was sorry — he was smashed to bits and was sorry for causing trouble.

I could hear that bastard laughing in the other room, and I thought, 'I'm going to get you hurt for what you've done.' As young as I was, I could take whatever he could dish out, but I couldn't bear to see any of the others get it.

I lay there for hours still holding little Kruger. I heard the telly shut down, we had one by then, and I think it used to go off at about eleven in those days. Still, I lay there until I was sure everyone was asleep. Then I woke up my brother, told the others to keep quiet, dressed us both and sneaked out of the flat. My mate Alfie had a go-kart made from an old pram, and he used to keep it tucked behind the rubbish bin on the ground floor. I got that out really quietly, laid Kruger on it and, pulling him along with a bit of string, set off to take him to my mum's mum, Nan Campion.

It wasn't that far, but it seemed like miles. It started to snow and it was pitch dark. About halfway there I saw a copper but I pulled the cart up an alley and hid until he'd gone by. Don't ask me why — it was just instinct, just something you always did. Eventually, we got there and the house was all dark but I banged on the door until I got Nan out of bed.

My eldest sister Linda was there, because Nan had taken her in when Dad died to make it easier for Mum.

My mum's brother, Uncle Fred Campion, was there, too. He was halfway down the stairs in his underpants, hair all sticking up. What a diamond of a man. From the day my father died that lovely man bought all our Christmas presents, right up until we were grown up. He never married, just looked after Nan and Linda. Now he's an old man and things have turned round. Nan's dead and Linda looks after him. I haven't seen him for years — you lose touch as you get older, but I'll always love him for what he did for us. Anyway, when they saw the mess Kruger was in there was hell to pay. Looking back, the scenes in my head are like fast-forwarding a video, all rushing and blurry.

I'm put to bed, Kruger's taken to hospital, the police are called and, best of all, as I hoped would happen, Nan sent for her brother, Jimmy Spinks. Why he wasn't called in years ago I don't know. I suppose Mum was ashamed of becoming involved with Jim Irwin and kept what went on to herself. Now I'd let the cat out of the bag, not for myself but for my brother.

My great-uncle Jimmy was one of the toughest men to come out of Hoxton. He was about 21 stone and 5ft 9in, built like an ox, with powerful arms and shoulders, and a fighting reputation that couldn't be bettered in those days. I'll tell you more about him in a bit, but right then, when he saw for himself what had been done to that child, he tore straight round our flat like a raging bull. The police had already been up to the flat and Mum had talked them out of prosecuting, so I expect that smug bastard thought he'd got away with it again. That was until Uncle Jim came through the door. I learned all this afterwards. He didn't knock, he actually punched the door open.

Jim Irwin just had time to come out of the sitting-room before he was battered, semi-conscious, back in again. Now remember, Uncle Jim was twice his age, but Irwin didn't stand a chance. As he got to his feet those massive fists put him down again, then out came the cut-throat razor. Whether he would have used it we'll never know, but he was more than capable and it wouldn't have been the first time. Mum, however, pleaded with him to give Irwin another chance. For Mum's sake he didn't use the razor, but told him to 'Fuck off' there and then or he'd, as Uncle Jim put it, 'end up with a face like mine'.

Now that was a threat because Uncle Jim's face had so many knife and razor scars that it looked like a map of the Underground. Irwin got the message. He might have been the business when it came to knocking the bollocks out of little babies, but fronted up by a real man that gutless coward went to pieces and buggered off without arguing.

Uncle Jimmy was a very tough man and in his day was the

Guv'nor of Hoxton. He was what they called a 'ten-man job', because to bring him down you would have to go ten-handed or turn up with a shooter. I've got to say I've heard that said about myself and I'm proud to think I've inherited that from him. He was a very hard man — a tearaway. He was in one of the gangs that worked the horse racing circuits, running protection. He used to mind the bookies and the number one bookmaker in that area at the time was a Jewish bloke called Lasky. Jimmy would mind all the other bookmakers on the street corners in that area. That was his block and he was a force to be reckoned with.

I looked up to Jimmy when I was a young boy. I used to love seeing him because he always gave us money and in those days there was little about. He always had money. Jimmy was very powerful and menacing, but a loving man to all his family, and always dressed immaculately — white shirt, tie, the big hat, the Crombie overcoat, and the pinstriped suit — the typical Al Capone gangster. He was the main man. I remember when my father died, Jimmy went round all the pubs and had a collection for my mum. That was in 1953 and he raised a load of money and handed over every penny. I think that probably helped to feed us until Irwin appeared on the scene. I don't forget things like that, even though I was only five years old.

My nan told me a story. She said her brother was down the Nile one day (an area of Hoxton named after Nile Street), when this geezer with a grudge crept up behind him and smashed him over the head with an iron railing. She thought it was one of the Birmingham mob from the Elephant and Castle, who he'd had an upset with. Anyway, Jim stayed on his feet and then knocked the hell out of the bloke before wrapping his white scarf round his head and walking to the hospital. When they saw the state of his head they called a priest, but Jim sent him packing, let them bandage him up, then discharged himself.

He had a run-in with the Sabini gang which got him banged up for a spell. The Sabinis were a force to be reckoned with.

They'd started in about 1910 and based themselves in the Yorkshire Grey, Clerkenwell. There wasn't an English man amongst them so they were known as the Italian Mob. Most of their business was done at the racetracks, so when Jimmy wanted to sort out a grievance he fronted up thirty members of the Hoxton Mob and headed for Brighton Racecourse. The battle that followed earned

Uncle Jim, as one of the ringleaders, five years in prison. That was in 1936, which in those days meant spending your time breaking rocks, not weight-lifting, watching TV or studying for a degree. I know he changed all the names, but when Graham Greene wrote *Brighton Rock*, much of it was based on what happened that day.

But Jim wasn't just a tough old villain; he looked after people. I'm often told of little incidents by his acquaintances, such as helping an old lady across the road, then slipping her a few quid, saying, 'There you are, mother, treat yourself,' or he would buy sweets for the local lads. Reg and Ron Kray would confirm that. Jim was in his local one day when an American film man, noting that he looked the business, offered to take him to Hollywood to act in films with Cagney, Raft and Bogart, but he turned it down. 'Son,' he said, 'I was born in the East End and I'm going to die in the East End.'

And he did. He was only in his early fifties when he had a brain haemorrhage. The funeral was like something out of a film — a proper gangster's send off. There were hundreds of shiny black cars following the coffin. There were television cameras, celebrities, pop stars and almost every major villain in London. The wreaths would have knocked your eyes out, all shapes and sizes. Jimmy Spinks was a legend.

So that was Uncle Jimmy. At the time, we didn't know anything of his reputation or his villainy. All we knew or cared about was that he had chucked out the bastard who had terrorised our home. If I'd known then that he was only out of the way for three months, I wouldn't have been so happy, but I didn't, so I was over the moon.

It was at about this time when I had my first paid fight, and I think I was as pleased with what I earned then as I was with some later fights which earned me ten grand.

Barry came home one day with a bleeding lip and Mum said: 'Now, what have you been up to?' Through his bawling he told her that Brian Hyams from downstairs had punched him in the face. Because Brian was older and bigger than Barry, Mum turned to me and said, 'Lenny, go down and sort out that bully.' So down I went.

He was the same age as me but a lot bigger. Still, I steamed in anyway. Bang, bang, bang, Now he's crying, and when you're that age it's the same as a knockout. So back up I go to tell my mum. Dead proud I am. Straight away she dipped into her purse and gave me three old pennies. But, in a way, the little pat on the shoulder she also gave me was worth more than the money.

Still, you couldn't buy a lolly with a pat on the back and that's what Barry, Kruger and I did. We shot round to Morgan's on the corner and got a little square ice lolly each. The owner, a mean old bugger, used to make them himself in his freezer, two sucks and they went white, but we didn't care. The three of us sat on the wall, the champion and his brothers, and sucked them to death.

Every kid passing by was collared by Barry and Kruger and dragged up to look at the tough guy who'd given Brian Hyams a thrashing. They were well impressed because he was a bit of a handful, but I think most of them were even more impressed when they heard I got paid for it. So, in a minor way, I became 'the Guv'nor' of Godwin House.

I was getting a fair reputation at school as well, but I never picked on anyone smaller than me. Come to that, I never really picked on anyone — they seemed to search me out to prove themselves tougher than me. I'd noticed that if you were a good fighter you had loads of friends — the more fights, the more friends. So I was always mixing it in the playground. Shirt-tail hanging out, knees and knuckles grazed, and the odd bloody nose. I loved it. Suddenly I was somebody who counted.

As often happens when you're a kid, after that first fight with Brian Hyams, he and I became mates; there was Brian, Alfie Hayes and Frankie O'Leary. We did everything together. We'd be in and out of each other's flats, though none of them wanted to come near mine if they thought Irwin might show his face. We'd spend hours together and we were always trying to outdo each other — who could run the fastest, who was the best swimmer, or who was the toughest fighter.

Alfie and I got into a fight one day with a kid about four years older than us — Roger Smythe, a right handful. He wasn't going to give up and neither were we, so we took turns in belting or being belted. When Alfie became tired he'd say, 'Come on, "Boy Boy", your go,' and I'd steam in until I got out of breath, then we'd change over again. What a tag team! I think it would have gone on all day had it not been for Alfie's big brother Freddie, who came round the corner and saw Roger off.

It wasn't all fighting, though. We thought we were the business when we formed a skiffle group and called ourselves The Four Lads

— Barry, Brian Hyams, Alfie and me. We were terrible. I remember going to Shoreditch Carnival once and entering a talent competition. We were belting out 'Diana' with the veins in our necks nearly bursting, seeing who could sing the highest and loudest. We came fourth — there were only three other acts. Those lovely times outside helped me cope with the horrible times indoors.

My favourite activity was visiting Alfie's flat — the one above ours. He had a great big, friendly family, about 13 of them in all. Most of them were older than us, but they weren't cocky at all. I used to love being in there. Some of the sons worked in the fruit market so the place was always loaded with apples, oranges, bananas — everything you could think of.

They knew what life was like for me, so in subtle ways they all tried to make things a bit easier for us. They were like a second family. Being working teenagers, they always slipped us a few pennies. Rosie Hayes used to work in a petrol garage, and she'd take me with her sometimes. I think I must have been in love with her in my childish little way. Of the older ones, Billy was my favourite. He had a lot of time for me. I don't doubt he liked me for myself — I think I was a likeable enough kid — but I have a sneaky feeling that he had a fancy for my mum. They were both about the same age and I've often wondered how life would have turned out if she had married him and not Jim Irwin.

Billy would sometimes take me down the market on a Sunday, or down Dog Lane — as its name suggests, it was a part of Petticoat Lane where dogs were sold. I'd walk up and down patting them all and choosing which one I'd buy, even though I knew I couldn't keep it. He'd take me in the café and I'd sit with his mates feeling really grown up, one of the boys. Sometimes I'd go out with him and his girlfriend Pat and it would always be great in his company. He must be sixty now and I haven't seen him for years, but I haven't forgotten him, or the others. Today, the sons who worked in the fruit market then are chairmen of the market now, even my old mate Alfie. A lovely straight family, all of them good workers, good people who brought a lot of happiness into a little kid's life when he didn't have a lot going for him.

While we were all enjoying our holiday away from our hated stepfather, Mum didn't seem all that happy. Then a bloke named Joey kept turning up. I thought, 'Fuck me, no, not again!' But it turned out he was bringing messages from Jim Irwin asking if he could come back. It's a pity Mum didn't put it to the vote, it would have saved a lot of misery. But she went to see Uncle Jimmy and pleaded with him to lift his threat from Irwin.

'For you, Rose,' he said, 'I'll leave him alone, but I still want to cut his insides out for what he done to that baby.'

She showed him some letters and promised that Irwin had changed and was sorry for what he'd done. So it was agreed that he could move back in.

So back he came and within a fortnight the beltings had started all over again.

He didn't seem worried at all about the threat of Uncle Jim coming after him again. I suppose he reckoned that Mum was so pleased to see him back that she wouldn't say a word outside the door. As for me, he marked my card with what he would class as a subtle warning. 'Grasses are scum and they end up with their throats cut.' So I made a habit of keeping out of his way.

I remember one time I was kipping upstairs with Alfie. I used to like that, because we could stay up late and his mum always did a nice spread for a bit of supper. At about seven the next morning, his dad shouted through, 'Make us a pot of tea, son.' Well, Alfie jumped up and I think he made a bit of toast as well, took it into his Mum and Dad, and then we sat on the end of their bed and had a bit of a joke with them. Lovely, ordinary family life. It didn't mean anything to Alfie because it was so normal, but it made me feel all warm and sad at the same time.

It couldn't have been more different from life in our flat downstairs. On a Sunday morning, you could always tell who'd been on tea duty in our house because they'd have a great lump on the back of their head. One minute you're asleep, the next minute ... whack. Now you're wide awake going 'What ... what ... what?' — Jim Irwin's just knuckled you in the head. He'd just stand there ready to put another one in, saying, 'Make the tea,' then he'd go back to bed. Spiteful bastard. I could go on and on about the beltings and vicious treatment we took off that excuse for a man, but when you're reading about it one punch is pretty much like the next. It's different when you're on the receiving end, though. I can't even say that he got tired of doing it, or that we got used to it. He didn't and we couldn't.

Only the people close to us knew what we were suffering. The rest of the world thought he was a hero taking on a widow and all her kids. Good old Jim, heart of gold. If only they knew the real man behind closed doors. A drunken, childbeating slag. And so my early years drifted away. Those years form a child's mind and set patterns for becoming an adult. What a waste.

Suddenly, I'm twelve, Mum's pregnant, Jim Irwin's in the money and we're on the move back to Hoxton.

This time we moved opposite my aunt Rosie Wall, a lovely woman, a real comedienne. All my aunts on the McLean side were comediennes, each could make you laugh until you had tears in your eyes. I thought the world of Rosie because she always talked about my real father. I'd sit in her kitchen listening to all the little stories she could tell me about him and it was like bringing him alive again.

Jim was still being handy with us, but he must have been up to some handy work elsewhere, because his expensive suits and flash car didn't come from a lorry driver's wages. It turned out that he'd been working with Ronnie Knight and a few others running the 'long firm' racket. The scam was that a few likely lads would get together and take out a short-term let on a warehouse. Then with some dodgy references and a few fancy letterheads they'd set up as distributors. All kinds of goods would be ordered in bulk from the manufacturers and paid for on the nail. The suppliers must have thought they were dealing with a right up and coming firm. It took a good bit of up-front money and a few months' work, but the end result was still worth it. All of a sudden, business would take off, on paper anyway, so orders would have to be doubled. The suppliers must have thought they'd got a right result, what with all the deliveries of TVs, washing machines and fancy gramophones to the lads at the warehouse — all on the knock of course, because this firm was very credit-worthy. Then ... wallop ... everything's sold off — all pre-arranged — to receivers all over the country. And all that's left in the warehouses are a few empty boxes, a load of cobwebs and a pile of bills sloping up to the letterbox. It would be a few months before the suppliers would get suspicious, so the villains could be well away, probably starting up somewhere else, before the scam was discovered.

Sometimes, when Ronnie Knight had a bit of business with my stepfather, he'd bring his wife to our house. He was married to Barbara Windsor then, who had just started the *Carry On* films, and was on the way to being a big star. I only met her the once, because I always seemed to be at school when they turned up, and then I was so nervous of Jim Irwin lashing out at me in front of them that I stood behind the settee like a big dummy. I might only have been a kid, but I was knocked out by how beautiful she was with that long blonde hair and how friendly and ordinary she seemed — not a bit stuck up as you would expect from a film star. I bragged about it at school for weeks afterwards. How we chatted and laughed and how she gave me a big kiss when she left … I wish. Most of the lads thought I was the dogs, but some of them needed a smack in the head before they believed me.

Years later, Ronnie and I met up and became friends, but as he and Barbara had divorced I never did get to know her. Funny, really, I used to look at Ronnie sometimes and think to myself, 'How could you have been mates with that bastard Irwin?' Then, one day, I came out with what that beast had done to me and the others. He just looked at me and said, 'Lenny, you're joking me.' I showed him the scars on my head, legs and arms and he swore he never had a clue about what was going on then. If he had known, he would have had the bastard done away with. I believed him because Ronnie's one of your own. Too late, by then, but it was nice to know he would have been there for me.

At home, Mum had my little sister Sherry and I loved her to death. Never mind that half of her was an Irwin, she was a little smasher and I never gave it a second thought. Funny, isn't it, that he hated me because I wasn't his, but I thought the world of his daughter? He spent fortunes on her, and still nothing on us, but I didn't mind.

I was about 13 then and knocking about regularly with a little firm of kids. There was Tommy Green, Andy Bradshaw and Joe Kyle. What a team. For starters we were just into the sort of thieving most kids get up to. Over the wall at the back of the sweet shop, pass over a dozen empty lemonade bottles, then nip round the front and collect the threepence deposit on every one. The same thing worked with off-licences as well. Because I was the biggest, I was always the one who was shoved to the front to do the business. One day, the others gave me a leg up over an 8ft high wall, and then to get out all I had to do was unbolt the back gate and bring out the gear. I dropped down, and within a few seconds found the gate padlocked from the inside and a huge great Alsatian looking at me with a big grin on its mug. I thought, 'Before I'm halfway up the wall this bastard's going to turn me into dog meat.' So I chucked this empty crate at it, opened the back door of the shop, shot through the storeroom, over the counter, and away. I can still see the look on the face of the little bloke who owned the shop. Never had time to open his mouth.

'Jump ups' was another good earner. We'd wait until we saw a lorry pull up outside a shop, let the driver take his first delivery inside, then we'd be up and in. You grabbed the first thing you set eyes on; it didn't matter what it was. In those days most of the lorries just had a big sheet down the back, not the metal doors today. We never got big stuff — it was mainly fruit or meat, but once we got about sixteen pairs of ladies' shoes. Anything like that, or full boxes of peaches or grapes, we'd fence off to an old character down the Nile. I won't mention his name in case he's still working, but if he is he must be about 90 now.

The trouble was nothing that was nicked could ever be taken home, and the money we earned had to be spent so that it didn't show. The reason was that our parents had a sort of double standard of what was right and wrong. I've already said that everybody in the neighbourhood was at some kind of villainy, some of it mild, a lot of it serious. Dad was a thief, using crime to put steam on the table. But just let them catch their kids up to any nonsense — it'd be a good hiding. It wasn't a big problem, though, all we earned went on the pictures, in the machines or into our bellies. We weren't into clothes, not like today where kids will kill for a pair of fancy trainers or a jacket with the right label.

We became more daring as time went on. My cousin Tony McLean had joined our little firm and he always thought big. It was his idea to start 'creeping'. It had many variations, but usually it meant going into a big office block and pretending that we had a message to give our mum or dad or uncle or whoever. Because we were kids, nobody thought much of it. Then when we found an empty office we'd collar anything portable that could be turned into a few bob — stationery, petty cash boxes, handbags, even typewriters if they weren't too heavy.

We didn't all go in, just two of us at a time. We were never nicked, although Tony and I were caught red handed once in one of the offices. I made myself look innocent and Tony pretended he was going to burst into tears. He was all choked up and said we were only looking for somewhere to have a pee and we'd got lost. What an actor! But it worked, though, and we got away.

A bit more serious was nicking wages from factories on a Friday. The set up was the same, really, but as the haul was in cash it was well worth the risk. We weren't stupid, though, we spread our little operation all over the place. Then as we picked up a few quid we could afford to travel out a bit on trains or buses. It couldn't go on, though. The law of averages said that, sooner or later, we would take a tumble.

It came sooner. On one of our trips out we were heading for Romford in Essex. The three of us, (Tommy, Andy and I) had just jumped on the first train that came in. We were in a carriage all on our own and, of course, we were messing about — we didn't know what to get up to next. Tom had the bright idea of nicking the pictures from the walls. That was in the days when every carriage had a couple of country scenes screwed up behind glass to brighten up your journey.

He took one off and was just starting on the other when Andy pulled the communication cord. Suddenly, it's as though the train has run into a brick wall and we ended up on the floor. We started shitting ourselves. We opened the door and jumped on to the grass bank, looked up and down the track, then somebody shouted, 'Oi, you little bastards!' and we took off up the bank, over the fence, and just ran and ran over the fields. So now we were miles from anywhere, covered in shit and mud and scratched from head to foot. Tom had lost one of his shoes.

We wandered about for hours, mostly walking behind hedges or in woods in case Old Bill was looking for us. Tom never stopped moaning about his foot, but he did look funny hopping along. It had just started to get dark when we came across a big garage, all lit up, with nothing else around.

I said to Andrew, 'Andy, do you reckon you can cream that place?' He said, 'No problem, just keep a look out for me.'

So while we hid in a ditch opposite, he sneaked over and tucked himself behind a van. After a bit, a motor pulled in and the bloke in the office came out to fill it up with petrol. It wasn't self-service like it is now. From where we were hiding we could see Andy, and as soon as the coast was clear he was in the office. Half a minute and he was out. We lost sight of him for a bit, then we saw him running like mad up the road. Still in the field, we started running after him, and we laughed and giggled. When we had a divvy up there was £69.00. We could easily afford a taxi to get home if we could find a phone or a village.

We were just heading for some bright lights in the distance, with all the money in our pockets, when a jam sandwich pulled up beside us; that's what we called a white police car with a wide red stripe down the side. We kept walking, pretending we hadn't noticed it, until another one, coming from the other direction, cut in front of us and we were lifted.

Because we were so young, they didn't put us in the cells, just in what appeared to be an office while our parents were sent for to take us home. Later on, we were found guilty at the court in Hertfordshire for stopping the train and for nicking the money, and all of us got probation, which was no big deal.

Though we were warned by our parents to keep away from each other, we did meet up at school and we compared the good hidings we'd got. I envied the smacked legs and bums the other two got. I had been punched and kicked, and sometimes now when I'm shaving, I can't help looking at the scar above my left eye. A nice little reminder of that time.

Still, it wasn't long after that that two incidents cheered me up and kept me smiling for ages — and one of them made me feel I'd got my own back.

I was sitting in the front room, flicking through the *News of the World*, waiting for my Sunday dinner, when an argument started in the kitchen. Jim Irwin had come home pissed and had laid into my mum. She was screaming and my little sister was crying. I ran through and he had Mum over the table, banging her head in the food she was getting ready. I was so wild I wasn't thinking. I ran straight in and punched him in the back shouting, 'Leave her alone, you big c**t ... if you want to fight, fight me.' My punch hadn't made much of an impression because he just turned round and said, 'Oh yeah ... you'll do,' and hit me four times in the face. Left, right, left, right, and I ended up in the passage, spark out. Well, nearly spark out, because I could still hear him, as though from a distance, shouting, 'Come on, tough guy ... get up if you wanna mix it.'

The fight had been knocked out of me, but at least he'd stopped hitting my mum. She put a plaster over my cut eye, gave me a cuddle and said, 'He didn't mean it, son, he's just had a few too many.'

See what I mean? Mum loved us all, but she still blanked the way that animal treated us.

About a week later, Nan Campion was round for a cup of tea. Jimmy Spinks was dead by then. We were in bed but she came up to see us. When she saw the cut on my head she just shook her head and said, 'You're just like your uncle, always fighting.' 'I ain't been fighting, Nan, ' I said, 'Jim Irwin gave me a belting.'

Down she went, and I lay there listening to her and my mum arguing and shouting. Irwin was out, so poor old Mum was taking some stick for trying to defend him. I found out what happened next from Billy Hayes from Godwin House, who was in the same pub when our nan came steaming in the door. She was a typical East End nan, a big strong woman who could have taken on Rocky Marciano.

Irwin was at the bar with all his mates. As the door burst open, he looked round and Nan punched him smack in the face. This big coward went white and tried to duck round the stool to get out of her way. As he turned his back, she picked up a big glass ashtray from the bar and did him right over the back of his head, splitting it wide open. It's a wonder she didn't kill him. She was hustled out, he was taken down the hospital, and the law was never involved.

When Billy told me all this it put a grin on my face as though I'd been razor cut from ear to ear. And every time I looked at Jim, I could see those ten stitches in the back of his nut, and I thought, 'Good girl, Nan.'

A little after that, something even better happened. At about six o'clock one morning, we were all in bed when we heard a banging at the door. Mum went down, opened the door, and suddenly Old Bill was swarming all over the place. I thought, 'Fuck me, I've got some hooky gear of me own stashed under the bed.' But I needn't have worried; it was Jim they were after, and once they'd got him they only had a quick look round. One of the coppers stuck his head round the door and said, 'All right, kids?' and I must have sounded as though I had a spike up my bum when I squeaked, 'Yes, thank you.' It was a close call; I was nearly joining Jim in the van. Next thing he's up in the court with a few others and they all got 18 months for fraud — what the busies call conspiracy. Time for the big grin again.

It was a nice holiday for all of us and not much worse for him either, because he didn't even do 12 months, and most of that time was at Ford Open, which was, and still is, a bit like Butlin's without the 'Goodnight, campers' sung to you at night.

Just after he got out it was my turn. The other boys and I were still nicking for a living. Ducking and diving. Real Jack the Lads. Then that law of averages I mentioned decided to level me off a bit. Funnily enough, it wasn't the thieving that caught up with me but a bit of bravado that went wrong.

This particular night I wasn't with Tommy, Andy, or Joe. I was with another kid called Charlie. He was a couple of years older than me and worked for a Jewish firm as a tailor. Well, he had this knife, a penknife. It was a lovely tool — it even had a thing for getting stones out of a horse's hoof. Bloody handy thing for a tailor's apprentice. Not to be outdone, I got myself a bayonet. I gave this kid two bob for it. The handle was all wound round with black tape and the edge was like a razor. It's funny the fascination kids have for knives. Well, I was no exception. I didn't see it as a weapon, more like a bit of jewellery.

Nobody could see what we were carrying but perhaps our cocky swagger down the road caught the Old Bill's eye. We had just gone past Woolworth's when two coppers stepped out and grabbed one of us apiece. They pulled us back into the doorway, turned us inside out, and that was it. They found his penknife and my bayonet, and we were well and truly nicked. They called up a motor and we were taken down Old Street nick. Processed up, laces out, belts off, then we were banged up in separate cells.

This is my first time and my bottle's starting to go a bit, but I thought, 'Fuck 'em. I won't let them have the pleasure of seeing it.' What a dump. It was like a public piss-hole, and smelled the same as well —plain brick all round, little window about ten feet off the floor, and a flush toilet in the corner. If you were banged up with someone else they couldn't see you on the bog because of a partition, but in the wall right in front of it was a peep hole so that the cozzers could have a sly look at your bum while you're sitting there. Bleeding perverts.

The only thing to read was a notice stuck on the wall saying, 'Any persons defacing HM property will be ...' possibly shot for all I knew, because somebody had torn the rest off. Every now and then the little square window in the cell door would open and a different face would peer in. I shouted to one of these faces, 'I know my rights ...

shouldn't I have a phone call or a cup of tea or something?' The window banged shut and this voice, disappearing down the corridor, said, 'Shut yer fucking gob.' So much for British justice.

My mum turned up with Charlie's mum and dad and we were bailed to appear at Bow Juvenile Court in 30 days. Mum was breaking her heart, but I told her not to worry because I'd only be down for a fine and a good bollocking when I went back.

Jim Irwin's first words to me when I got home were, 'Did Old Bill give you a belting when they got you down the station?'

I thought, 'Hello, here we go,' but I said, 'No,' anyway.

'Right then, I'd better sort you out,' and he did. 'Fucking teddy boy' — punch — 'Thug' — punch — 'Disgrace your family' — punch. He'd just done 11 months behind the door and he was belting shit out of me for getting myself nicked. For the next month I didn't see the light of day after four o'clock. It would be straight home from school and into bed. I began to hope I'd get sent down just to get away from it all.

Then the day arrived. I wore my best pullover and my hair was slicked down with Brylcreem. Anyone seeing me would have thought I didn't have a care in the world. What they wouldn't know was that my bum had been glued to the toilet seat since half-five that morning.

So we turned up. Jim Irwin didn't show, thank God, so there was Charlie and me, his mum and dad and my mum. We all stood in this great big room, wood panelling and chandeliers everywhere, all shuffling our feet and talking like we were in church.

Charlie was called in first, and I could tell by the tight-arsed way he walked that he was feeling like me. Ten minutes later and he's back out again grinning all over his face. As he was ushered past us by a teacher-looking bloke, he whispered out of the side of his mouth: 'Three quid fine.' Result, my son!

Then it's my turn. Being Juvenile Court, the courtroom wasn't like the ones you see in the pictures or on the telly. It was just a big posh room, like a library without the books. Down the middle there was a dining table about 30 feet long that you could see your face in, and all round it were carved chairs with high backs.

In the biggest chair was a bloke in a blue pin-stripe suit and beside him were two old girls in flowery dresses and glasses, and they were all looking at me as though I was something on the bottom of their shoes. They let Mum sit down, but I had to stand in front of them while they read papers and mumbled to each other. Then I got the lecture: dangerous weapon ... vicious thug ... streets not safe ... society will not tolerate ... and so on. I wasn't really listening. I just kept my eyes on the pigeons crapping on the window sill outside.

I must have gone into a bit of a daze, because the next thing I knew, the bloke in the suit was saying, 'Three pounds,' and Mum started crying and shouting, 'Oh no, please no.' I thought, 'Hold up, Mum, I can nick more than that tomorrow.'

They were all looking at me as though I was stupid because I must have been smiling or something. One of the old girls said, 'If, by the smirk on your face, you imagine three years in an approved school will be some sort of a holiday, then I suggest you think again.'

Bloody Hell, what did she say? Three years? I was stunned. I looked at Mum and she had her hanky over her mouth, and I looked back at those three mugs and I could see in their eyes they knew they'd got a result.

What did they know about me and what sort of life I'd had? Did they care that I'd been belted nearly all my life, abused and knocked about, and known nothing but fear, terror and pain? No. They'd go back to their cosy little houses in Croydon or Barnet, proud of their day's work protecting society. Back home to worry about real life like the daily papers being late or the milk not being delivered — fuck them.

Because he was a tailor, they'd swallowed Charlie's story that he used his knife for work. Were they mugs or what? Me, because of my little bit of previous, they treated me as though I was Jack the Ripper.

Anyway, I was locked in a back room while they sorted things out, and after about half-an-hour they let my mum in. She was still crying and I said something I've always regretted. I told her to pack in the tears because she was showing me up really badly. Tough guy, eh? She didn't say anything but just tried to stop crying. I can still see that hurt look on her face and all these years later I just want to cuddle her and say, 'I'm sorry.'

The system sent a coach round all the juvenile courts picking up the kids who had been remanded, so we had to sit there for about four hours, staring at the walls, without even a cup of tea. I know I said I was hoping to go down to get away from Jim Irwin, but that was when I thought it wouldn't happen. Now I felt different. The coach arrived too soon and I was taken out the back door. Mum just had time to say, 'Be brave, son, be strong for me,' then I was bundled aboard.

As the coach pulled out of the yard, I wiped the condensation off the window and looked back. Seeing that little figure of my mum standing there in the rain with her shoulders all slumped, still crying and giving a little wave, I felt my own eyes filling, so I mouthed, 'Love you, Mum,' then turned away to face whatever was coming.

CHAPTER TWO

Stamford House is a remand centre in Shepherd's Bush where they assess you before deciding in which unit you'll serve your term. It was a bit like a very strict school. Everything was done on the double — march here, march there. First, I was taken to reception. You're not allowed to talk to the other kids, you just have to stand there in a line while they sort through your papers. Then, on the trot, we were taken to whichever house they had decided to put us in. Mine was Amby House, for the youngest, the 12–16-year-olds.

All your personal possessions are taken away and stuck in a big envelope, then all your clothes. You get a towel and a bit of soap and you've got to have a shower. Once that is out of the way, you get dressed in the clothes they give you and you are well and truly part of the system. Once you put on that rough grey shirt and short pants, you not only feel a prat, but it seems as though you've lost your identity, and that effectively knocks any fight out of you. Not that there was any in me; it had been a long day and I was missing my family already.

Tea was bread and jam, and then, because it was our first day, early bed. The dormitories were just a long room with lines and lines of beds. Again, we weren't allowed to talk, but had to get into bed straight away, and I was glad about that because I wanted to shut it all out.

I lay there with the blankets pulled right up to my chin and slowly let it all sink in. It seemed like a distant dream being in my own house early that morning. I pictured my mum standing crying at the court house and I thought of my nan and my brothers and sisters — would they all forget me? Then I thought of Jim Irwin. His beltings and abuse had driven me out of our home and into trouble so it was down to him I was here and I hated him for it.

In the beds all around me frightened kids were scrunching their faces into their pillows and crying themselves to sleep. But I just stared at the blue light in the ceiling that was always on, and I burned with rage.

I felt hot, then cold. I wanted to jump out of bed and smash everything to bits. My arms and legs kept jerking as my mind raced through ways I'd like to kill that bastard who'd ruined my family. Then, when I eventually fell asleep, I dreamt of my dad and he was singing 'Yellow Rose of Texas' and the pain woke me up. I was a tough guy, but in the dark, in the middle of the night, I was just like all the other kids as I pulled the pillow over my head and let myself go. That was my lowest point.

After that first night, I came to terms with the life there and it wasn't so bad. Don't forget, I'd known some rough times up until then, so I was no kitten. Nothing could be as bad as what I'd suffered at home. If Stamford House had an old school tie, most of the villains in London would be knotted up with one. Charlie Richardson and Ronnie Biggs are two chaps who spring to mind. It wasn't Oxford or Cambridge, but it turned out some likely lads. It wasn't a prison so they didn't bang us up and we didn't have to work. We had to do lessons, though, and that was hard for me — I hadn't put in a full week at school for years. What most kids feared wasn't the screws — or teachers, as they liked to be thought of — nor the system in general. What they really worried about was other kids, the tough, violent kids. And there were always plenty of them.

About a week after I moved in, this little, effeminate kid in the next bed to me said, 'Lenny, I got something to tell you.' Now I'm a big lad, and this kid's about the size of tuppence, so I reckon he's looking for a minder.

'Lenny,' he said, 'the Daddy is telling everybody that you're a cockney poof.'

'What do you mean, fucking "Daddy"?', I said. 'Who's that?'

'It's that Scotch boy in the next house, the tough one.'

I realised that by 'Daddy' he meant 'Guv'nor'.

'Well, you pass the word down the line that Lenny McLean thinks he's a haggis-eating c**t.'

That was a Friday. On Saturdays we were all allowed to play in the orchards in the grounds. You weren't allowed to climb the trees, but you could play cricket or football, or lay and have a kip. That's exactly what I was doing when I looked up to see a big kid of about 16, standing right over me, surrounded by a gang of others.

He looked down at me and said, 'So you're the tough guy who's browning all the little ones in Amby.' I knew who he was because of that 'hoots mon' voice, and I never even got up. I just put some leather in his bollocks while I was still lying on the grass.

As he went down clutching his nuts, I leapt up ready to give him some more. Then I was grabbed from behind. Luckily I didn't back-nut whoever it was, because it was one of the teachers.

'Right,' he said, 'you know the rules.' I didn't, but he soon put me right. 'If you want to fight, it's in the ring only, so three o'clock in the gym or you're on report.'

I didn't know it at the time but this was a regular Saturday afternoon event, the official way fights were settled — boxing matches in the main hall and everybody would be there to watch. So that's what happened. At about four, we're in the ring; plimsolls, shorts and gloved up. Referee as well. Professional stuff.

As we touched gloves I whispered to Jock, 'How's your maraccas?' That got his temper up, so he wasn't thinking. Me, I'm as cool as a cucumber. The first round knocked the temper out of him, and the second spilled enough of his claret for them to stop the fight. His nose was bleeding and his lip was cut and all the other kids were cheering. Even the teachers were clapping.

Once we'd been cleaned up, we both had to go to the main desk to get our prize, which was an apple or an orange — the winner had first choice. I chose the orange, and didn't it taste sweet! Now *I'm* the Daddy.

Did the Jock get his revenge by creeping up on me in the dark with half a brick? No, he didn't. Like all kids everywhere, once the fight was out of the way we became the best of pals.

The pair of us got into a bit of trouble one day and we were due for a right bollocking, so I said: 'Fuck this ... let's have it away.' I'd been there for about three months so I knew the layout and the ropes, so getting out was easy as pie. Straight after roll-call we just walked out. Remember, Stamford House wasn't a prison, so there were no bars or barbed wire, nothing. It was about eight o'clock on a summer's evening, and still light, but we'd got no money and we're miles away from the East End. We didn't even know where we were heading. Perhaps in my mind I was taking Jock to Nan.

Dusk fell and we were still walking. Hours later dawn was breaking, and by this time we were limping down Old Street. Not suspicious, are we? Both in grey uniforms wandering about at half-four in the morning. Then one of life's little coincidences popped its head up. We were just passing Old Street nick, about 20 minutes from home, when down the steps walked the copper who had nicked me for the bayonet in the first place.

He looked at us and we looked at him. I had blisters up to my arse and we were both absolutely knackered — it was a waste of time even thinking about running away. So, like a pair of lambs, we followed him back into the nick. The coppers were as good as gold. They gave us a cup of tea and a couple of smokes each, even though I was under age. Then they phoned Stamford House to pick us up.

That little trip out cost us both six of the best, two on each hand and two on the backside, as well as loss of privileges, which meant no telly and no cinema in the main hall on Fridays. It didn't do our reputation any harm though, because all the other kids treated us like gangsters.

A month after that incident I got my allocation through for approved school proper. So I'm on the move again, this time to Redhill, further north. It didn't make a lot of difference really, it was Stamford House all over again. What did help was that my reputation had preceded me through kids who had been shipped out earlier, so I was halfway to being the Guv'nor without raising a fist.

In all I did 18 months. I was 15 — not a kid any more. I'd grown a few inches and the stodgy grub had filled me out. So when I was released, I felt ready for the world.

When I got back home to Hoxton I felt strange and awkward. Everybody made a fuss of me, except Jim Irwin, of course. The best welcome home he could manage was, 'Hope you've learnt your lesson.' Mum said, 'Please don't start again, Jim,' and he just pointed and said, 'He's the troublemaker,' as though I'd asked for all the beltings I'd had over the years. Still, he didn't raise his hands, so I thought that perhaps I'd grown too big for him. That was naïve. I might have been a handful for kids about my own age, but I was no threat to a man over 6ft and weighing in at 20 stone.

But, for the time being, things were quiet. I'd reached school-leaving age while I was away so it was time to get a job. It wasn't my idea, but Mum was old fashioned like that. After about a fortnight, she got me fixed up with a job in the print. A friend of hers had a husband working in the same print works, a handy person to know really, because the print has always been a bit of a closed shop.

The Saturday before I started work Mum dragged me down to Burtons the tailors and got me suited up; two-piece, latest colour (royal blue), and it set her back 18 guineas, and that was a week's wages for a working bloke then. She should have saved her money, because the job didn't last 18 days. Come to that, it didn't even last a week.

I had never been so bored in all my life. I was supposed to be learning indexing and how to put books and papers together, but as reading wasn't my strongest point it was a bit of a struggle to say the least — especially as the going rate was only £2 10s a week.

Well, I messed everything up. I know I wasn't trying too hard, but everything I touched got itself in a muddle somehow, and I was getting some grief from the manager. We hadn't started off on the right foot because on the first day he said, all snooty, 'I've marked your card, McLean. I know you've been in jail.' Cheeky git. By Thursday I'd had enough, so when I saw this manager going to the bog, I crept up and tied the door handle to a pipe, so he couldn't get out.

He banged, he hollered and he swore, and I dared any of the others to let him out. After a bit, one of the office girls came down and undid the rope, and he came out like a greyhound from a trap. His face was bright red and he was sweating like a pig. 'Right, who did it?' he shouted. Nobody grassed me up, but eight pairs of eyes all swivelled in my direction. 'Get your cards, McLean, and don't expect any wages.'

'Stick 'em up your arse,' I shouted back, 'and yer poxy two and a half quid.' I felt like smacking him, but I wasn't that daft. I was still on licence from approved school. Fuck his money, I was well covered. Three mornings running I'd passed what they call quires of papers over the wall to Tony, and he'd delivered it to a local fence by the name of Tommy. He's dead now, poor old sod, so Old Bill can't touch him.

I'd got my eye on a nice load of lead as well. In those days, they printed books and manuscripts using lead letters and numbers, then afterwards they scrapped them. This scrap was all piled in a lean-to near the fence, saying, 'Lenny, take me home.' I'd be back. I told Mum I'd been victimised because I'd been inside, and she swallowed it. Sorry I lied to you, Mum, but it saved a lot of aggravation at the time.

She was going to send the suit back but I said I'd get some bits and pieces of work and stand the five bob a week myself. As it turned out, the lead we got a few weeks later easily covered the bill. How could anybody be expected to work all week for peanuts, when you could nick twenty times as much in a fraction of the time?

Tony and I became really busy; we were a good team, and getting a bit too big for creeping which was a pity because it was a good earner. Still, as usual, Tony came up with some good ideas for grafting a few quid. There was a little place down a back street off Commercial Road. Tony's mate, who had a Saturday job with one of the big shops in the main road, said it was extra storage space for the shop and was stacked up with electrical goods. There wasn't a bit of security. No lights, no alarms, nothing. We said, 'Lovely, we'll have some of that.' This wasn't a game we'd tried before, but if we could rob a few quid out of it, we were game for a laugh.

We arrived there at about nine at night. If you go too early there are mugs all over the streets. If it's too late, Old Bill's got their eyes peeled for anything that moves. So nine's about right, and I'm dying to know why old clever bollocks has brought a big tin of syrup and a roll of brown paper.

So we were down the alley and over the wall. It was dark but not so dark that we can't see what we're doing. The back door was covered in sheet metal but the windows weren't meshed up or anything. Tony messed about with the paper, holding it up to one of the windows then tearing bits off.

'Get the lid off that tin,' he said to me. So I whipped it open and passed it over.

He poured the syrup over the paper then spread it out with a bit of old wood. Next minute, he stuck the whole lot on the glass, picked up a bit of metal and banged it straight in the middle of the window and the whole lot just dropped down in a sticky puddle. Never made a sound. Tony picked a few bit of glass out of the edge of the frame and we were in. Yeah, we had gloves on. Didn't watch Z-Cars for nothing.

It was like Aladdin's cave inside; boxes everywhere, washing machines, TVs, even cookers. Every time I flicked my lighter I saw on another piece of expensive gear. The problem was, how were we going to shift it? We could hardly walk down Commercial Road with a fridge under our coats.

'Grab the small stuff,' Tony whispered, 'then we'll worry about it outside.' So I balanced a load of toasters in my arms and stacked them by the window. And while I was doing it I thought, 'We could get five years for this and all for two bob.'

Anyway, I jumped over the wall in the alley and Tony started passing over the little boxes, when a voice said, 'What's going down, boys?' I nearly jumped out of my strides. I whipped round and a torch blinded me. The same voice said, 'Lenny McLean, I might've fucking known.'

I said, 'Put the light out, you mug, or I'll do you.' Do him? I couldn't even see who it was.

Tony kept dead quiet on the other side of the wall. The next minute, I heard the click of a latch and this old geezer's coming out of the place over the alley. He clocked the little pile of toasters at my feet and gave a chuckle. 'In the big stuff now, eh, boy?'

I said, 'Yeah, I've just nicked a warehouseful, and what's it to you?' He said, 'Nothing, boy, nothing, but when me and your dad, your real dad that is, was doing a bit of business, we sussed moving the gear before we nicked it.'

Thank fuck for that. He was a mate of my dad's.

'I'll tell you something else, you ain't nicked a warehouseful. All you can get away is about a dozen of them,' and he kicked one of the boxes. 'Tell you what, I'll get you a bit of help and we'll cut it up. All right?'

So that's what happened. Tony and I kept our heads down while Old Jackie Taylor did the business. Ten minutes later, a Commer van backed up the alley, and we loaded it up with whatever was small enough to come out of the broken window. We couldn't get the door open.

The two blokes with the van couldn't have had a nerve in them because they broke into song every now and then. They didn't have a lot to say for themselves but the way they moved soon told me this wasn't their first caper. It wasn't their last, either, because in '72 or '73 I heard they both got an 18, but that was in a bigger league than our little job.

A week later, we picked up £200 each off of old Jackie. It had crossed my mind that we might have got stitched up, but I should've known better. If the old bloke was a mate of Dad's, he had to be sound. Thinking about it afterwards, I could see that Tony and I had been right prats. We went tearing in without giving it too much thought. All right, it was sweet as a nut but that wasn't down to us. Still, it was a bit of experience. We'd know better next time.

I was about 16 then and I thought I was the dog's bollocks. I suppose you could say I was running a bit wild. I could handle myself if I had to, there was plenty of dough about, and I had some good pals to waste the days and nights away with.

I tried a few jobs here and there, to keep Mum happy more than anything else, and to keep my stepfather off my back, but none of them ever worked out. Same old thing every time. I couldn't stand being told what to do. I'd had enough of that all my life, so if the boss or foreman came on strong, I'd fly off the handle. I never actually put one on any of these people, because I was young enough to still have a little bit of respect for people who were, as far as I could see, older and a lot weaker than me. When you're that age anybody over 30 has got one foot in the grave.

Because I was getting to be a big lad for my age and, as I said, could handle myself, I was growing more and more confident. The trouble was confidence, in my case, having been beaten down for so many years, meant aggression. And I really think it was then that my personality took on that 'time bomb waiting to go off' that people mention when they talk about Lenny McLean.

I've got to say I gave myself a bit of variety, what with all the different jobs I tried: driver's mate on the brewery wagons; humping stuff around on building sites; and I even had a spell of being a plumber's mate. You'll notice only the work was different — the amount of brain needed was the same wherever I went. Don't get me wrong though, I wasn't stupid. If I'd been born in St John's Wood or Knightsbridge, I think I could have gone places, but to be honest I don't think I can say I was a victim of circumstances like you read about in the papers. The truth is, I didn't give a fuck. So I gave up pretending to live a normal working life and, after a while, Mum seemed to accept that's how things were. She didn't condone what I was doing, she just never mentioned it. I've said it before — she was a great one for blanking anything she didn't want to see or hear about.

Most of my time I spent with the chaps, and only went home to sleep; generally I didn't even do that. And though I knew she didn't want it that way, it made things easier for Mum, because although Jim Irwin still picked on my brothers and sisters, it was mostly when I was around that there were terrible fights. Years later, when it was too late, I wished I'd spent more time with my mum while I had the chance. But with my life stretching out in front of me, I thought she'd be there for ever.

Tony and me used to spend a lot of our time down Hoxton Market, having a crack with whoever was down there, chatting up the girls, or sitting in the café talking about birds, boxing or what we'd get up to next to bring in a few quid.

We'd just had a knock back on what should have been a nice little earner. Always looking for that bit extra, we had by-passed Tommy the Talker and took our latest bit of thieving to a fence we hadn't used before. We're talking good money here. Gold bracelets, chains, earrings and stuff like that. We'd gone back the same night to pick up our wages, and suddenly he's forgotten who we are. He's got a minder with him so he thinks he's Jack the Lad. 'Go on, boys, fuck off, I'm a busy man, I haven't got time to play games.' I'm nearly 16 and this prat thinks he's dealing with a little kid. I went towards him and the minder cut in front of me. So I belted him as hard as I could on the point of the chin and he went down like a sack of spuds. I got hold of the other bloke and screamed at him, 'Are we getting our money or are you having some of this?' and I've got my fist stuck under his nose. Needless to say, Tony and me came out of there with a nice bit of dough. Working it out afterwards, I think we got a bit more than we were due. Lesson learned that day — stick with your own.

It didn't take long to blow the money from that little job, so after a bit we were sitting in the café again, both well skint. 'See that geezer over there,' Tony said, 'the one with the glasses?'

'Yeah, so what?'

'He manages a shoe shop ... let's give him a tug.'

Our plan was to get a bit friendly, then go round the shop with him and try to nick a few pairs of shoes.

We plonked down beside him and he said, 'You're Lenny McLean, aren't you?' I gave him a look and said, 'Yeah, and this is my cousin Tony — how's business?'

'Don't ask lads, don't ask, it's right down the pan.' Then he started to whisper, 'I know you two all right, but keep it to yourselves ... I've dropped myself in the shit.'

I said, 'If it's money trouble, why don't you dip in the till?' He just gave a sick laugh.

'Already done it. I cleaned the till out yesterday and thought I could double it and I've just done the same this morning. All down the pan.'

Turns out he likes a bit of a gamble — horses, dogs, flies crawling up walls, it didn't matter as long as he could get some odds on it. Tony and I had a bit of a chat between ourselves, then I said to the shoe bloke, 'How's your bottle?'

He said, 'If I can get this sorted, sound as a pound.'

'Right then,' I said, 'when do you bank your takings?'

'Friday at two o'clock.'

'OK, where do you bank them?'

He told me.

'Lovely. On Friday, take what you've got down the bank and it'd better not be an empty bag. We'll jump out of that alley down by the corner, grab the takings, and have it away. Then you can tell Old Bill and your head bloke that it was all in the bag, When it's quietened down, we'll cut it up.'

He said, 'Lovely, boys, don't let me down.'

'And don't you fucking let us down,' I said, 'because we don't let anybody rump us and get away with it.'

We popped in the shop the next morning, got him to one side, and said, 'If we've got a bit of running to do we'll need a decent pair of baseball boots apiece.' He looked a bit cross-eyed, but we got them. We were taking the piss, really.

Come Friday, Tony and I were all geed up and fidgety waiting up this alley. Two o'clock, half two, ten to three, bloody bank shuts in ten minutes. We're just thinking he's blown us out when we see this prat sailing right past us. I had to stick my head out and shout, 'Oi, back here.'

Back he came. He didn't have his glasses on because he knew what was coming, but he didn't know how hard it was going to be. To make it look right I gave him a good belt on the forehead, and he went down without seeing it coming. He was spark out, so Tony grabbed the bag and we legged it. We ran like a couple of greyhounds, ducking this way and that, and didn't stop until we got to the canal. We just lay there for a bit getting our breath back.

I know I said we grabbed a bag, well, it wasn't. It was one of those security briefcases, and the arsehole had locked it. We jumped on it, battered it with a brick and even tried to cut it, but that bastard stayed shut. In the end, we took it over to Tommy and he keyed it open. The man was a pro. When it was open he didn't try to look inside, he just handed it over. I pulled two tenners out, said, 'Thanks, Tom, you're a pal,' and we took off. When we counted up there was £410 and some silver so, with Tommy's drink, not counting the kites we threw away, we'd lifted £430 plus. Good stuff. Later on, we sent a girl we knew round to the manager with a little packet because we couldn't go near him. He was happy, we were happy. Good result.

It was only natural at that age to want to impress a few of our mates. Let them all see that Tony and I were a couple of Jack the Lads and a bit tasty when it came to pulling a few clever strokes. The next thing we knew, the word's down the earhole of a local bloke by the name of Joey Norton. No, he didn't go to the law. He turned up at the shoe shop and told the manager that he knows the robbery was a set-up. He knows the two McLeans were involved and if he didn't give him the keys so that he could go in that night and clear the place out, he'd put us all in the frame.

What's the manager going to do? He's a straight bloke. I know he did the business with us but he was in trouble. Basically, he was a straight. Nice little house, wife, two kids, two weeks in Skegness every year — you know what I mean. So his arsehole drops out. That piece of shit Norton gets all pally then. 'What I'll do is clear the shop, but when I'm going out I'll smash the door and everyone will think it's a break in.'

He gets the keys, does the business, then carefully locks up after him. Now Old Bill's not always stupid so this time they've got the manager banged up and they're giving him the old rubber truncheon before his kids have gone to school next morning. It's all over and we're in Old Street nick by dinner time.

A month later, we're up at the sessions and poor old Mum's got to face it all over again. This time she's with my grandmother, Nanny McLean, who raised Tony from when he was a little kid. My uncle Bob was there as well — a lovely man you could depend on when you were in trouble. Uncle Bob, Bobby Warren, wasn't a stranger himself to being up in court. He was a quiet man who never took liberties with his own, but back in the Fifties he'd got a seven, along with Frankie Fraser, for doing Jack Spot. At the time, Uncle Bob worked for and was a good friend of Albert Dimes, who controlled most of Soho. Jack Comer, or Spot as he was usually known, was one of the top five gang bosses at that time. Him and Dimes were always at each other for one reason or another. Then they had this knife fight on the corner of Frith Street, Soho, and both of them ended up in hospital. It was a messy business with this one doing that one, then somebody else would get some, so it wasn't just the fight that got Spotty the slashing.

Norton the grass was up in court as well, but he never lifted his head up. He couldn't look at me or Tony, and there was no way he was going to catch Uncle Bob's eye.

The manager, because he wore a shirt and tie, got a fine. Norton got 18 months' prison, and we got Borstal, which meant being bussed straight off to the Scrubs.

CHAPTER THREE

Unlike before when I was green and the separation from my family was a terrible shock to the system, I surprised myself at how I accepted the situation. Over the last few years, I'd had words with a number of lads who'd spent a bit of time in Wormwood Scrubs, so I wasn't completely in the dark about what to expect. I was even ready for the 'bend and spread' routine once you've been through reception, when a screw checks your khyber in case you've got a gun or a razor tucked up there.

First, you're classed as a YP (young prisoner) if you're under 21. If it's your first time in prison, they class you as a star prisoner and that separates you from the ones who have been inside before. Those in charge reckoned that anybody who had been inside before was beyond help or hope, so we weren't allowed to talk to them, or them to us, in case they corrupted us stars. Apart from that little difference, the screws treated us all the same.

When they banged us up that night I found I was about six cells along from Tony. There were two to a cell, and I was sharing mine with this thick country boy. When this swede wasn't farting he was snoring. In the end, I woke him up, got him by the throat and told him, 'If you don't shut your fucking row I'm going to do it for you.' He never made a sound for the rest of the night! I found out next day he hadn't slept a wink.

Before we got locked in the following day, I nipped into Tony's cell. I said to him, 'When your cell mate comes up tell him to get his gear together and piss off up to my gaff because I'm moving in with you. Tell him I'll see him all right if he keeps his mouth shut.'

Nobody said anything and it was great for about a week, then one night when we're locked up, one of the screws comes looking for the kid who should've been in with Tony. He'd read the name card on the door, opened up, and was bawling out a name that wasn't McLean. Panic stations. All of us, kids included, were quick-marched up to the Governor's office, where we got a right bollocking and three days' bread and water each. Give the kid his due, it wasn't his fault, but he took it on the chin. I give him ten out of ten for that. Good stuff.

Unlike Stamford House, this place had a lot of hard cases. Half of them were after your food, money or fags and the other half were simply interested in belting any of the kids for a bit of fun. So I had to fight. Not only for myself, but for Tony as well. I classed him as a brother more than a cousin and I'd looked after and protected him since we were kids. Knowing I was always behind him, he used to take a few liberties with all the other blokes. He knew none of them could dig him out because they were all frightened I'd belt them.

When I was number one in the kitchens dishing all the grub out, everybody had to be in full kit and all lined up neat or they couldn't be served. Not Tony. He'd come waltzing in about seven, still in his slippers and dressing-gown, march past all the others, and sail up to the top of the queue and pick up his breakfast. They would all go crazy, muttering and giving him the eye, but they'd be looking at me at the same time. I used to say to him, 'If I get discharged before you do, this lot are going to kill you.' He'd just give that grin of his and say, 'I know that, Lenny. That's why I'll make sure I'm right behind you when you go out the gate.'

He was a live wire and just a funny, funny kid, not a fighter. But, for me, Borstal meant fighting, and being stuck in the chokey. Come out after two days, fight again, more chokey. I was up and down like a bride's nightie until we were ghosted off to the seaside to Hollesley Bay Borstal on the Suffolk coast. It was miles from anywhere and, as we got nearer, I was thinking that there was no chance of me walking home from this place. Still, it was a great improvement on the Scrubs, and more like Stamford House. We weren't in cells any more and things were much more free and easy, and having Tony as a pal made life seem a bit more like home.

What wasn't so cosy was the fact that we had to work, and I do mean work. The Borstal wasn't just a nick, it was a working farm, so they could make bloody fortunes out of us.

We were up at six and straight into the showers. Once your towel was off you made sure you kept a tight grip on your soap, which you had to buy out of your own wages if it was a decent bit of gear. You had to keep looking over your shoulder as well because if somebody had a grievance that was when they timed their move, when you were vulnerable. After your shower, it was a quick breakfast before lining up to march out to wherever you had been allocated.

My first work party was out in the fields digging carrots. It was freezing cold and the ground was like iron. Your hands were so cold you didn't notice the blisters until night time, when you suffered agonies. One morning I said to a screw, "Ere, guv'nor, if you got yourself a machine you could dig the whole field in half an hour.' He gave me that look straight out of the screw's handbook, squinty eyes looking round each side of the peak on his cap. 'McLean,' he said 'You are a fucking machine ... keep digging.'

I'm sure they had it in for me. I think they all used to get together in the screws' tearoom and work out what shitty job to give me the next day. Then they came up with a blinder.

'Fore party tomorrow, McLean,' I was told. 'Lovely,' I thought, 'better than digging carrots.' I soon found out that fore party meant working with the pigs — and our little set-up was proud to own about 1,500.

They were all in their own little cubicles and all you could see for miles was great pink backsides. The nearest I'd ever come to a pig in my life were the trotters Nan Campion used to boil up for Saturday supper. Now, all of a sudden, I've got acres of them making me dizzy just looking at them.

I soon learned that a pig has two important bits. The front end, which you stick food in, and the back end that pours out twice as much as you put in the front. The front end also had a nasty habit of snapping at you if you got within range. Most of the time that wasn't a problem because guess which end McLean was in charge of. Dead right. I didn't only shovel shit all day, barrowing it for about two miles to the pit, but I also dreamt about shovelling it at night. So my days and nights became a nightmare. I was actually pleased when one of them took a bite out of my leg and I was allowed to stay home for a week. Funny how you settle in. We used to refer to the unit as home when we were cold and tired. How do these farmers do it? They must be mad. Where there's muck ...

While my leg was healing, they put me in the library. Nothing clever, just moving books around and bits and pieces. I'm just thinking this will do me until I've done my time, when they must have had another meeting and, bang, I'm out in the potato shed. This time, Tony is with me. Up until then he'd been on a nice cushy number on a shoe-making course. I told him I reckoned he'd pulled a stroke somewhere down the line to get that job and he laughed and gave me a wink.

Sometimes we'd be picking potatoes, other times we were in this big shed grading them into different sizes. It was hard, but having Tony there made it a lot easier, because things are never as bad when you can have a laugh. At one end of the shed there was a big opening in the wall about six foot up, so when nobody was about, Tony dragged some crates over and climbed up to see what was on the other side.

He burst out laughing and shouted down: "'Ere, Lenny, there's two horses next door having a shag.' I thought, 'This I've got to see,' but by the time I got up it was all over and the male one was standing there, blowing clouds of steam out of his nose. We both stared. The horse had an old bill about five foot long and it was practically touching the floor. 'How would you like one like that, Lenny?' Tony said. I shoved him off the crate and told him, 'I have!'

He climbed back up again and pulled out the front of his jersey, filling it up with the biggest spuds he could lay his hands on. I hope the RSPCA don't read this, but then he lobbed these taters at the horse's dangling old chap. Every spud he lobbed was missing by a mile, then, lucky shot, one of them caught that poor horse right on its bell-end. It went mad. It jumped up in the air, all its legs went stiff and it screamed like a woman with a mouse up her drawers. It reared up and ran round on its back legs, then started battering the walls with its feet. Lumps of boards flew everywhere, and the whole place shook. The only reason it didn't bust its way out was because all the screws came running to see what the racket was about. They quietened the horse down and nicked us. There was no point in denying what we'd done, it was pretty bloody obvious. That bit of a giggle earned us one month's loss of pay and loss of all privileges, but we didn't lose any remission, so it could have been worse.

Another laugh we had was over soap. Tony didn't smoke, so he'd save up his wages and buy the best Palmolive soap, the one that lathers up and smells a bit tasty. Me, I'd rather have a smoke so I made do with White Windsor.

Because he was in the boot room and I was on the land, I used to finish about half an hour earlier, so I'd rush back and have a nice bath or shower and use his Palmolive.

One night I was laying on my bed, having just had a bath and smelling like a poof. In came Tony and he said, 'Len, every night I go to have a shower my soap's shrunk by about half an inch.'

I said, 'It'll soon match the size of your dick, then.'

'No, Len,' he said, 'I'm serious. You're using my soap, aren't you?'

I kept a straight face and just kept denying it. A few days later, I was having a rest after my bath and Tony came in with a few others and they were all laughing. 'Enjoy your bath, Len?' asked Tony.

'Yes, thanks, what's the fucking joke?' I said.

'I'll tell you. I know you've been at my soap, so every night I've been soaking it in the piss pot. Didn't you notice it had gone yellow?'

Dirty bastard. I chased him all over the place threatening to punch his head in, but I wasn't too serious. I could take a joke against myself.

In order for me to get out and about, I put my hand up and volunteered to join the Army cadets while I was inside. I suppose they thought we'd straighten ourselves out and then afterwards we'd join the Army full time. No chance. It did make a break, though, and I used to get a buzz from marching through the town on Sundays. One eye ahead, the other swivelling round looking for crumpet. It didn't last long, like most things I had a go at. They kicked me out when I had a set-to with some lads who were taking the piss while we were marching. So I joined the gymnastics classes, where Tony was, and in no time I'd taken up the con's favourite hobby, weight-lifting and training, and I took to it like a duck to water. So what with my temper and the toned-up muscles, I was even more of a handful than ever before.

As you gradually serve your time, they move you to different blocks and houses. They're all named after saints, so somebody had a sense of humour. We started in George House, then Patrick and finished up in Andrew, where me and Tony palled up with a very likeable kid called David Fraser. Dave was one of your own, out of a good London family, and the three of us stuck together. Like Tony he was a right comedian, always ready to get up to something for a laugh.

David had about three days to go before he was due to be released. Tony and I had about seven weeks. We were all in the television room once and we'd just watched *Dr Who* or *The Monkees* or something, when the news came on. The first thing up on the screen was an update on what the papers were calling 'The Richardson Torture Trials'. This trial had been going on for about six or seven weeks, and now it was all over. I can remember the exact date because it was 4 April 1967, five days before my eighteenth birthday.

It all went quiet as this face on the telly said Charles Richardson, 25 years, Edward Richardson, 10 years, and Francis Fraser and two others, 10 years each.

I looked over at David and he'd gone dead white and was biting his lip. Then he spotted some stupid slag smirking all over his mug. Dave picked up a chair and he was going to do the prat, but we all grabbed hold of him and told him to leave it out or he wouldn't be going home. He was so wild we had to sit on him until he calmed down. He screamed, 'I've got to do him. That's my dad going down and that c**t thinks it's funny.'

I said, 'Don't worry, we'll iron him later.'

The bloke who laughed had only been with us for about a week, and he didn't know who David was, and he certainly didn't know who I was, but he found out. He was a big bastard but he cried when we caught up with him and said he hadn't meant any harm. We did him anyway. Ten years is nothing to make a joke about. I told Dave to keep quiet if there was any trouble or he'd lose his remission. If it came to it, I'd put my hand up and swear I was on my own.

But there was no comeback. The mug might have said he had fallen downstairs, I don't know. David was well pleased and on the day he went home he had four ounces of Old Holborn brought in for me. I haven't seen him since that day, but I've heard about him over the years. From what I hear, he's done his fair share behind the door. The last time was in 1984 when he was handed out a 14 for holding up the director of an airline company, with his family, in Hyde Park Gardens. So, with a bit of luck and if he's kept his nose clean, he should be getting on with his life outside by now.

Which was what Tony and I were looking forward to back in 1967. When you go away, it's not just your freedom that's put on hold, but your life and your mind. The outside world becomes sort of distant and blurry. You think about home, your family, friends and what you might be doing if you weren't away from them all. But it's more a dream than reality.

I'd seen more of Mum and some of the others when I was in the Scrubs, but with Hollesley being nearly 100 miles from London, just the travelling could take all day and it cost a bomb. I always looked forward to visiting days, but when they came round I couldn't wait for them to be over. Suddenly, there was nothing to talk about.

Now that it was time for the release I'd thought about for the past 20 months, I started to get nervous. What struck me was the anti-climax of it all. When you're sent down there's a right fuss. Police, courts, no time to yourself, rushed here, rushed there and watched all the time. Come your release day, they quietly open the door and shove you out. Well, not quite. A couple of the screws did have the decency to drop us off at Ipswich Station, but that was all. No brass band, nobody out front waving us goodbye. Just a quick 'Bugger off and don't come back.'

As we left Ipswich well behind and the train roared towards

London, I looked out at the woods, little streams and green fields, and I thought, 'Stuff the countryside — we're on our way back to the East End.'

You would have thought that once I was back in London I couldn't wait to get home. But it wasn't like that. We pulled in at around six o'clock, I said ta-ra to Tony, then I just wandered about for a bit. I'd forgotten the smell of the place. Not a nasty smell, in fact it probably wasn't a smell at all, but as I breathed in I was sucking in the feel of crumbly houses, people and everything that was part of where I belonged.

Wandering through the market where they were all packing up, it was as though I'd never been away. 'How you doing, Len?' 'Where you bin lately, Lenny?' ''Ere, cop this bag of apples, mate.' I don't remember if I let on or not. A lot of them must have thought I was on something, but I wasn't, I was just drugged up on freedom and being home.

Not long after, I'm at my house and there's Mum. She just stood there looking at me like I was a ghost, screwing her hands in the pinny she was wearing. For a second, it was like we were strangers, then I grabbed hold of her and cuddled her to death. She's crying and she's laughing, both at the same time. I gave a couple of twirls, still cuddling her, and danced us both up the passage until she was screaming like a young girl. I hadn't realised just how much I had missed her.

Young girl she wasn't, though. When she was making a cup of tea I looked at her and saw this little old woman. She was 38. Her face was lined, she was thin, and that lovely blonde hair was slowly turning grey. What had we done to this woman who had never had a bad thought in her life, or done anybody any harm? I wanted to blame Jim Irwin, but I couldn't kid myself. A lot of the wrinkles and grey hair were down to me. So I gave her a cuddle and said, 'I'm sorry, Mum.'

I was well pleased to see Lorraine and Kruger and my little half-sister. Not that I ever thought of her as anything other than my real sister. She was six then and she followed me round and round the house showing me pictures she'd done, prattling about school, and telling me what her dad had been up to. I thought, 'Darling, you don't know half of what that bastard's been up to.' But I wouldn't have said that to a little baby.

Barry was gone and the house wasn't the same without him. At 17 he'd decided enough was enough and had emigrated to Australia. It broke his heart to leave us all behind, but Irwin made life so unbearable he couldn't take any more. He'd come down to the Borstal a few days before he went and the governor had allowed me an extended visit. He could be a hard man that governor, but give him his due, he was fair where it counted.

We had a good talk that day, Barry and me. A lot of it was about how Jim Irwin had screwed up all our lives. Then it was time to go. Because we were both men then and very conscious of not showing our real feelings, we just shook hands and said our goodbyes. Then as he left the hall I thought, 'Fuck it,' went after him and gave him a good cuddle. I didn't see him again for five years, and that was going to be a sadder time than this. He still lives in Australia, working in the water industry and doing well for himself.

Jim Irwin kept out of the way that day, so it was a nice sort of family get-together, though I think he was in the back of all our minds. Uncle Fred came round to see me and wished me all the best, and slipped a few quid into my hand as he was going. Smashing bloke, he wouldn't see me potless and it kept me going while I was looking round for some way to earn a few shillings.

I reckoned Irwin was up to something, because he didn't show up until a couple of days after I got back. It was about eleven in the morning, so there was only Mum and me there. He just walked in and stuck his arse in the armchair, not so much as a hello or kiss my bum. Not even to Mum. I thought, 'You ignorant pig, I'd like to smash you to bits.'

Nothing was said for ages until Mum went out of the front room. Then he looked up and said, 'You've got a big lad.' I said, 'Yeah,' and he leaned forward and said, 'Don't ever think you're big enough to take me on because if you do, what I start with my fists I'll finish with an iron bar.'

It was funny in a way, that I could swallow that sort of shit indoors, yet outside I could be a violent lunatic if I was challenged or mugged off. I wasn't frightened of Irwin any more, so it could only have been the love and respect that I had for my mum that stopped me from hurting him and I know I was capable of doing that. I just gave him some eye and walked out of the room. Now I know I'm definitely home.

I put Irwin out of my head and I soon got back into the swing of life again.

CHAPTER FOUR

I'd never been a drinker, and where I'd been for nearly two years at the age when most kids get a taste for a jar or two, the strongest drink you could get was lemonade. Still, I was a quick learner with anything that wasn't work, and in no time I was a regular piss-artist. What a mixture — my evil temper and alcohol. Now that I've got more sense I think drugs are a terrible thing. Anybody who takes them is a mug, and those bastards that deal them and make money out of kids are nothing better than slags. But, back then, we were all a bit naïve as far as drugs were concerned. There wasn't the publicity about how bad they were. They were just a bit of a laugh. So we'd all take what they called 'purple hearts' then and, when we were buzzing, go round all the clubs in the West End — the Tiles, the Flamingo, Twenties, anywhere we could get a drink — pull a few birds and have a good time. We never went out looking for trouble, but being five likely lads we seemed to attract other groups who wanted to take a pop. At some of the clubs we never even got in the door. Flying high or out of our brains with drink meant we weren't ideal customers. The doorman would pull a face and ask us to go elsewhere. We'd give him a bit of verbal, out would come the bouncers, chucking their weight about, and it would all end in a right tear-up.

For our spending money and a bit of excitement we got into a bit of 'after-hours window shopping'. After we'd done our rounds of the clubs on a Saturday night, we'd jump in our motors (mine was a green Mini Cooper), and tour round the high-class shops in Oxford Street or Regent Street. When we found the right pitch we'd chuck a metal milk crate straight through the glass and cream the display. We had less than a minute to do the business. The alarm would be ringing and the police would be on their way, but we didn't give a fuck. Cashmere jumpers, fur jackets, suits, posh dresses, whatever we could rip off the dummies. One night, we couldn't get this tasty suit off the dummy quick enough, so we flung the whole thing in the motor and drove off with its legs hanging out of the window. It looked like a kidnapping.

Another time, a mate turned over a high-class store in the West End. We got a load of good gear out of the window, mostly suits and posh dresses. After we stashed the stuff, we arranged to meet young Barry who always got us good money without aggravation for anything we asked him to move. We cut him in on a percentage so he wasn't doing us any favours. Barry got there first, then I turned up but my mate didn't show. After about two hours sitting there waiting, Barry said to me, 'That prat ain't going to show, so why don't I flog the stuff and we'll cut it up between us two?'

'What did you say?' I said.

'We'll cut up the money and fuck him.'

'No,' I said, 'fuck you,' and I belted him straight in the mouth, breaking his jaw. That's all he got out of the job because me and my mate shared the split. What a slag, he'd rob his own.

Nicking the stuff was the easy part, but we didn't see any dough until it was flogged off. That Barry could piss off as far as I was concerned, so anything tasty we had was passed on to Tommy the Talker. We were quite busy and shifting a fair bit of gear, so if Tom ever got a bit loaded up we would slip round Hoxton or Roman market and do a few deals for ourselves. We were making good money and spending it like water, so come the weekend we'd start grafting all over again.

Back in 1968, the clubs didn't turn out until about four or half-past, so by the time we'd done some work and tucked away the night's takings in a little lock-up we used as a slaughter, it was well into the next day.

This particular Sunday, it seemed like I'd only just closed my eyes, when I got such a bang on the head I thought the ceiling had come in on me. It hadn't, it was Jim Irwin and he was shouting, 'Three o'clock, you lazy bastard, and still in your pit. This ain't a fucking hotel,' and he was bringing his fist up to give me some more.

I've bashed up half the bouncers in the West End and this bastard's whacking me like I'm six years old. I chucked the covers back, shot out of bed just in my Y-fronts and I'm like a fucking madman. The look on his face, in that second before I smashed it, will stay with me until the day I die. It was like traffic lights changing. Anger, surprise and, I'd like to think, fear. He fell backwards against the door and I swung another to his head but before it connected he slumped to the floor and I split the door panel instead.

If the bedroom hadn't been so cramped and I'd had more room to move I would definitely have seriously harmed him. As it was, Mum had heard the commotion, run up the stairs and pushed her way in. Irwin came to when she touched his face. I think for a second she thought I'd killed him. But he shoved her out the way, got up and staggered out holding his mouth. Mum put her arm round my shoulder. She didn't say anything, just gave me a squeeze to calm me down. I was still shaking with rage. I wanted to finish him off.

I said, 'Mum, that is the last time he ever lays hands on me or you or any of the others, because I'm ready and I'll fucking kill him.'

She said, 'Len, I don't blame you for hitting him, he's had it coming, but please, son, for my sake, don't hurt him any more.'

What could I do? That slag had battered me since I was five. I had given him a bit of a slap and the woman I respect more than life itself was asking me to leave him out. No contest.

But after I got dressed I went downstairs and into the kitchen where he was dabbing his nose with a flannel. He looked up and said, 'You made a big mistake just now, boy.'

'No, you c**t, you made the mistake,' I replied, 'and if I didn't love that woman through there so much I'd be biting your face off right now.'

He just said, 'Fuck you,' and pushed past me. I wish I could say that I battered him until he screamed for mercy and swore he was sorry for what he'd done, but that's just for films. Real life is never so black and white.

I liked to imagine that after our little disagreement Jim Irwin was nervous of being around me. When I was indoors he was out. When I was out, back in he'd go. It might have been coincidence. I felt sorry for Mum stuck in the middle. All of us kids hated the very sight of him, but what did we know of adult relationships? There had to be some sort of spark between them because with three of us bringing in some money she didn't need to depend on his charity. At about that time, he started working up north, in the rag trade, having got himself into the business of making bed-quilts in a little factory. He was away for most of the week, so I started to suspect that he was test-driving the quilts with the bird he was in partnership with but I wouldn't upset Mum by saying so.

Time crept on and the lads and I were getting older and wiser. We started going our separate ways, mixing with different people and giving up what we had begun to see were juvenile pranks. Most of our stunts were good capers, but we were at an age when we could be looking at serious bird for what was really schoolboy mucking about.

About then we all chose the various paths we were going to go down. Some decided that the straight road was the way to go. They'd had a good run so now was the time to settle down. Others took up some serious villainy on their own, or teamed up with some of the well established local firms. Me, I didn't make any decision one way or the other. I would take it as it came.

My reputation as a fighter was gradually spreading further and further. If a bit of aggression was needed for frighteners on a job, or a bit of business, my name would be put forward. People knew I wasn't just another thick-headed thug, but somebody who could be trusted to use his nut for thinking as well as breaking jaws. I never did favours, though. If they wanted me on the firm, I had to be well paid.

Life wasn't all about fighting and getting pissed up, though. I did have plans in other directions. Don't get the idea that because I'm always out with the lads and talking about me and the boys that I haven't got any time for girls. I'd had my share of birds, but what with the strained atmosphere at home and violence wherever we went, girlfriends didn't last too long. Then, one night, I was in the Standard in Kingsland Road having a drink and a talk with the governor's son, Sid. The door opened and in walked this little angel, and Lenny took a knockout.

She was a tiny little thing, about 17, blonde hair, beautiful face, and a tiny bum that would've fitted into one of my hands. I can even remember what she was wearing and I bet not many blokes could say that looking back nearly 30 years. She had a beige suit on, red shoes and a red handbag.

Sid and I both eyed this little dream up and down, and I said, 'You know what they say about girls who wear red shoes.'

He said, 'You mean red hats, don't you?'

I straightened my tie and said, 'Oh, bollocks, who cares? I'm going to give her a pull anyway.'

When the girlfriend she was with went out to the ladies' room, I slipped over and gave her a bit of the McLean charm. I said, 'What's your name, darling?' and she said, 'Valerie, and yours is Lenny McLean.' I was well chuffed that she knew me but I didn't let on, just gave her my film star look and said, 'Why don't you park your mate up and let me take you up West?' She gave me one of those looks that birds like to put on and told me, 'I couldn't do that, I couldn't leave her on her own and, anyway, I might be seeing my boyfriend in here later on.' I sussed she was giving me a story. I could see by the look in her eyes that she was more interested than she was letting on, so I just gave a shrug, dead casual, and said, 'Well, I'll be in here next Saturday, meet me then if you change your mind and I'll buy you a drink.'

I couldn't believe how I acted all the next week. I was like a lovesick kid, mooning about and counting the days until Saturday. There was no guarantee that she'd show, but it couldn't hurt to consider the possibilities.

Come Saturday, I was suited and booted and in the Standard at opening time. I never took my eyes off the door for the next hour. Then it opened and in she came, on her own, and even better looking than I'd remembered from a week ago. Her first words after the initial hello were, 'Are you going to behave yourself if I go out with you?' I pretended to be shocked. 'Don't worry, babe,' I said, 'I'll keep my hands in my pockets all night.'

She giggled at that. 'No, I don't mean that, but I've been hearing all about you. Everybody says you're always fighting.'

'Me, fighting, never. Just you tell me who said that and I'll belt them.' She giggled again and I knew I'd cracked it.

I took her to the Royal in Tottenham, and we had a great time. She said she would like me to take her out again and after I left her that night I went home clicking my heels together, well pleased. I told Mum all about this beautiful girl I'd met and I must have gone over the top a bit because she laughed and said, 'You're in love, son.'

'Don't be daft,' I said, 'that stuff ain't for me.' She just stood looking at me with a little smile on her face. Then we both burst out laughing. She was dead right. She'd spotted what I hadn't really thought about, but now that I did, I had to admit, yes, I was in love and it was a nice feeling.

I said, 'Mum, don't say nothing to Jim. You know him, he'll try and dig me out and I'll have to unload him.'

'I won't, son. But one night, when he's not around, bring Valerie home for tea, I'd like to meet her.'

Val and I went everywhere together, pictures, clubs and pubs, and day trips to Margate or Southend. I took her home to Mum and they got on like a house on fire, and, naturally, then Val's parents want to meet the fella who's taking up all their daughter's time. I suppose it must have been about two months after I met her that she said, 'My Dad suggested that as we are going to be very late home Saturday night, it would be all right if you stopped over, then they could meet you.'

So that's what I did. We had a really good night out and it was early Sunday morning before we got back to Val's house and we had to creep about a bit because her mum and dad were in bed. I got my head down in the spare room and fell asleep telling myself that I had to make a good impression on these people. Now I don't know what Val had said about me or how she had described the sort of bloke I was, but when I rolled downstairs next morning at about ten o'clock, the look on her parents' faces said that I wasn't quite what they'd expected.

What you've got to understand is that she came from a straight family — good people. Then out of the blue their little girl has brought home this big lump of a bloke, and he's sitting there eating toast, drinking tea and babbling on about life in Borstal. I was nervous, I suppose. I wanted to impress the parents of this lovely girl, and every time I opened my gob something stupid popped out. The room seemed to grow colder and colder, and if I wasn't so young, full of myself, and blind, I'd have noticed that Val's mum and dad were becoming less friendly and more po-faced with every word I said.

Val had disappeared by now. The strain was too much — she sat on the stairs listening, biting her fingernails and praying for me to shut up. After a bit she dived in, grabbed hold of me and dragged me out. I can't say her parents blew kisses from the door.

It was the first time she had taken me to meet her people and show me off and I had blown it. Anyway, she didn't want to go home for a while so we had a bit of a walk and ended up in the park. Being kids, all we'd done so far was have a good time and plenty of laughs, we hadn't really got round to sitting down and finding out about each other. So we sat and talked. It turned out she was one of the Smiths out of Bethnal Green, a really well known family which has been in the rag trade for years and years. Good people, good money-getters, and always have been. She told me her dad had died when he was only 23. Her mum had remarried, so, like me, she had a stepfather.

Because of my experiences, I jumped straight in. 'Bet your stepdad's a proper bastard.'

She looked vaguely puzzled. 'No, he's not, Len, he's a nice man, a proper dad.'

I felt stupid for opening my mouth.

'What made you say a horrible thing like that?' she said, so I told her about Jim Irwin. She could hardly believe what I was telling her, but, in time, she'd see for herself that I wasn't exaggerating.

After a little kiss and cuddle, Val told me I'd better not come round to the house for a bit. And so it didn't make things hard for her, I kept out of the way. It wasn't easy but I kept myself busy with a few little jobs. Weeks later, I bumped into her in the market and I arranged to take her to a party at the weekend. She said that she'd had a lot of stick indoors, but it had quietened down, so she didn't think going out with me again would be a problem.

We enjoyed the party and I took her home. I was just giving her a kiss on the doorstep, when the door opened and she was dragged back inside by her mum. One of her high heels broke off and she started to cry. I said, ''Ere, I've brought a Chinese supper for all of us.' Her mum just screamed out, 'Bugger off ... we don't want you round here.' 'Well fuck you, then,' I shouted, and slung two carrier bags of grub right at her. Then the old man stuck his head out of the front room and I yelled, 'Don't you start or I'll belt you.' I stepped back, picked up some flowerpots and smashed all the front windows.

In the meantime, somebody's called the police. I think it was the bloke who lived opposite, but I can't really blame whoever grassed me. Old Bill came mob-handed, but I'd cooled off by then, so I just put my hands up and quietly got in the van. Sitting in Old Street nick gave me a bit of time to consider the 12 months I'd get for assault and criminal damage. What a total arsehole I was. At 19 years old, I should have known better. But an hour later I was back out on the streets. Those ordinary, straight people had told Old Bill to forget it.

I'm not proud of what I did. I was right out of order. Now that I'm older I picked up those double standards I mentioned earlier. I've mixed with some rare people all my life. I have made good friends with people I met in Borstal and prison, and palled up with villains who have made headlines all over the world. But if some kid, like I used to be, turned up on my doorstep with his heart in his hand for my young daughter, I'd boot his arse down the road. If he came back, I'd fucking murder him.

So my lovely Val's parents didn't want to know me for a very long time, but she, bless her heart, loved me, and suffered earache from both sides so we could be together. It's strange how life repeats itself. She had to suffer like my mum — stuck in the middle. Still, whether they liked it or not, Val and I courted for about 12 or 14 months. I was 20, Val was 18, and when we decided to get married, Mum was well pleased. I suppose she thought it would settle me down.

I wish now that I'd given Val a proper wedding. You know, church, fancy clothes, posh do afterwards — it's a girl's dream, isn't it? But the best I could manage at the time was the business at Mare Street Registry Office over Hackney way, and a bit of a knees-up at Mum's place.

We found a place to live in George's Square, round the back of Old Street. We rented two rooms in a little terraced house. I don't know about rooms, they were more like cupboards, and they were in a right state. I couldn't decorate and I was no handy man, so I went to see Uncle Fred Campion. That diamond of a man spent weeks and a load of his own money on doing the place up, and all he took for wages was a kiss off Val. When he'd done, it was like a little doll's house, and there was just me and Val, and she was my whole world.

Bloody hell, we hadn't been tucked up in our little love nest for a week when she said, 'Len, I want you to get a proper job.'

I said, 'Doll, for you I'd fly to the moon.'

'Len, just go to work, that'll be enough.'

So I got myself fixed up in a clothes factory in Kirton Grove, not far from home. Money wasn't all that, but I soon gave myself extras. My job was to pack parcels of clothes, mail-order stuff, women's coats, dresses, jumpers, all kinds. Last thing at night, I'd have to load up the van and take them down the post office, but before I got there I'd made a little detour and off-load half of them at home. Val would unpack them again, burn the packaging and flog the clothes all over the place. Nice little fiddle.

As soon as complaints came in about people not getting what they'd ordered, Lenny was looking for another job. I couldn't believe it, I stepped straight into the same sort of number in another clothes place in north London. But this was even better. The boss was an absolute prat because he asked if I minded working at night on my own. Talk about sticking the cat in with the budgie, it was fucking magic. I didn't even have to hump the clothes around, just dropped them out of the window to my mate and he carted them away in his van. Job didn't last long, though — I can't think why — so I was back to ducking and diving for a bit.

CHAPTER FIVE

I mentioned my reputation as a fighter had spread beyond Hoxton. Well, I got a call one day from a guy in Woodford. He said, 'Lenny, I want you to do a favour for a pal of mine. His name's Dougie.'

'I don't do favours,' I said, 'but as long as I get well paid I'll go ahead and see him.'

It turned out that Dougie had just picked up a big council contract. There were loads of flats to be painted and decorated, which meant he had to employ a lot of men. What he wanted me for was to mind him in case any of the blokes decided to take a pop at him when he wouldn't pay them for, in his opinion, rough work.

It seemed fair enough at the time because I know that building workers can get a bit stroppy if things don't go their way. What I didn't realise was that Dougie was a right bastard. The reason he wanted me around was so that he could screw the painters out of wages they'd worked bloody hard for. These were family men grafting to feed their kids, and I didn't feel happy about my role. We'd go round the sites with the wages and Dougie would be telling different blokes, 'I'm not paying you for this ... not paying you for that.' They didn't like it, but they'd look at him, then look at me standing behind him, and just swallow it.

He started to get a bit flash because of me, so I'd already got the hump when he came up with the idea of teaching me the decorating game. He said, 'When you're not minding me you can be picking a trade up,' like he was doing me the biggest favour in the world.

On the Monday I was in a place in Mare Street. I was perched on top of a ladder with a four-gallon bucket of sugar soap wedged between my knees, and I was scrubbing the bollocks out of the ceiling with a sponge as big as a loaf of bread. This filthy black water was running down my arm, through my vest, twice round my niagaras and out the soles of my plimsolls. But I stuck at it. I didn't expect to be hanging flock wallpaper on my first day. Then Dougie showed up. 'Hold up, hold up,' he says, 'you've missed half of it.'

I said, 'Do what?'

'You've left big dirty patches all over.'

I've done no more, I've tipped the whole fucking bucket of dirty water right over him. I've come down the ladder like a monkey and belted him in the mouth. This idiot's hired me as a minder because I'm the toughest money can buy, and he's got me doing this shitty job as though I'm some sort of skivvy. I didn't do my nut, just gave him a quiet seeing to. I belted him senseless — not just for mouthing off, but for taking the piss out of me and all the other blokes.

I was beginning to think that work was nothing but aggravation. Val didn't give up, though. She knew that if I wasn't working, I was going to fall back on a bit of thieving, and then get myself nicked.

Anyway, I've got home at about half-eleven, black as Newgate's knocker. Val pulled a face so I dropped on my knees and gave her a couple of verses of *Mammy*, just like Al Jolson. It didn't work. She was still pulling a face. 'You've got yourself the sack, haven't you?'

'Love of my life,' I said, 'it was just a difference of opinion ...'

'And you belted him.'

'Well, yeah, I did give him a little slap.'

She gave me one of her looks. 'Oh, Len, when are you going to pack up fighting?'

She went off shopping in a bit of a huff, so I got in the bath to clean myself up. I was just drying my hair when she returned and she was all happy now. 'I got you fixed up with a job down Essex Road,' she shouted through the bathroom door. I looked at myself in the mirror and thought, 'Fuck me, now what?' I shouted, 'That's lovely, sweetheart, what is it?'

'I saw an advert down the shops for a window cleaner, so I called in and they said you could start tomorrow.'

'Good stuff, babe, good stuff.' I just sat on the bog and groaned to myself. Her heart was in the right place but fucking window cleaning — leave it out.

She was right, though. I couldn't sit about on my back-side doing nothing. The rent had to be paid, and on top of that we'd only just found out that she was pregnant. So that's going to mean a pram, baby clothes and tons of gear for the little fella. Funny really, I never thought for one minute that our first baby could be anything but a boy. I'm over the moon, proud and excited about having another little Lenny in the house.

I didn't mind the window cleaning, as it turned out. We started at six and finished by twelve. It wasn't hard work, though I was never happy climbing up too high, and those cradles on blocks of flats gave me the shits. Especially when one of them broke and a bloke was killed. I was going to chuck it in after that, life's too precious, but the firm must have thought a lot of me because they made me a foreman. That meant I didn't have to clean windows any more. My job was to go in early, get all the sheets out, give them to the blokes, then the rest of the time go round checking up on them. I didn't worry about that, though. Once they were all out of the yard I'd go home and back to bed. At the end of the week I'd get the sheets back in, draw the wages and settle up with the men. If they had days off I'd still book them in. But what I did was buy a load of wage packets from W. H. Smith, empty the firm's packets and make up new ones, this time with deductions. There were a lot of workers on the firm so on a good week I could clear a monkey, plus my own wages.

Then somebody worked out what I was up to and grassed me up to the bosses. They didn't pull me in the office and sack me, they sent one of them round my house on a Saturday morning to do the business.

I opened the door and there was this suited-up mug standing there flanked by two policemen. He said, 'Mr McLean, you're sacked. Here's your cards.' I growled at him. Now you don't sack somebody with the law minding you, so there had to be a few back-handers flying about. These coppers are bang out of order and they could be in a lot of trouble if I squealed. So I've got a licence to see the three of them off.

My fuse got very short and I shouted at the boss, 'You gutless c**t,' and I planted one on him. The two coppers ran off. The boss picked himself up and legged it down the stairs. I was going to chase after the three of them but I didn't have any trousers on, so I thought, 'Bollocks to it. I've had a good run with the job — let it go.' I ripped up the insurance cards I'd been given and went back in the bedroom and said, 'Babe, I've had it with working for muggy straights. I don't fit in with them and none of them know what life's about. I'll graft for you and the baby and you'll never go short, but never ever ask me to take a proper job again.'

She never said a word, just looked at me with those lovely blue eyes. One minute I'm at the front door and I'm a madman. Now I'm all the other way — choked up just looking at her lying there with her little lump making a football in the blankets. I climbed into bed with her and we had a cuddle, and I said, 'We've had the bowl long enough. I'm going to fill it with cherries for you because I love you.'

Two weeks later Val was taken into Bart's Hospital and our baby was born. It was 15 April 1971 and he weighed in at 7lb 2 oz. In my life, I've known hard times that could break your heart. But there have been wonderful times, too. Top of the list has got to be when I met Val, and right up there equally was when my boy was born, and a year later when my lovely little girl Kelly popped into the world.

It's funny how women take it in their stride. Of course, they're proud and happy, but a bloke has to go over the top. You don't find women doing cartwheels all over the place shouting, 'Look what I've done,' and you don't see many women dancing on the bar top buying drinks and cigars for everyone. No, I looked round the room and those young mums all had the same look, sort of queenlike. They all knew they had done the business, and let the old man do all the crowing. After all, it hadn't been easy for him.

Val was no exception. She lay there like a little blonde princess. She was tired, looked like she'd just run a mile, but she was sparkling at the same time. And she'd changed. I couldn't have put my finger on it if I'd tried, but she was different. And the little doll she was cuddling — what can I say? He had red hair and his face was all screwed up and he was the beautifullest baby in the world.

She held him out to me and I felt big and clumsy with this fragile piece of life cradled in my arms. I couldn't say what was going through my head, there was too many things, but I did think that perhaps Dad was looking down and he'd be as proud as me.

I thought it would be nice to name him after me, but Val wasn't struck on that. She said, 'One Lenny McLean in the family is more than enough. I want to call him Jamie.' So Jamie it was.

Suddenly I've got a bit of conflict going on in my head. I've got a wife and family now and they've got to be looked after, not just with money but with some sort of sense of responsibility. Do I knuckle down to a regular job, pack up getting into rows, and take a load of shit from some mug boss? Or do I go the other way to earn a crust?

For a start, I had torn my cards up, but I suppose they could be replaced. On the other hand, my dad never did us any harm with his ducking and diving and probably a load of things we never knew about. So fuck it, I put the word out that I was looking for a bit of 'work'.

I've already told you that I was well known for being a hard man and for being reliable. So when this character Freddie Davis, who worked out of North Road, got in touch he didn't have to ask me for references. Fred was a bank robber like other people are master builders, masons, or first-class joiners. It was his trade. He knew nothing else and he wanted nothing else. Of course, he made mistakes, who doesn't? But if a joiner slips up and cuts too much off a piece of wood, he gets another piece and starts again. He doesn't get a sentence of seven years. That was what Fred had just done when he got in touch with me. He hadn't lost his bottle, it was just the downside of his chosen work so he shrugged it off and, being skint, was ready for some more.

I wasn't the only one he'd organised. He'd rounded up two other good men, but I won't name them because they're still working. He'd got a job sussed out in Hastings on the Sussex coast. I told him there were about a hundred little earners ten minutes away, but he said he had his own reasons, so that was that. It was his job. We had a meet in a pub over the other side of the water, The Black Prince near Dartford, I think, and we set off from there at about seven o'clock. It took us about two hours — there was no motorway then, and anyway we didn't want a pull for speeding. He'd already put us in the picture. We were going after a bank, but instead of bursting through the door with the high risk of getting caught inside, Fred wanted to be a bit clever and subtle.

His information had the manager down as a poofter who lived on his own, but even if he was living with somebody, whoever it was was going to be a pushover. No women, no kids, sweet as a nut. The idea was to get in the house, grab the manager, and hold him all night. In the morning, two of us would slip into the bank with him and wait for the time lock on the vault to open. Piece of cake.

It was just getting dark when we pulled up about a hundred yards away from the manager's house. So first off we're having a smoke then, fuck me — I think we're lifted before we've even got out the car — Old Bill comes past in a little panda car. It slows down and they give us some eyeball. Fred's got a big map spread out over the steering wheel and he studies it enough to set it on fire. We all held our breath, then, thinking that we'd got ourselves lost, they drove on.

The car was nicked but we knew it wasn't hot yet, so we were clear on that. With the motor tucked up a rough track near the house, one of the lads and I made our way along the road, up the drive, which was nicely overgrown with bushes and trees, and crept under the window. Looking through the gap in the curtains we could see a man, a woman and, fucking hell, two kids watching television. Suddenly it's all blown away. Fred, if you paid good dough out for your information — you've been rumped and so have we. The sight of those kids and it's finished. What are we, animals? No. It's one thing putting the frighteners on grown people, but babies? Leave it out. I'm not giving you bollocks about villains with hearts of gold, but you've got to draw the line somewhere.

While I was working on this book, a case appeared on the telly and it was exactly the same set up, except, this time, the slags carried out the job, terrorised the children in the house, and got away with it. I sat and watched it and thought, How can you be proud of yourselves after pulling a diabolical stunt like that?

It wasn't just me; the others were good stuff and wanted to pull the plug as well. So that was it. We pulled out and set off for home.

All our faces were as long as paper kites and Fred kept moaning over and over again, 'They said he was on his own ... they said he was on his own. No family, no dog, not even a fucking budgie. They swore it.' I don't know who 'they' were, but they deserved straightening — what a cock-up.

We were just pulling out of St Leonard's, heading for the London Road, when Fred said, 'Pull up at that off-licence and I'll get some fags and some crisps.' In he went and we sat there talking about him while he was gone. Then he came out and he opened the door, shouting, 'Go, go, go,' like that geezer in *The Sweeney*. Our driver, who knew Brands Hatch racetrack like the back of his hand, which was why he was on the job, took off like a rocket — never even asked why. We were in a Triumph Stag, a tasty motor in those days, and it went like the clappers. When us in the back scraped ourselves off the rear window, I said, 'Don't tell me, Fred, you didn't pay for the fags.' He gave a fucking great laugh and said, 'No, I never, and I creamed the place while I was there.' As he said that he flung a load of notes over the back into our laps.

Jesus Christ. We were doing 100 mph up this road, that silly old prat was laughing his head off, and we were covered in pound notes. I said, 'Fred, you've done a wrong 'un.' He looked round and said, 'What's up, Len?' I shoved his hat over his eyes and said: 'You forgot the crisps.'

We cut the money up and got a hundred and forty quid each. I had to mark Fred's card, though. I put him straight. 'Fred, you are a lovely man, but that stunt you pulled back there could've got us a ten stretch and all for fucking pennies. If there's a next time, do me a favour and leave me out, there's a pal.'

If you were working in the early Seventies you might think that was a nice little earner for a day's driving about, especially as most blokes didn't take that home in a fortnight. But work it out — if we'd been nicked our wages would've added up to something like thirty pence a week while we were away.

I never told Val what I was up to that day. She'd stopped asking how I was bringing the housekeeping in. She knew but she didn't want me to spell it out.

One of the same blokes on that job got in touch a bit later. He said, 'Lenny, we've nicked a load of penguins and we need a hand to shift them.'

I said, 'Leave it out, what do I know about animals.'

He said, 'No, the chocolate kind.'

'Just joking, why don't you bring them round then. I love them. I'll eat the lot.'

'Lenny, pal,' he said, 'even you couldn't manage this lot. Meet me in the Green Man.'

So him, his brother and I all shot down to Hertfordshire where he had the stuff hidden up in a barn on this famous actor's property. He's dead now but I'll leave his name out because his kids are all in the film game. This barn was like an aircraft hangar, and inside was the biggest container lorry I have ever seen in my life. It must have been a hundred feet long and it was packed solid with boxes and boxes of these biscuits. What we had got to do was transfer that load into two other lorries and deliver them to a big café on the A10.

We set to. We were laughing and eager and talking about what we'd spend the money on. By the evening I had eaten two boxes of those bastards. I was feeling a bit unwell, and it looked like we hadn't started yet. I said to my mate, 'I wish the law would hurry up and give us a raid because I'm absolutely bolloxed.' We didn't finish until early next morning and I don't remember the delivery. I went out like a light as soon as we pulled away from the farm. Cash was on the nail and we cut up eight grand between us. Well worth the graft. Next time you read about a little tickle like that, think about the poor sods who've sweated their cobs off — it's not all roses.

One night I was getting dressed to go out on a job with some of the chaps. I pulled on a black roll-neck and all of a sudden I couldn't breathe. My face went bright red and I said to Val, ''Ere, babe, this jumper don't half seem tight.'

'I ain't surprised, Len, you got your head through the fucking sleeve.' It was a good job she told me, or I might have choked to death before I got to work.

I was in The Fox in Kingsland Road one day when Fred Morris, a well-known bloke in the demolition game, gave me a pull. He said, 'Business is good, but I'm getting loads of aggravation from plastic gangsters trying it on. There's this wanker, with a new East London name behind him, that wants his bricks and stuff for fuck-all, or else.'

I said, 'Don't worry, Fred, if you see me right I'll sort it. When's he due?' He told me he thought the geezer was going to show the next morning. I said, 'I'll be there.'

Next morning, I tucked myself in the caravan they used as an office and I sat drinking coffee, having a smoke and keeping an eye on the gates.

A tipper lorry pulled in and this big fella jumped down, all boots and no fucking brains. I watched him as he went over to Fred. They started arguing and Fred got poked in the chest by this mug's finger. They came over to the caravan and Fred said to him, 'My partner wants a word.'

As he put one foot on the metal steps I've chinned him. Down he went like a bag of shit. But I picked him up and did him again; four of them and he's unconscious. Once I start I don't stop. He had blood coming out of his ears and nose, and his forehead was split open. I was going to give him some more but Fred grabbed my shirt and pulled me back. 'Enough, Len, enough, don't kill him.' So to get rid of some steam, I picked up a lump of concrete and flung it through the windscreen of his lorry. We brought him round, slung him in the back of the tipper, and parked him two streets away. Never saw him again.

There was a big notice at the front of the compound saying 'Beware of Guard Dogs'. Some prat painted out guard dogs and wrote in 'Lenny'. Gave us all a laugh.

Fred squared me up nicely for that bit of business. Then he come up with, 'How about a hundred notes a week to keep an eye on the place?'

'Lovely,' I said. So I was on a retainer. A few hard nuts tried it on, but I soon saw them off. Word must have got around and it went nice and quiet. That started Fred thinking he was throwing his money away, so my £100 suddenly becomes £50. I didn't draw up every week. I used to let it run up, so when I was expecting to pick up 600 notes, I got 300. No problem, I kept my mouth shut. I had a quick think. Do I belt him or box clever? I went for the last one.

A couple of days before, I'd stuck my nose in one of his warehouses and clocked about six ton of copper. Once he rumped me, that made my mind up. So I phoned up a pal of mine who was in the scrap game, Ronnie Norris, and told him to bring his big lorry and meet me at the yard. He knew where to go because a while before I'd got him some sub-contract work for Fred cutting up miles of double-skinned pipes all lagged with asbestos. I'll tell you more about that in a bit.

We cut the padlock off the gates and drove in. We did the same in the warehouse, backed in and loaded up. It was two o'clock and they started work at six-thirty, so we sweated our nuts off. We got away just before six, parked up in Ron's yard, and I went home to bed. At half-eight, there was a bang on the door. It was Fred with two foremen.

I said, 'What the fuck do you want? You've got me out of bed.'

He was doing his nut. 'What do I want? You've nicked all my gear.'

It wasn't obvious, was it? I was still black from all that copper that I hadn't had the strength to wash off. So I said, 'OK, Fred, you're right. I have nicked all your gear and I'm keeping it, so piss off.'

He's pleading now. 'It's got to go back.'

I'm getting wound up. 'I've told you, fuck off. You've taken the piss out of me with the wages and, anyway, me and Ron worked all night and it was bloody hard work. So you can fight me or you can call the law.' Give him his due, Fred was one of your own. The law was out of the question and he wasn't going to take me on. I noticed the two foremen had moved down to the bottom of the stairs.

'Len, please take it back and I'll sort it.'

'Sort it now,' I said. So he pulled out a wedge of notes as thick as a Bible, peeled off a grand, and said, 'What a fucking liberty. I'm buying my own stuff back.'

We never fell out and I've done favours since, but only when he's in desperate shit. He doesn't seem to like me going near the yard, though.

I cut up the wedge with Ronnie and he did better out of it than me because I was already owed £300 from Fred. It was only money, though, and if I knew then what was to happen I'd have given him the lot.

A couple of years later, when I was making a name fighting, I got a call from his wife Pat. She said, 'Lenny, Ron's bad in hospital and he wants to see you.' I shot up there straight away and when I saw him I could hardly talk for a bit because that big man had turned into a seven-stone skeleton. His eyes filled up when he saw me.

'Len, mate, I'm done for, I'm dying.'

I said, 'Shut up, you'll be up and about in a couple of weeks,' and I squared up to him. He clenched up his bony fingers into a fist and tried his best to shape up to me, but he couldn't even raise his arms.

I gave my nose a good blow, sat him up, and cuddled him. And I thought to myself, 'Please, God, I hope it wasn't that asbestos job that done in his lungs with cancer.'

I said, 'I want you ringside when I fight Roy Shaw, and when I've beat him I'm taking you out for a steak dinner. Fatten you up a bit.'

He stroked my hand, he didn't have the strength to pat it, and he said, 'You'll murder Shaw, Len, but don't bank on the steak dinner.'

A week before I took on Roy Shaw, he died in his sleep. He was 45. My Val loved him, and he was a great pal. God bless you, Ronnie. We still miss you.

After about two minutes I've done all the money from the scrap copper and I'm looking around for something to fill the pot up again. I don't know where money went in those days, though you've got to remember that when somebody tells you they've picked up a grand here, two grand there, for a few hours' work, that might have been the first tickle for a month. Anyway, I've blown my bit of dough, Val wants a new coat, and the kids are looking for new shoes again.

I was in the Widows, a little drinker in Bethnal Green just behind the Blind Beggar, when a couple of Rastas walked in. All hair, woolly hats about two foot high, beads, the lot. They had a quick word with the governor, then they looked round at me. I gave them a bit of a growl in case they were thinking of starting something, but they came over anyway. We got all that 'Hey, man, how they hanging?' crap out of the way and the biggest one said, 'Some people we know need a minder for a few hours and the word is you're a very tough man with your fists.'

'You look big enough to do your own heavy stuff,' I said.

He gave a shrug. 'I agree, man, but I don't do that sort of work. I'm in business, I do other kinds of things.'

I was polite but I told them I was too busy what with this and that, so they let it go. Don't get me wrong — I'm no racist, in fact loads of my pals are black fellas and they're as good as gold, but there was something funny about these two. Couldn't put my finger on it, but when I get a gut feeling, I go with it.

Don't forget, when I get offers to work, it's on the other side of the fence. It's not decorate a couple of rooms, bang a few nails in, or taxi someone to the airport. It's something heavy with a fair bit of aggravation. So I never, ever take chances.

As I said, I turned them down and forgot all about it. I could have done with the work, but you can't be too careful. A couple of days later, I was in a different pub when this pikey-looking geezer introduced himself, threw up a couple of names, and offered me a bit of work. These pikeys aren't proper gypsies, though they like to think they are, but most of them are straight enough to deal with so I didn't get a sense that it might be a bit iffy. There was no reason why I should — I got these offers all the time. He seemed sound enough, what with the names and everything, so I heard him out. Three grand in cash if I watch his backside while he does a deal with a little South London firm to buy a load of bearer bonds. Straightforward, so we set it up for the coming Friday.

The meet was to be near the Dartford Tunnel, well out of the way of any nosey-parker. It is different now, what with the motorway and bridge, but then it was like a trip out into the country, and the waste ground where we were to meet is now a shopping centre on about five acres.

I met this pikey, Bill, not far from where we were going, got in his motor, drove the rest of the way, and parked up. Twenty minutes later a big Ford Executive pulled in and flashed his lights. Out we got. Bill was holding a bag of money. 'Hold back a bit,' he says, 'but if you see it looks a bit iffy, get in quick, and put them down.' Getting out of the other motor were two blokes, the same set up as us, one doing the deal and one minding. Usual stuff.

Bill handed over his parcel and as he put his hand up for the other package — flash, bang, and he's gone down. As I jumped forward and grabbed the gun before it was pulled round on me, the other bloke jumped in the motor and started it up. I only managed to get one belt in before the geezer I took the gun from scrambled up from the ground, dived in the car, and it screamed off.

I flung the gun at the motor and ran over to Bill. He was screaming and crying and holding his side. Now I was raving mad. I didn't give a bollocks about the deal, it was nothing to do with me, but this slag had nearly got me killed. I got hold of him and dived down his pockets.

He had a wallet stuffed with notes, so I took the lot. I gave him the choice; fill me in on what had just gone down or stay there and bleed to death. It turned out he was fronting for the Rastas and it was a drugs deal, not bearer bonds. I'd guessed as much — I had taken on a straightforward minding job with good heart and this shit's gone down. I never can tell what I'm getting into.

He was still crying for me to take him to a hospital, so I slung him in the back of his motor, fuck the blood on the seats, and drove back to where I'd left my car in a little lay-by. He had passed out by now, so I parked him up, put all the lights on, and scarpered. At the first phone box I came to I dialled 999, told them where the geezer was, and put the phone down. I didn't want to be involved in any more shit.

Does that sound heartless? Well, it was, and I didn't give a toss. As I was driving along I felt cold sweat running down my face, thinking about my wife and kids and how close that drug-dealing bastard had come to ruining their lives.

By the time I got home I had calmed myself down. It wasn't finished yet but I was using my nut. Keep cool. Keep calm. Val was dozing in front of the telly; the screen was blank and giving out a sort of musical hum because it was after midnight. Do you know, I didn't have a drop of blood on me. Driving along I felt like I was covered in the stuff. Val's sleepy, 'Hello, luv, how did it go?' was so ordinary and homely I couldn't believe what had gone down just over an hour ago. Still, I couldn't disbelieve it either, because when I emptied the wallet that little stash counted up to over four thousand. I cut in it half and dropped one of the bundles into her lap. She just said, 'Thanks, Len, I'm going to bed.' Bless her, she didn't ask why, where, or what. Not disinterest — just trust. She was the housewife, I was the money-getter, and that was that.

Before I got into bed, I looked in on the kids. Jamie in bed, Kelly in her cot, two little ginger heads sticking out of the blankets. I gave them both a little kiss without waking them and shivered when I thought again what might have happened, not for me but for these little innocents. Some bastard was going to get it.

I checked out the papers for a few days but there was nothing about the Dartford business. I put the word out through a few people I could trust for them to keep an eye out for those Rasta slags. It took nearly a month before I got the call that put them in a club in East London. You think I'd cooled off? You don't know me.

I was there in ten minutes. The place was nearly empty. Three punters — the two I wanted and the bloke behind the bar. They'd have had more chance if somebody had let a wild dog loose on them. I slipped into both of them at once. I broke their jaws with the first swipe and as they went down warned the barman he was next if he touched the phone. I could have stopped there, they were well damaged, but what the hell, they nearly made my Val a widow. Anybody who's seen one of my bare-knuckle fights will know what I gave them. This wasn't a straightener, it was all in. With both of them still on the floor, I punched, belted and kicked them until they didn't move. I gave the barman a look and he put his hands up. 'Didn't see a thing, mate. Blokes who done them was masked up.' I gave him a nod, said, 'Mind how you go,' and slipped out. I was satisfied. When word got round, slags would think twice about taking me for a mug.

A little end came to that story about 18 years later. I'd done a bit of work for a firm over Catford way. In fact, I'd done a lot of work for them over a few years, so we were quite friendly. We were talking about various things we'd got up to, and I told them how I nearly got blown away. One of them, a bloke called Jimmy, gave a big laugh and told me he knew who it was that took a pop but that he's been dead for years.

It's a small world. There's me all pally with a geezer who was a mate of the bloke who nearly killed me. It might seem strange but I never really had the needle with the other firm. What I'd been well pissed off about was being taken for a mug without knowing the score. About a week after the shooting, and luckily while I was still carrying a good wedge in my back pocket, I was driving down Hackney Road with a pal of mine when we got a tug. An unmarked car pulled us over for a dodgy brake light. What a load of bollocks. That stuff's always left to old plod, not plain clothes. Never mind, we're as good as gold. We've got to be. In the boot there were two boxes of blank insurance certificates, and a handgun in the glove box. The joke was, it wasn't even my gun. I'd taken it off a slag who had tried to use it on me months ago, and had forgotten all about it.

We both sat there like we had ice lollies stuck up our bums, looking straight ahead, dead innocent, while they walked round the motor. These two aren't really looking at the motor, just walking round for a bit of show. I was just thinking that this was simply for them to break the monotony between tea breaks, when we were asked to step out of the car.

Yes, sir; no, sir; three bags full, sir. We hopped out and one of them started looking through the motor. Now we were in deep shit. The paper in the boot's not worth a lot but the gun could see us off for a long time. Still, he might miss it. Some hope. He opened the glove box, rooted round, then shut it again. The next minute, he and the older one got their heads together. Here we go.

If I'd thought about it, we could have done a runner as soon as they waved us down, but now it's too late. The older one came over, took me to one side away from Jimmy, and said, 'This brake light could be a lot of aggravation for both of us. I could get you nicked and give myself a lot of paperwork.'

I wasn't thinking. 'What, you're going to nick me for a fucking poxy light?' He just gave me a look. 'Lenny, I know of you, you're not a c**t. Which way's it going to be?'

I said, 'Like that is it? Well, come round my gaff tomorrow and we'll sort something out.' But as I spoke I already had my hand on the roll in my pocket.

'No, Len,' he said, 'we'll square it now or forget it and you can take a pull, but remember, there are two of us. Want to shake on it?' Bastard — I never answered, just stuck out my hand and palmed him my last £700.

I could see in his eyes he was weighing up the roll of notes and I thought, 'In future, I'm going to carry a wad of notepaper wrapped in a tenner.' The wedge must have felt right because he gave me a nod, stepped away, and said, 'Thank you, sir, you can proceed.' As he got in his motor he called over, 'Don't forget to get that light seen to, and give your kid his water pistol back, somebody might think it's real.'

See what I mean? Easy come, easy go. Now I'm potless again. I've often wondered how they picked on me — they knew something. Coppers never take backhanders off muggy punters. Forget all that crap about sticking a £20 in your driver's licence when they give you a pull, it only works in the pictures. They'll only take from those who know the score and then they won't consider anything under £500.

Somebody said coppers could be trusted in those days and they were right — trusted to be bent as arseholes. But if you made a deal they stuck by it. Today, a lot of them don't want to know, and those who do will bugger you anyway once they've got your money. That was the first time I'd had to pay my way out, but it wasn't the last.

I shifted the certificates to get a bit of dough back in and the gun ended up in the river. I made up my mind to get rid of the starting handle tucked under the seat of the car that I kept in case of trouble. If I didn't, the cozzers might realise that Cortinas don't have starting handles. If it suits Old Bill and they catch you carrying a piece of pipe, pick-axe handle or whatever, without good reason, they'll do you for carrying an offensive weapon, a bit like my bayonet and Charlie's penknife all those years ago.

So that's how life was in the early Seventies — up one minute, down the next. Some days, I could have five grand in my bin — others, five bob. But I loved it.

And all through these ups and downs my Val stood beside me 100 per cent. She would have loved me to go to work proper and be a straight guy. But I couldn't do it. I wasn't going to work all my life for the system then when I'm 65 get thrown on the heap without two bob to my name. I always got a good living and we never went short. It had its risks but what hasn't? I fought everybody, but mostly I fought against certain types in the straight world and the system. Fuck the system.

Everything was going well for us. We had a nice little flat, the kids were growing up lovely. Jamie was nearly four and Dad's little sweetheart Kelly was nearly three. Good kids, no trouble. Val seemed to become more beautiful as she got older and the three of them were my world.

Linda was still living with Nan and looking after her and Uncle Fred. Barry was doing well in Australia. And for the same reasons as Barry, Lorraine, who was never called anything else but Boo, had gone to America with a mate of hers. And my little brother Kruger, who wasn't so little any more, had just married a girl out of Hoxton.

At home — funny how I never got out of the habit of calling Mum's place home — things were a lot better than they had been when I lived there. This was mainly because Jim Irwin spent most of the week living with some bird up north. Sherry was about twelve, a smashing kid who still followed me around the house whenever I went over to see them. Which leaves Mum, and she was worn out.

She'd put her whole life into bringing us all up. She'd always been kept short of money so it was a struggle. The money had been there, she just never saw much of it from Irwin. She never gave herself a second's thought. She was just a proper old-fashioned mum; family was everything. As long as they were all right that's all that mattered. She put everything into everyone else's life and took nothing out for herself. And because she'd prematurely aged with the constant struggle, that piece of shit Jim Irwin was shagging some bird up north; how's that for a punch in the mouth for any woman? She never mentioned it though, kept it all inside. She never complained about her health either, although she had asthma and related problems. She just suffered in silence in case it upset us all.

A bit later she was taken into Hackney Hospital for a check-up and a bit of a rest. Then, one night, I got a call from the hospital that the doctor wanted an urgent word. I flew up there, but before I could see Mum the doctor took me to one side and said, 'Mr McLean, your mother's a very sick woman.'

I said, 'Well, do an operation or something.'

He just shook his head. 'I'm sorry, it's gone beyond anything we can do.'

I couldn't take it in — he was making a mistake. 'How many years are you talking about — two, three?' I was shaking him now.

To give him his due, he wasn't just a white coat. He looked upset himself when he said, 'I'm afraid we're not talking in years, but in hours.'

Hours, oh no. Please, God in heaven, don't let this happen.

I couldn't face her straight away. A nurse got me a cup of tea and chatted to me until I got my strength back. Then she took me into Mum. She lay in the bed and there was nothing of her. For a second, my heart stopped. I thought she was gone already. But when I whispered, 'Wake up, Mum, it's Lenny,' she opened her eyes I saw a look pass across her face, then she took my hand and said, 'I thought you was your dad.' I cuddled her as gently as I could and we both broke down.

In a way, I was lucky. Not to lose my mum, but that we had the chance to talk before the end. She told me not to feel sad for her because she was going to see her Lenny again, my dad. She said, 'You know, I never loved anyone else all my life but that man,' and she was sorry for all the trouble Jim Irwin had caused. I shouldn't have come out with it at a time like that but I couldn't help it.

'Mum, I'm going to kill that man stone dead for what he's done to you and us.' But she made me promise never to hurt him. How could anyone be so forgiving? I said, 'Please, mum, don't make me say it,' but she held both my hands, looked straight in my eyes and said, 'Do it for me, not for his sake, for me. Just promise.' So I did. That lovely, lovely woman was thinking of someone else right to the end.

The doctor was right. My mum slipped away before morning. I'd never known pain like I felt then. I felt empty. I'd lost my mum. I felt I'd lost everything. I had to fight against the hate that was always inside me in case I broke my promise even before she reached heaven. How could God let all those people live until 80 and 90, but take my dad at 28 and mum at 42? There couldn't be a God.

Eventually, all the family turned up except Barry; he hadn't come from Australia yet. Lorraine had flown back from America. We were all upset and crying. Even Jim Irwin broke down, and for a moment I felt sorry for him. Mum never loved him properly, but yeah, I think he loved her in his own way and now he was broken up. But the feeling passed when he tried to give me a cuddle and the hatred flared back up. I made a bit of a scene. I couldn't believe this man who'd never been anything but a fucking horrible beast.

'Lenny, son, we've all got to stick together as a family now that Rosie's gone.'

I just shoved him away. I marked his card. I said, 'Listen, you mug. I've just lost my best friend, someone I loved more than life itself. The only reason I'm not hurting you right now is because I promised her on her death bed that I wouldn't hurt you,' and while I talked I poked him in the chest. 'You've never been worth nothing to us. We've all hated you because you're a gutless, child-beating bastard. Mum never loved you either ... she just took you on to pay the rent. Now the best thing you can do is fuck off and leave us in peace, because every time I look at you I want to knock you spark out.' I suppose I was out of order causing a row, but he made the hate spill out of me. And while I ranted, this great big bullying giant, who had battered me unconscious so many times, stood with his head hanging down, crying like a baby, with tears running down his face.

Mum was cremated at Finchley and not long after the funeral Jim Irwin packed his gear and all Mum's jewellery, and moved in with a relation of Mum's in Hertfordshire. He took little Sherry with him and the idea was that they were going to be lodgers for a while. This relation was a widow, and perhaps she needed a bit of extra rent money. But not long after they were married. And I thought, 'What a liberty!' I didn't blame my aunt, but that fat git treated my mum bad and wore her out with worry, then when she died he started on her sister. I didn't like it, but it was nothing to do with me.

I didn't know it at the time, but two years later Sherry got pregnant at 14, and Irwin, being his own horrible self, slung her out of the house. As far as I know, he has never set eyes on her or her baby since that day — and that's his own flesh and blood.

About six years later my sister Sherry came to visit me. She was about 20 and her little baby was six. She had this drug addict with her who I had no time for, but she was in lumber so I let it go. I let them stay the night then I stuck 200 notes in her hand to sort out her bit of trouble and I gave another £200 to Val so she could take them down the market and rig the baby out. That was done. We had a kiss and cuddle. I wished her all the best, and off they went. By this time I realised that Sherry was on the gear just like her boyfriend.

The next day, Val found a load of jewellery missing; rings, bracelets, some of it good stuff, the rest my little girl's bits of cheap kids' stuff. It didn't matter, though. Forget the value, you don't thieve off your own.

I went down to Hertfordshire and found out where they were living, and followed them up. They both denied touching our gear, then I smacked it out of them both. And I mean smack. I know when to hold back. They both admitted it and I gave them a right roasting. I told her I never wanted to see her again, that we were finished. It was no good me remembering that little girl who used to follow me all over the place, that little baby I loved so much. That was then; now she was a screwed-up adult, but I wouldn't allow her to screw my family. I haven't seen her since. Sticking that shit up her nose she might be dead by now, and if she is, I'm sorry, but it's out of my hands. Put another notch on your stick, Jim Irwin, for fucking up another one.

Mum's death was the one thing I could never imagine. I said before, you think you've got a mum for ever. It doesn't matter where you go, what you get up to, good, bad, or bloody evil, you've only got to go home, open that door and there's Mum, same as always. Who do you run to when you've grazed your knee as a kid, or you've had a knock back as a grown up? Who do big, tough men cry out for when they're lifed off? Mum every time.

But it had happened. I knew she was at rest now, so I tucked her into a little corner of my heart and got on with my life. Watch over me, Mum — but not too closely.

CHAPTER SIX

It was about this time I thought I'd leave out the heavy stuff for a bit. I was still available for the right job but, let's face it, I'd had a bloody good run. I hadn't been nicked since I was a kid. I don't care how good you are, it's very difficult to earn your living having it away and not get a pull every few years. So while I was on a roll, I thought it was about time I got myself into a different game. What I was looking for was a nice regular earner. Something where I didn't have to knock my bollocks off and something not too iffy, so I wasn't looking at a nicking every five minutes. I came up with working myself into the minding game.

I picked out a decent little drinker — no minders and a good turnover. This was the Victory in Kingsland Road. I was known in there, but I started going in a bit more regularly. I gave it a while, then I got four lads to kick off with a good brawl — you know, break a few glasses, knock the tables over while they're giving each other some. Then like the seventh cavalry at Saturday morning pictures, McLean jumps off his stool and breaks it all up. Chucks the kids out, straightens up the tables. Nice one, Lenny — drinks on the house. This is for starters. Give it a couple of nights, same again, different chaps. I had given them their drinking money so they can have a fight in the first place, so they're not doing me any favours.

The governor's well pleased again. 'Lenny, I don't know what the place is coming to. What are you drinking?'

'Forget the drinks,' I said, 'give me a pony a week and I'll mind the place for you.'

'Lovely, Len, you're on.'

Nice little pension. The thing was, though I started the aggro in the first place, if genuine trouble started I did what I was paid to do, so it wasn't really such a rip off. Once word got around that Lenny McLean had a place under his wing, troublemakers tended to go somewhere else. But I didn't have to sit in the boozer all night — like I said, the word was enough. So I pulled the same stunt in a few other pubs — it never failed, and I pulled in a pony from each one. I had to do a bit of running around at night to show my face at each one, but it was worth it for the dough.

Most of the time my name kept trouble out, but there were always a few tearaways; tough kids and plastic gangsters who wanted to make a bit of a name for themselves. A bit like the Wild West — who's going to bring down Jesse James? Nobody took Lenny McLean down, though. I can't blame them for trying. When I was younger, I did the same myself. New face on the manor, let's try him out. Sometimes I could have three fights in one night. Short and sweet.

Then as quick as this nice little number started, it dried up, when I got a visit from Old Bill. It seems that the bloke running the Basing House in Kingsland Road reckoned I was demanding money with menaces. If the law had anything on me, I would've been pulled in, so I thought they were trying it on.

I flared up a bit. 'Do what, you c**ts? Every one of them clubs and pubs came to me and asked me to look after them for wages. What's the game, are you two looking for a pension out of me?'

They said, 'No, Len, this is official. We've been told to give you a warning. You're hurting too many people and wherever you are there's nothing but trouble, so take a tip and move out of this manor.'

'Or what?' I said.

'Or you'll find yourself well fitted. You know the score, we know the score, so fuck off to the other side and stop taking the piss.'

They definitely couldn't pin anything on me or else they would have pulled me, that's why they were a bit heavy on the threats. Still, they had my nuts in the wringer, so I had to tell Val that we were moving.

On top of all the removal expenses, I had to lay out a long one. 100 pound notes, and I didn't begrudge one of them. This cash was a drink for some up-and-coming youngsters to redecorate the Basing House. Apart from the usual chaos and smashing the inside up, they finished off by putting dustbins and crates through that grassing bastard's windows. Serves him right for dropping me in the shit because he was too tight to pay what was due to me.

So we moved out of Hoxton and over to Bethnal Green again, to 51 Allen Road. It was the best move I ever made.

I'm soon skint again. I've paid out fortunes, I've got no work, and there's no little fiddles about. On top of that, my motor gave up on me just as I was coming out of the Blackwall Tunnel. There was oil, water, and fuck knows what pissing out of it and about ten miles of traffic building up behind me. In those days, I wasn't too clever about paperwork, MOT, insurance, driving licence and all that cobblers, so I stuck two fingers up to all those mugs behind me and started walking home. The car wasn't worth anything and wasn't registered, so it couldn't be traced back to me.

Now I had to find some new wheels, otherwise I'd be scuppered for doing a bit of business. So I ended up at a little car site in Kingsland Road. This fella mainly dealt in vans and lorries, but I knew he took in part exchanges and knocked them out on the cheap.

His name was Kenny Mac and he was the size of tuppence, but could he give some old fanny. He wanted 60 notes for a Cortina that had had the clock turned back twice, the tyres were smoother than my bum, and there was a weed growing out of the back wing. Still, it had a fresh MOT and, 'On my life, mate,' he assured me the last owner was a nun. Did he see me coming or what?

We settled on £47.50, all the money I had in my pocket at the time. Well, all right, it wasn't, but if these dealers think they can get a few extra quid out of you, they'll turn you upside-down and shake it out of your pockets. As I pulled out of the yard, he said, 'Don't forget, it's guaranteed until the end of the road.' I thought he was joking. I put up with this heap for a couple of days, then I got a pal to tow it back to the lot.

I'm steaming, the motor's steaming, and this Mac fella's grinning all over his mug. To give him his due, he had some bottle. I said, 'You've taken a diabolical liberty flogging me that motor. Just because I give you shit money don't mean I want to buy a shit motor. Only time it goes is when you push it.'

I'm putting on a bit of an act because I've taken to this little bloke, but I still want my money back. He said, 'Put up a bit more money and I'll fix you up with something a bit decent.'

'I'm potless,' I said. Like I told you, you've got to graft a bit cagey with these blokes.

'Tell you what,' he comes back with, 'I've heard about you. You're a bit tasty with your fists, so if you want to pick up a few quid, why don't you have a fight?'

I said, 'That'll do me, come on then — how about a straightener?'

'Hold up,' he said and he backed up the yard. 'Do you think I'm off my head? I don't mean with me, I mean I can arrange something for you, do us both a bit of good.'

Anyway, we sorted the car business. He let me take a nice little Escort on spec and said he'd give me a bell when there was something fixed up. He didn't hang about. I got a call that night saying he'd arranged a fight with some gypsy bloke. £500, winner takes all, and Kenny would put up the money. He stood right up on his toes when he told me, 'You lose this one, Lenny, and you'll have to take me on, because where money's concerned I'm a wild man.'

'Yeah, in your dreams,' and I lifted him off the ground and gave him a cuddle.

Gypsies are fighting men. It's a way of life. But they don't just fight for the sake of it, they're always proving something. My son's a better fighter than your son, my cousin can murder your best. They do it with their dogs and their fighting cocks and there's always got to be money on it. The money's not the important thing. It's the prestige and the bragging that counts.

Val was a bit worried, but I told her, 'Babe, I've been fighting people all my life and nobody's come near me except that fucking Jim Irwin when I was a baby. Well, I'm not a little kid any more, and just because it's for money don't make any difference.'

I got down to Kenny's car site about half-seven. The big gates were all closed up. I gave a shout and some kid let me in then locked up again. There was a big crowd of gypsies all standing around and they all turned and gave me the once over. Around the back of the site on the waste ground there was a big gypsy camp. They did a lot of dealing with Kenny — horses, lorries, motors — that's how he knew them. I think he was a bit of a pikey himself though he didn't look it.

He'd set up a bit of a ring. Nothing fancy, we'd be scrapping on the dirt, but he'd marked out the area with gas bottles for corner posts, and tied a bit of rope between each one. The spectators were a bit one-sided. In my corner was a kid of about 13. Kenny was the ref. In the other bloke's corner there were about 50 men all telling him what he should do when it started. Arms were waving about, they were pushing and shoving, but I've got to hand it to the other fighter. He ignored them and just stood with his hands at his sides staring at me, trying to get my bottle going. Some hope.

He was about 6ft and 17 stone — a big bastard, hard looking and full of himself. At about that time I weighed in at 16 stone and stood 6ft 2in — twice as hard and bloody handsome with it.

Kenny shouted, 'Righto, righto, keep it down, we're ready for the off,' and he gave one of the empty gas bottles a kick. Ding. The gypsy came tearing out of his corner like his arse was on fire. I was a little bit slow coming out, and he swung a curving right-hander at my head. I went through his guard and smashed him full in the face with everything I've got, and he went down. I couldn't believe it. I mean, I know what I can do but, fuck me, I thought a monkey was going to be harder to earn than this.

Talk about lose interest. One minute all the gypsies are behind their fighter, then when he's spark out they all piss off back to the camp — all except one old bloke who's trying to bring him round, his dad I suppose. I didn't give a bollocks either. I just left him there and went to pick up the wedge.

Kenny handed over the 500 and I said, 'Hang about, what about your cut and the motor?' He gave that big daft grin of his. 'It's all yours, mate. I done well out of the side bets.' Side bets, eh? I had a lot to learn about this game.

So Kenny Mac, as his mates called him, and I were in business. Not a very legal business, but when was anything I did legal?

I'll put you in the picture about the fighting game. There's boxing proper. It's all licensed and strictly regulated by the British Board of Boxing Control. Everything's legit and above board, well, in the ring anyway. Behind the scenes it's as shitty as any business, no matter what they tell you. Boxers are vetted for health and background. So if you've got a metal plate in your head or a criminal record for violence, forget the licence. Once they climb in the ring, boxers have to stick to the Queensberry Rules. On the other hand, unlicensed boxing is what it says. Unlicensed. It's still legal as long as it's in a ring, supervised and both boxers wear gloves. Though quite often, when tempers flare up, the rules go out the window.

Bare-knuckle fighting is in a class of its own and definitely illegal. There are only two rules and that gets sorted before the off. One is the straightener — that's a stand-up fistfight and as near to a boxing match as street-fighting could ever get. The other is an all in, where anything goes — kicking, gouging eyes and, if you're that way inclined, biting your opponent's nuts off. Bones are broken, ribs caved in, some fighters are blinded, and every now and then somebody dies. But everyone involved thinks it's worth it.

The prize money is out of all proportion with the time it takes to earn it. The only drawback is that the loser gets nothing, not even expenses or a few shillings for plasters. But none of the fighters put up, or take a challenge, expecting to lose. Every one of them thinks they're the business.

Me? I never doubted that I was the best. My training in taking punishment had started when I was five and had gone on for a dozen years. I've read that karate experts sit for hours just thumping the heel of their hand on a block of wood. Eventually, that hand is a solid weapon that can't be hurt. That's me —pounded and belted until I don't feel a thing. Ask anybody who's seen me fight. Does Lenny ever back off? No. He keeps moving forward all the time. Does Lenny ever react or flinch when he's taken a punch? No. He feels nothing. Just dishes it out. Anyone taking me on was putting a loaded gun to their head, but it never stopped them trying because they thought, 'One day he'll be put down and I want to be the one who does it.'

A bit later, Kenny's fixed another bout. The same money, same set up really, but a different bloke. This one's a bit older and no novice judging by his lumpy knuckles and flat nose. Noisy bastard though; he said he was going to tear my head off, rip my guts out and break my back. I thought, 'Shut up, you c**t, your bottle's going already.' Ding. In goes Kenny's boot to the gas bottle, and we're off.

This is supposed to be a straightener, but he's kicking like a donkey, then stamping on my feet, and he hasn't even thrown a punch yet. I swung one into his derby and he woofed like a dog. I followed it with a really low one, right in the assets. Got to hand it to him, he didn't drop his guard but his eyes crossed for a second. His team are doing their nut. 'Finish him, Sean. Kill him.' Their shouts seemed to perk him up and he came at me in a flurry and planted one right between my eyes. Fucking hell, he could throw a good one. But he never got his guard back quick enough and I crouched and sunk two into his ribs. He fell forwards on to his knees just as Kenny gave the gas bottle a belt. End of round? Was it bollocks! I jabbed one into his throat and one into the side of his head, and he just laid forward, nose in the dirt, arse in the air. I'd done it again.

What I'm pleased about isn't that I've won a fight. I never expect to lose, and I've had hundreds. It was the fact that there were these mugs queuing up to stick a monkey in my hand for five minutes' sparring. Good stuff, Kenny, set them up.

On another occasion, he said, 'Len, the fair's over Leytonstone next week. We'll get ourselves over there and drum up a challenge — could be some good dough in it.'

'Lovely,' I said.

I told you Kenny knows all the gypsies and tinkers, so it's not like they think we're a couple of mugs. It took about five minutes after we got to the common, where the fair's blaring out the music, and we had a deal. Ken said, 'Give us ten minutes, Len, while I sort the money out, then meet me over the back where the generator is.'

I wandered around, had three hot dogs, a go on the rifles, lost a few bob throwing a load of bent darts, and was just giving a couple of young birds a bit of the McLean charm when up comes Kenny all red in the face. 'Fucking hell, Len, I said ten minutes. They're all waiting.'

I said ta-ra to the girls and followed Ken round the back of the caravans and into this monster on two legs. There were about 20 pikeys surrounding this bloke who looked like he should be in a cage. I swear he was 6ft 8in and about the same across. His boat had been shifted around so often he didn't look human. I whispered to Kenny. 'Hope you got a better deal than 500.'

He said, 'We'll walk away with two grand from this one. He ain't as tough as he looks.'

I said, 'How do you know?'

I just got that big grin again. 'I don't, I'm just trying to cheer you up.'

We all moved back away from the flashing lights of the rides, and they formed a large ring. No formalities, no bell. Just, 'Go on, boys.'

I steamed straight in putting all my weight behind four or five solid belts. Every one connected on his arms. I tried to come up under and do his ribs in but I couldn't get round those massive arms. It was like he was holding sandbags up in front. He threw a couple but his eyes gave him away before he even started to swing.

I tried again. Bang. Bang. Bang. This time I got through and put a nice split in his forehead; good bit of claret. Then he grabs me, pins my arms to my sides, and nuts me full in the face, trying to get his teeth into my nose. I could smell his breath — a mixture of shit and beer. I brought my knee up into his sack and he let go with a surprised look on his bloody face. Got you now, you bastard. I slammed into him, but he'd got those fucking great arms up and I'm punching sandbags again.

Round and round we went. I had him sussed now. He's not a fighter, he's a steamroller. He wanted to tire me out then drop 20 stone on top of me. He's got the right idea; I'm knackered. It's dead quiet except for faint music from the fair. There's no cheering encouragement, just a ring of brown faces watching us both with cold eyes. Kenny's looking worried. Fuck it. I shouldn't have looked round;

he's caught me with a right-hander full in the side of the head. My head's ringing, I've gone deaf on that side and now I'm really pissed off. This has gone on for long enough. I had to take a risk.

I turned my back on him, raised my arms in Kenny's direction and said, 'When are you going to ring the fucking bell?' At the same time, I spun round and, as I'd hoped, the big animal was so surprised at me turning my back he dropped his arms. Everything I've got went into a straight punch to the heart. He fell backwards and down like a falling tree.

After Kenny had dropped me off back home and divvied up the winnings, he patted me on the arm and said, 'We done well there, old son.' I'd had the bollocks battered out of me. I had lumps, bumps and bruises, and he's sitting there as cool as a cucumber talking about 'we'. I didn't have the strength to argue, so I just gave him a friendly tap on the chin and agreed, 'Yes, mate, we did,' and went into my Val.

On the strength of that little earner Val, the kids and I had a bit of a holiday. Nothing flash, just a bit of time in Clacton — laying on the sand, getting a bit of sun, watching Jamie and Kelly making sand castles and running in and out of the sea. I thought, 'It seems a 100 years ago that I was doing my little bit of bird up the coast at Hollesley.' Everything had changed — Jim Irwin was out of the picture, my family had split up and were living all over the place, and where was my cousin Tony? We were so close and now I never saw anything of him. And Mum, God bless her, how many times did I forget and think about calling round for a cup of tea? Then a little hand put a live crab right in the middle of my chest and brought me bang up to date again. Lovely days to remember.

So things were looking up for me. I was offered bits of work here and there, nothing heavy, but it was bringing the money in. Kenny reckoned that after the last do I should cut down on the beer and shape up a bit. I wasn't keen on either of these two ideas because I never hung about long enough in a fight to get out of breath. I know the last one dragged out longer than usual but that was a one-off. I ask you, how many blokes do you come across built like two brick shithouses?

He kept on though, so to shut him up I went down his gym, as he called it. Nobody else would have. It was just a big old shed in his yard, full of straw and horse shit, and the training facilities were a bag of sand strung up from the rafters.

I know I kept larking about and taking the piss, but Ken's heart was in the right place. He took everything so seriously with that stopwatch of his. Ten minutes round the yard, ten minutes on the bag, five on the bench (well, bale of straw). I couldn't go a second over the time, or a second under. It was bloody torture.

Still, it was for my own good and giving me a good wind. Bit on and off, though. Too much like hard work. I told him, 'I'm a cobble fighter not a fucking Olympic contender.' What I didn't know, because Kenny had kept quiet about it, was that he'd taken up a challenge from some tinkers and he was making sure his investment was safe by getting me fit.

I had a few more fights down the car lot and one over at Blackheath when the fair was on. But we were back on the 500s and they were nothing special. I smashed my way through all of them, though.

A friend of mine, Danny Kylie, came to see one of these fights and when it was all over he pulled me to one side and said, 'Len, my dad's just taken over a nut house in Commercial Road called the White Swan, and it's fucking murders every night — shootings, stabbings, the lot. I'm getting worried he'll get done himself, so can you go over and look after him?' I went over there that same night, had a bit of a chat with his old man, and we struck a deal. If I kept the peace I could keep the door money. Good dough in them days.

Fuck me, it got worse for a bit. I was a new face on the manor so every Jack the Lad in town turned up to try me out. I fought them all and bashed them up, even the tastiest amongst them. I didn't need the publicity but my reputation went up in lights when this mug pulled a gun on me.

The barrel of a gun doesn't look much on the films but you try looking down one when it's between your eyes — the fucker's like the Blackwall Tunnel. Some of these kids are all show, you get a gut feeling about whether they'll pull the trigger or not. This one was just playing cowboy. I took the gun out of his hand and broke both his cheek-bones with it, then tucked it in my pocket. I'd chuck it in the river like the other one on the way home. Guns I don't need. My fists are my weapons and if the day ever comes when I need a shooter to get myself out of bother, I'll be ready for the knacker's yard.

I was at home getting ready to go to work at the Swan when Danny's old man rang me. This was about half-seven. He said, 'I've had a Scotch bloke in here mob-handed and looking for a bit of protection money. I think it's the same firm that did that publican with axes last week.'

I said, 'Are they coming back?'

He said, 'Tonight, and they want the cash.'

I was on the door later on when four blokes came in. They didn't know me, they were polite, 'How you doing?' and all that bollocks. They paid their money so I let them in. But I followed them up.

They made a little ring round Bill, the governor, and they started giving him some verbal. All I could see were these padded shoulders going up and down. Bill gave me the nod and I took three of them out with belts to the back of the head. They've gone down — didn't even know it was coming. I held the Scottish bloke against the bar and told him nobody gets a tanner out of this gaff except me and my mate. As he's trying some of that 'Hold on, Jimmy,' shit, I pinned his arms to his sides, looked at Bill and said, 'Go on, son, help yourself.' And Bill did him across the nut with half a bottle of whisky.

We dragged them outside and dumped them on the pavement. They must have ended up in the hospital because it wasn't long before the police were at the door. They said, 'You should both be looking at a section 18, but we know what this firm's been up to. Take a warning, though, don't go at it too strong.'

Later in the week, a message filtered through the grapevine that Jimmy Boyle, one of Scotland's hard men, was sending some of his firm down to get us sorted. One of the blokes who worked in the pub, who was also a bit involved, said to me, 'How do you reckon we should handle it?'

I said, 'Fuck 'em. We'll let them have it.'

His solution was to go off and come back with enough guns to start a war. He's got some handguns, three 12-bore shotguns, and a 20-bore. I didn't know there was such a thing — it would've brought down an elephant.

I said, 'Look, Baz, you know how I feel about them fucking things, what's the game?'

'I've got to make him right,' he said. 'We ain't all built like you, Len, me an' the others are going to feel a lot safer with that lot by the door. You got to think, we might be on our own when they turn up.'

I said, 'OK, it's no skin off my nose, but if the governor finds out that you've brought shooters into his pub he'll do his nut and sack the fucking lot of you. You know how straight he is.'

'Don't worry, Len, we'll park them up where he won't see them.'

So to keep him and the others happy, I let him hide all those guns in a cubbyhole by the main doors and things carried on as normal. In the next few days, while we're waiting, I've got this young kid who comes in the club, Freddie Fox. I couldn't let him right in the club, because he'd been barred for causing aggro and fights. To be honest, he was a

Challenge me – and regret it.

Top left: My father in his twenties.

Top right: My mum at a family party.

Bottom: Me *(second from left)* and the Hayes family on the loose in Hoxton!

Top left: Me aged eight.

Top right: When Kelly *(right)* and Jamie *(left)* came along, family life was just perfect.

Bottom: My father's pauper's grave. He was a wonderful man.

Top: On holiday with Val.

Bottom: At a charity dinner for the Ex-Boxers Association with *(from left to right)* Frank Fraser, Charlie Richardson, me, Alex Steen and *(standing right)* Bruce Wells and *(standing left)* Jack Lavinsky.

Top: A pre-fight chat with two well wishers.

Bottom: Me and Charlie Kray at my pub, aptly named The Guv'nor's.

Top: Psyching myself up!

Bottom: Hard day at work in the office!

In my prime.

Top: On the way to the Old Bailey for my murder trial.

Bottom: Me as Eddie Davis in *The Knock*.

nice enough kid but he could be a bloody nuisance. He could come in as far as the coconut mat just in the doorway. We'd stand there while I was working, having a chat and a smoke.

This kid never stood still; he's fiddling here, fiddling there, next minute he's opened the cupboard and he's sizing up the armoury. 'Fuck me, Len,' he said, 'what are you up to?' To shut him up I told him what was happening. He goes home and tells his father, and we've got a spot of bother. I didn't know Freddie's dad, but I understand that he spoke to someone and eventually it got to the ears of another man I didn't know but had heard of, by the name Ritchie, a Scot himself who is a good friend of Arthur Thomson, the top name in Scotland. Ritchie got in touch and said he'd make a few phonecalls. It turned out that the whole business was a lot of bollocks. Some mug was throwing names up to put the frighteners in. It didn't come to anything, but you were there, Ritchie — good stuff.

Some time later, I learned that Jimmy Boyle, even though he was in prison at the time, really did send down one of his firm to find out what was going on and to sort things out. I won't put a name to the man who came down from Glasgow, but his instructions were to give the first Scottish geezer a seeing to for putting up Boyle's name without permission and for leaning on friends of friends on the firm. I believe he ended up in the same hospital as before.

A bit of time went by and Kenny told me about the fight he had set up. It was to be at Epsom, Derby Day. Some geezer was coming over specially from Ireland and the prize was £4,000. I said to Ken, 'Are you carrying that sort of folding?' and he said, 'Don't worry, I've spread it around a bit, but I know you won't let us down.'

Come the day of the races, I was feeling proud. Top of the world. To tell you the truth, though, I might as well have been on my own on the way down, because I hardly got two words out of Kenny. I guessed he was thinking about all that dough if anything went wrong and I suppose I should have got the hump over his lack of confidence in me, but I didn't. Let's face it, nothing's guaranteed. Even the odds-on favourite can take a tumble at the final fence; it doesn't mean it's not a great runner. Tell you what, though, I've never in my life gone into any fight thinking that there's a possibility that I might lose. I've always been 110 per cent behind myself.

It took us about an hour in the motor to get down to Surrey. By the time we got to the other side of Croydon, we were in a different world — beautiful it was, all little country lanes, fields and trees. A lot of East

Enders wouldn't give tuppence for all that wide open space; they'd think they were on the moon. Not me though, and as we we drove along, I thought, 'One day I'll buy a little cottage somewhere like this for my Val and the kids, away from all the aggro.'

What with Kenny not saying much and me dreaming away, I nearly forgot why we were down there. But as we drove out of Epsom and up on to the Downs, I was back on the ball again and ready to go.

There were a couple of travellers already waiting for us at the arranged place. I gave Kenny a minute with them to sort out the business, then I got out of the motor and followed them further on to the Downs, where I could see half-a-dozen trailers parked up. The way they'd set them up made a nice little private ring, so we'd have plenty of time to square things off if Old Bill stuck his nose in.

I didn't want any messing — straight in, straight out. So off comes my jacket and shirt and I'm into a bit of quick shadow boxing to loosen myself up. An Irishman from the other team slipped over and said, 'Would you want to say hello to Paddy before yis start?'

I gave him a look. 'Say he-fucking-llo? 'Scuse me, pal, but I take it you're joking. In half a minute I'm going to knock seven bells of shit out of your mate, so, no, I don't want to say hello.'

You've got to understand how I'm grafting here. If I have a few words with the guy and he turns out to be sound, it's going to take the dairy off my feelings. When we're fighting, I'll be thinking, 'He ain't such a bad bloke, I'll take it a bit steady,' and that's no way to think when there's four large at stake. No, what I have to do is hate — and I mean really *HATE*. From the top of my head right down to my ankles. This man in front of me has interfered with my wife, he's interfered with my kids. Bastard.

So that's what I'm doing when Paddy Bury steps out from behind one of the trailers and shapes himself up, ready for the off.

I suppose we were pretty evenly matched; roughly the same build and about the same age, but does he hate like I do? No, he doesn't. Kenny gave me a slap on the shoulder and I was into Bury like a fucking lunatic. I gave him such a flurry of short vicious jabs that he must have wondered where they were coming from. He backed up to give his head time to clear, but I kept after him. He tried to nut his way out of it, but as he put himself off balance I stuck two blinders into his ribs, then, as his guard came down, hit him full-square on the point of the chin and down he went. I'm not going to let him get up again. As he struggled to get on his feet I hit him on the side of the head and he collapsed on the ground spark out. Three minutes start to finish. A bit one-sided? Of course it was, just like most of the fights I have.

By the time I got myself dressed and Kenny had sorted the pay out, my hands were looking a bit puffy but, apart from that, not a mark. As we walked away, Paddy was just sitting himself up on one arm. He looked well cross-eyed and by the dribble running from the corners of his mouth I'd bet a pound to a pinch of shit that his jaw was busted both sides. That's the luck of the draw. A nice day out and a nice little earner for three minutes' work.

What I could never understand was reading about bare-knuckle fights they had years and years ago that went on for a couple of hours. It strikes me that they couldn't have been going at it too strongly. If a man's fighting for that long with unprotected hands, they'd be smashed to bits and his knuckles would be up around his elbows. As far as I can remember, the longest cobble fight I ever had was about five minutes.

While we were at the races, I was introduced to Ritchie Anderson, the Scotsman who'd helped out when we thought we had aggro at the White Swan. I'd spoken to him on the phone but hadn't met him until then. He was a decent bloke, knew his way around and was well in with some sound people. He said, 'I heard about the fight just now. I'd have been over but I couldn't leave the pitch. You're as good as I'd heard. Me and you could do some business. Keep in touch.' And that was that. We blew a few quid on one of Kenny's certainties, the three-legged one at the back, and headed for home.

It went a bit quiet for a while and we didn't get any challenges. Plenty down the Swan, but there wasn't any money in that, just wages on the door. My name was being put up all over the place now, so I was a bit surprised when we got a tasty offer from the gypsies living behind the car lot. I thought I'd wiped out all their boys. Still, it didn't matter where it came from; I was ready. A couple of days before the fight, Kenny and I were sitting in the caravan he used for an office, when this tinker and his half-dozen backers came in to check me out. Well, they didn't say that but that's what they were up to. Arrogant bastard, full of himself. This was another one who was going to break every bone in my body.

To give him his due, he looked a bit handy, but didn't he know it. His mouth was getting my back up but I didn't say anything. I just let Kenny do the business. He agreed that this was going to be an 'all-in', and I thought, 'Lovely ... this *leery* get don't deserve a straightener.'

On the day of the fight, I'd wound myself up. I don't mind somebody having a go at me, but I don't want to hear what they're going to do before we start. So when I walk up the yard I'm in a pretty evil mood. Hennessey, or whatever his name was, was leaning against the caravan giving his mates plenty of old rabbit. He looked at me, looked back at his mates, and I just caught the last bit — 'fucking wanker'. That's all I needed. Stuff the ring. I tore into him there and then and didn't even take my coat off.

My first couple of belts threw him back against the caravan and his head bounced off the window, smashing the glass. A couple more knocked him clean over the tow bar and he went down. He's on all fours and he sort of half-turned and looked up at me, so I kicked him in the face. He rolled over and put his hands over his face, but that didn't protect him because I knelt on his chest and punched the back of his hands until the blood was running out from under them and he stopped moving.

By this time, we had got ourselves up between the caravan and the shed. He lay there moaning. All the other tinkers pushed past me to help their boy, and Kenny said from behind me, 'You got to the off a bit soon, mate ... they ain't put their money in yet.'

'Don't worry,' I said, 'these lads won't rump us. Right, which of you six mugs is still holding the bet money?'

One of them said, 'Fuck your money, you took him when he weren't ready.' I shoved Ken out of the way with one hand and knocked the other fella out with the other. 'Don't tell me to fuck the money,' I shouted at him, but he was already spark out. That was it — they all came at me at once.

The space we were in was only about 4ft square so the five of them couldn't mix it all at once, though they tried. I nutted the first one bang in the mouth and his false teeth flew out. He stumbled back but with the others all trying to get at me he got pushed forward so he got another one. Then I just waded into them all. The last one standing put his hand up in a sort of surrender, shouting, 'Leave off, you'll get your money.' The punch in the mouth I gave him taught him to keep his guard in place.

They're all over the place — lying down, sitting down, and one's leaning against the shed. I just said, 'Bring that dough over tonight or fucking else,' and walked away with Kenny.

They came back that night — not with the money but with shooters. Luckily, there wasn't anybody on the site otherwise it might have been worse than it was. They blew a load of windscreens out and peppered the sides of a few decent motors, then fucked off before the law turned up.

Kenny phoned me at about four o'clock in the morning and told me what had gone down. So I dressed, got in the car and drove over there in twenty minutes. Kenny didn't want to know about going after this lot, reckoning it would only cause more aggravation for him. But, as I told him, if he'd been living on the car lot he'd be dead now, so he should just tell me which caravan the main tinker was in and I'd sort it. Stroke of luck — this geezer lives on his own, so no wife or kids to worry about.

Have you ever noticed how flimsy they make caravan doors? Wouldn't keep a cat out. I climbed over the fence, crept through all the caravans until I got to the right one, and then ripped the door clean off. The bastard's got my fingers round his throat before he's half out of bed.

When you see these tinkers round the streets, you wouldn't think they had a pot to piss in. Don't believe it, it's all front. Stick your head inside one of their trailers and the quality gear will knock your eyes out. Most of the silver and porcelain on display wouldn't look out of place in a top antique shop. In public they want to look fuck-all. Amongst their own they want to look top dog.

I said to him, 'I want ten large out of you now or, on my lad's life, I'm going to smash you to fucking death.' And I meant it. This is where deterrents like hanging and long sentences fall down. I wasn't thinking, 'Oh dear, I'll get into serious trouble for killing this man.' It never entered my head; it did after, but not then. 'Come on, c**t, get it now.'

He got off the bunk and I could see his legs were like jelly. He dug around in a fancy cut-glass cabinet and pulled out a roll of notes. He only had seven grand. I told him, 'I'm going to walk you round this site until I've got the lot, so start thinking where we're going first.' What a state he looked. He was stark bollock naked, he'd pissed himself and was shaking like a leaf. Then he remembered he had another stash down by the stove. He thought I was going to rob the lot, but I just took my three and flung the rest on the floor. This was a debt, not a robbery.

Before I left, I marked his card. 'You boys are all hard men, I know that, but don't even consider making this into a war you can't win.' Then I smashed up a shelf full of china that probably set him back two grand. Spiteful bastard, aren't I?

I settled with Kenny and we didn't have any more trouble from that lot. In fact, they pulled out not long after, but they took the word with them because nobody tried to rump us in that way again.

I think I've mentioned that I've never been a liberty taker. I've hurt a lot of guys in my life, but they've asked for it; either for money on the cobbles, or in the clubs or pubs where somebody fancied their chances and offered me out. But like everything, there's always an exception, and this incident is the one and only.

There was a guy by the name of Jimmy Briggs, a good money-getter and game as a bagel. I was driving down Roman Road and saw him walking along, head down and looking a right misery. Mind you, he hadn't been long out of a ten stretch; he got nicked on a robbery. All the others got away, but Jim didn't try and do himself any favours, he kept his mouth shut and did the full lot. Good stuff, Jim.

So I gave him a toot on the horn and over he came. I said, 'You've got some face on you. What's the matter, lost a tanner?'

He said, 'Hello, Len, you gotta be joking, I never had a bleedin' tanner to lose, I'm skint. Trouble is my boy's in Stamford House and I can't afford to get down to see him.'

'No problem, Jim, I've just had a result. Cop this pony, and buy him some fags and sweets and I'll run you down there.' Silly sod got all emotional, but I've got time for people who look after their own like he did.

We had a decent visit with his boy. It seemed funny being back in the old school, though. Afterwards, we stopped in a pub, had a few bevvies, then another. We sank a few more in Riley's up the Angel and finished up in the Green Man back in Hoxton. We'd had a good day, we're laughing and singing and well tanked up. Jimmy started chatting up this bird. She wasn't my cup of tea, all tits and peroxide, a bit too flash really.

Anyway, we'd met up with a few more mates by now and decided to go back to Riley's. I said, 'Come on, Jim, we're off somewhere else.'

'OK, Len,' he said, 'with you in a minute.' No problem. Then this bird sticks her oar in.

'He's not coming with you, he's staying with me.'

I gave her a bit of a funny look. 'Do what, sweetheart? Jim makes his own mind up.'

'I don't care,' she said, 'he's fucking well stopping with me.'

I wanted to give her a smacked arse, but I held back. ''Scuse me, you saucy prat, don't you swear at me.'

Then Jim has to open his gob. 'Don't you have a go at my bird, Len, or I'll put one on you.'

His bird? He's only known this woman for five minutes and he wants to fight for her honour. 'Jimmy,' I said, 'we've had a lovely day. We've seen your boy. I've fronted you so's you could treat him. I bought your drinks all day. I don't begrudge you a penny, but you're going to spoil it all for that piece of skirt?'

What does he do? He swings one at me. Now I'm mad. I'm very pissed and I've lost my rag. I pushed him away but he tried to dig one into me again. That's it. I got him by the neck and dragged him outside. I let him go and he kicked me, so I hit him on the chin. He went arse over bollocks and when he jumped up I could see from the way his jaw was hanging that it was broken.

He stood there spitting blood. I've lost my head by now. I punched him twice in the face, broke his nose, hit him again in his jaw and he went down. As he lay there I flung myself across him and punched his head half-a-dozen times

Now I've broken my own thumb and little finger so I can't punch him any more. He was choking on the blood from his jaw, so he arched upwards, pushed his head back and as he did that I nutted him right between the eyes. I'm ashamed to think back on how I battered that man. I know he started it and I know he was big enough to look after himself, but I went way over the top. I knelt beside him and looked at his bloody face; then I was aware of screaming, shouting and kicks and blows raining down on me as people from the pub tried to stop me doing any more damage. But I was sickened and finished.

I came to my senses, punched everybody out of the way, and fucked off in the motor. I found out later that a few blokes carried him to St Mary's Hospital, which was only 20 yards away. While the porters were rushing about like lunatics, Jimmy died on the trolley. Lucky for him and very lucky for me, the doctors managed to bring him back to life. His jaw was broken in five places, his nose and a few ribs were broken, and his skull was fractured from where I nutted him, but, thank God, the surgeons managed to patch him up.

Some slag phoned the police and put my name up. At six o'clock the next morning they crashed through my front door mob-handed. They were looking for a wild animal so they came with the riot gear. I was still half pissed but I didn't have any fight in me. Ten minutes later I was banged up in Shepherdess Walk nick. Not the first time and definitely not the last, but it never got any better.

They kept at me all the time but I just denied it. I'd had a good shower when I got in and my bloodstained gear was stuffed in the kids' rabbit hutch out in the garden at home. This wasn't a murder charge yet so they hadn't turned my gaff over.

In the end, I said I wanted to speak to whoever was in charge of this case. A CID officer came down to my cell and immediately said, 'Putting your hand up are you, Lenny?'

I said, 'No, I'm fucking not! I just want to mark your card about Jimmy. He's a lovely man, he's your own. He don't talk to you people. Right, tell me what you want to nick me for?'

The CID bloke said, 'We'll do you for attempted murder and a section 18, and we'll get it.'

I said, 'You know what will happen. You'll get me in front of the magistrate then you'll get me to the Bailey. Jimmy's going to stand up and say, "That man didn't do it — Lenny's my pal!" — case dismissed. Don't waste your time, don't waste mine.'

He just walked out and slammed the door.

And that's what happened. Not quite, it didn't even get to the magistrate. They let me go on bail. When Jimmy recovered he denied I was involved and they couldn't get him to budge, so the law was buggered.

What can I say? I know I can be an evil bastard when I lose my temper, but if it hadn't been for the drink I could have controlled myself. I couldn't change my temperament but I could knock the booze on the head. From that day I haven't touched a drop — not even Christmas, birthdays or weddings. And I'll tell you something else. When I'm in a crowded club and I order lemonade or an orange juice, no one takes the piss. Nobody thinks I'm a pansy — I don't know why.

In future, when I'm being a raving lunatic, belting seven bells of shit out of someone, it will be because I want to. I'll know just what I'm doing. I won't be in a drunken haze, I'll be controlled. I don't suppose I need to point out that Jimmy and me never spoke again after that, though I did read in the papers that he'd got better and gone back to work, because it said he'd got nicked doing the Bank of Cyprus.

There's a little story here. Some chaps robbed the London Electricity Board in Ilford. A copper, a bit of a hero, tried to tackle these lads and copped a bullet in the leg. They all got away. Naturally, Old Bill are doing their nut, so they pull in George Davis, Mickey Ishmael and a pal of mine, Tommy Hole. Davis got a 20, the other two were acquitted. So a big campaign fired off to get Davis out, and if you were round London in the late Seventies you couldn't help noticing that catchy slogan: 'GEORGE DAVIS IS INNOCENT — OK' painted everywhere. I used to see it on rooftops and think, 'Fuck me, how did they get up there?'

So they let George out. Eighteen months later he was caught red-handed on the Bank of Cyprus with Mickey Ishmael, my mate Jimmy and a few others, and they all ended up behind the door.

Another pal of mine who was nicked on the same job was Freddie

Davis, no relation to George. Years later, I used to go round to his house when he was dying of cancer and try to give him a bit of comfort. Before he got too bad he would get out of bed and we'd have a little spar. It broke my heart to see him, wasting away and still game. He was always a good money-getter, but because he'd been ill he didn't have a penny. So the other chaps and I arranged a benefit for him in Connie Whitehead's pub, the Crystal Tavern. It went well and we raised about £6,000. Unfortunately, he died before he could appreciate the money, but it helped his wife and paid for him to have a wonderful send-off. God rest him.

Going back to the ruck we had on the car site, Kenny was doing his nut. He had the right hump. I said, 'What's the matter with you? We nicked enough off the gyppos to pay for the motors that got shot up.'

'Don't matter,' he said, 'it's too much aggravation. We're going to have to knock off fighting in the yard.'

It didn't matter a fuck to me where we took on the fights as long as we were well paid. So we started going a bit further afield. One of the places we went to was almost in Scotland — Appleby — where they have a well-known horse fair every year. The gypsies came from all over the country, not just to trade horses but to have a bloody good show off. Travellers I've spoken to say never buy there because prices for everything are sky high. The sellers know that it's a big thing for the gypsy buyers to pull out a bundle of notes as thick as a mattress and let everybody see they're doing well and can afford anything. We weren't buying but we were after some of that folding, so I took on three gypsies that day, creamed the lot of them and was back home by eight o'clock that night.

Around this time I've laid off the villainy for a bit. I had been picking up good dough with the bare-knuckle fighting, and I was still minding the clubs — not so much for the money but to keep my finger on what was going on.

We started hearing things about a geezer called Harry Starbuck over in South London who was a bit tasty as an unlicensed boxer. He'd had about 30 fights and won them all with knockouts. I put myself about and found he was under the wing of one of the guv'nors over the south side, Eddie Richardson. I didn't know him personally at that time, but I knew him by reputation. I gave him a bell, and I said, 'Eddie, I've been hearing things about one of the fighters in your stable and I've got ten grand here that says I can paralyse him.'

I had already introduced myself and he knew who I was. He went quiet for a bit, then he said, 'Len, we're making a good few quid over here out of Harry — he's the business. If you come over here you'll do him, I know you will, then we're ten grand out and we've lost our pension. So thanks for the offer, but no thanks.'

I didn't want to leave it alone. If there's a bloke out there who can put down six men who have been taking the piss out of him, he's a tough guy and I want him to see that Lenny McLean is tougher still. I don't hide from anybody. A lot of fighters and world-famous boxers pick and choose. They're not mugs — they take challenges from people they're pretty sure they can beat. Not me. I'd take on King Kong and beat the hairy bastard.

Eddie won't budge though, so I left it that when he wanted to call it a day with Starbuck, I'd slip in, do the business, and we'd both make a nice few quid and a load more on side bets.

A year or so later, I was in the Green Man with Danny Kylie, Billy Sutherland and Chris Hawkins. Stuck on the wall was a big poster advertising a match between Donny Adams and Roy 'Pretty Boy' Shaw. I said to the others, 'See them two. I could do them both in the same night.'

Then the governor of the pub stuck his bit in. 'Take a friendly warning, son ... that Roy Shaw is a lunatic.'

I give him a look. 'Shut up, you c**t. You're looking at a worse lunatic.' He said, 'Yeah, I know all about you, but I know Roy Shaw as well.'

This bloke had just taken over the Green Man from a pal of mine, Lennie Gower, a bit of an entertainer and singer. Lovely man. This new bloke wasn't all that, always putting names up. He reckoned he was well in with everyone. Didn't like me, though; I made him nervous. Anyway, he says, with a bit of a sneer on his face, 'If you want, I'll put the word to Roy.'

I said, 'You do that. I've got the money and he can have it on the cobbles or in the ring, with gloves or bare knuckles, either way I'll do him.' With that I stuck a few darts in the poster, and we slipped away to another club.

I didn't go to see the Shaw–Adams fight, but I was told afterwards that Shawey had done the other bloke in about ten seconds. First punch and he had knocked Adams spark out and earned himself about 16 grand.

I was talking to another bloke and he told me that Harry Starbuck had been to see one of my fights. When it was suggested he challenge me, he said, 'Fuck McLean, he's a nutter. I've got more sense.' In his way, he was showing me respect. I never met him but I understand he's a gentleman, very polite. And one thing I like is polite people.

A few days later, Roy Nash walked into the pub where I'm sitting. Good man Roy, out of one of the best families.

He got himself a drink and me a lemonade and said, 'How's it going, Len?'

I said, 'Lovely, Roy. Glad you've come in, because I think you could do a bit of business for me.' I asked him to arrange a challenge between me and Roy Shaw.

He's given it a bit of thought then said, 'Leave it with me. I'll be in touch.'

Time went by and nothing happened. Roy Nash is a busy man and all I can think is that he was over-run with work in running his business because he didn't get back to me about my offer of a fight. It must have gone right out of his head. Looking back, I sometimes think that if he'd got something sorted, then come along with me, he might have ended up going to the top of the fight game instead of Frank Warren.

Still, it didn't matter as word got round on it's own, like it does in our circle. I was minding the club one night when Roy Shaw walked in. Tough-looking geezer, those close set eyes of his make him look really mean. He had another bloke with him I didn't know. This other fella was nice and relaxed and introduced himself as Joe Pyle. He said, 'You know who this is,' nodding at Shaw.

'I know him,' I said. Roy sat down and never said a word. He was like a volcano ready to go. He didn't look like he was with us, he just stared into his own world with those fucking eyes.

Joe said, 'How much you putting up?'

I said, 'I've got people with three grand for this one.'

'Right, that'll do. He's got a couple of fights to put out the way, then he can take you on.'

Roy and I sized each other up for a minute. Then he said, 'Make sure you're there.' Then they were gone.

Now I don't want to give the impression that Roy Shaw's some sort of mental case. I don't suppose he's any nuttier than I am. But he had a way about him where he sort of shut himself off — saw and heard what he wanted to hear. I didn't know much about him then so I thought I'd shoot down to his next fight and check out the opposition.

We found out he'd taken a challenge from a bloke called Lew 'Wild Thing' Yates, and it was going to happen at the Ilford Palais, so Kenny and I got tickets and drove down there. Shawey could draw a fair crowd. The place was packed with about 1,500 people. All the front rows were taken up with villains and well-known faces. We found ourselves sitting behind Alan Lake, Diana Dors' husband. Yates is a bit of a giant, well over 18 stone, and he's got this shaggy black beard that makes him look like a cave man. When Shaw gets in the ring he looks like a midget next to him. Talk about Popeye and Bluto.

Bang, they're off. Shaw goes at him like a Rottweiler and puts him on his knees. Yates stays there until a count of nine and gets to his feet. In the second round he wakes up a bit and gives Roy some lovely belts to the head — remember, there's 18 stone behind his fists — but Roy didn't even back up. Seconds into the third, Roy tears into that beard and rips up the face behind it. Yates is finished. He's down on one knee leaning against the bottom rope, and his blood's running everywhere.

Then Shaw's dancing all round the ring, pumping the air and shouting out for challenges. Some young bloke, Kevin Paddock, jumps in and it's off again.

I said to Kenny, 'I'm going up to do him.'

He said, 'Leave it for tonight, Len, that Pyle bloke said he's going to fix you up.'

'Yeah, I know, but it could be fucking months — hold me coat, I won't be long.'

As Paddock hit the deck I was out of my seat and barging my way down through the crowd. I was over the ropes shouting and hollering to wind Shawey up so he'd take a pop. Then I was surrounded by all his corner. His manager, Joe Carrington, wants to have a go at me but I don't want to fight him so I just shove him out the way. Then Joe Pyle's got me by the arm and he's saying, 'OK, Lenny, that's enough, leave it out. You've got your challenge, but not tonight.' So I left it and went back to my seat. The crowd's doing their nut — whistling, shouting, and banging their feet. I don't know if they were for me or against me but I put up two fingers anyway.

CHAPTER SEVEN

From what I was told about his background, Roy Shaw deserves a good gee. Like me, his dad died when he was young. He didn't suffer the violence I did, but his early years were the same as mine; bit of thieving, dishing out violence, approved school, Borstal, prison. Before he got tripped up by the law he'd taken up the gloves, something I never even fancied, and boxed his way through ten professional fights. — 10 wins, six KOs. Like I said before, once you've got a criminal record that's your licence down the pan, so Roy had to give up any plans for a career in the licensed ring. So he thinks, 'Fuck 'em,' and starts taking his wages out of banks and security vans with the help of a shooter. His biggest and last robbery was a nice little earner of £90,000 from a van in Kent. Then he was grassed up and got a 15. Did he settle down and serve his time? Did he bollocks. He fought every week of the way. If he wasn't fighting other cons it was the screws. Once, when he got a bit upset, he ripped a piece of metal off his bed and smashed his way through his locked cell door. I never heard of anybody else ever doing that.

Nothing they could do to him slowed him down because he was so full of hate for the system, and I can understand that. The screws did his head in so many times with their truncheons he had more scars than hair, and he still wouldn't let up. So they ghosted him off to Broadmoor. Not because he was a lunatic, but because there was no way they could control him.

A lot of straight people get the wrong idea about places like Broadmoor and Rampton. They think anybody sent to one of those places has got to be a mass murderer or a perverted child killer. Well, that's not always the case. If they're like Roy, too tough for the system, they'll be sent to a secure hospital so they can be drugged into submission. If a con has a nervous breakdown while he's serving his time, he'll get sent there for treatment, nothing more, then returned to normal prison. Well, Roy worked out that they could bang him up for ever in Broadmoor Hospital, so he kept his head down, behaved himself, and was returned to the prison system and finished his time. That's when he took up unlicensed fighting. In his case, legal robbery.

After I was put in the picture about this guy, I had to give him a lot of respect. He'd suffered, he'd fought against the same fucking system I hate and he's come out the other side. He had to be good stuff. Respecting the way he'd handled his life didn't mean that I'd changed my mind about tearing his head off. If he was putting himself on offer, Lenny McLean was going to take it up.

All my camp who had stuck their money up for the side bet were all giving me some earache. 'Come on, Len, you've got three weeks, get yourself in shape, lose a few pounds and shape up a bit.' Were they joking or what? I could put away a dustbin-lid sized plate of steak, eggs, mushrooms and tomatoes, top it off with half-a-dozen cream cakes, and never put on an ounce. That wasn't going to change. And as for training, I'd never done it in my life, unless you count what Kenny made me do, and that was a waste of time. I did cut down on the fags, though.

Come the night, Chris, Danny, my cousin John Wall and I all drove up to Sinatra's Club. They'd put a ring up in the middle of all the tables. I was sent off to this big dressing room and I was sitting there when Joe Pyle came in, stuffed two crêpe bandages and a pair of gloves in my hands and told me to get them on. This was something different for me. Gloves were for fairies.

Had Pyle pulled a stroke? He'd given me magic gloves. Every time I closed my fist, these gloves would spring open — they'd been fucking doctored. It didn't matter, I'd manage. I got in the ring with Johnny, then all the lights went down and we heard that Gary Glitter record belting out of the speakers, 'Come on, come on'. Now John's an ex-pro but he turned pale and he said, 'Look at this fucking raving lunatic coming down.'

I said, 'Keep calm, John, you ain't fighting him and you know what sort of lunatic I can be.'

Down he comes, shoving people out of the way and knocking

chairs over. He might not have been a nutter but he was some showman who knew how to sell himself. He was chucking himself all over the place swinging his arms around. He jumped over the three ropes and stood there jumping and bouncing up and down. Me, I'm just leaning in my corner thinking, 'You should be saving your breath, you're going to need it.'

The MC was the famous stunt man Nosher Powell, and he introduced Roy 'Pretty Boy' Shaw as the hardest man in England — challenger, Lenny McLean. I was just telling John that my fucking gloves keep bubbling up and bang, the bell's gone.

I steamed straight in and belted him, but the gloves aren't doing me any favours. I wanted to rip the bastard things off because they were breaking my fingers. Round one — waste of time.

Round two wasn't much better, but as I couldn't get a decent punch in to slow him down he'd wedged me in the corner and for the full three minutes he smashed me on the head and chin. Round three, exactly the same. To give him his due, he could throw a wicked punch, but I could take every one. Bang, bang, bang. He's giving it everything he's got; he's desperate to put me down. He'd be the first one who ever did. Come the fourth round and we're both absolutely knackered — me from taking his punches and not being able to retaliate and him because of his non-stop throwing of them.

I don't know if you've had a fight as an adult, but if you haven't then let me mark your card. The average person couldn't sustain a real fight for much more than a minute. Adrenaline is pumped into your body but it's short-lived, then you're left drained. So don't think it's strange that we were done in after ten minutes.

Halfway through the fourth I was still laughing at him and calling him names and that was making him wilder and more exhausted. Ding, the bell goes; the ref's called it a day. I don't want to make excuses and I don't want to take anything away from Roy. He gave me some punishment that would've flattened anybody else. But he couldn't hurt me and he couldn't put me down. I've got to hold my hand up. I wasn't fit — I was used to the damage I could inflict with bare knuckles inside the first minute. The gloves didn't help but I let myself down by not being ready.

Before I left, I had a word with Joe Pyle and told him to tell Roy that this business wasn't over yet; I'd be back to finish him next time. Joe just laughed. 'Good boy, Len, get yourself some money together and you've got yourself a return.'

We came out the back of the club and were walking across the car park when suddenly there were three hefty-looking blokes barring our way. Full of beer, piss and wind, they've got themselves psyched up watching the fights all night and now they think they're Tarzan or Cassius Clay. One of them put on a voice like a fairy and was dangling his wrist. 'Ooh, I think these gloves are doctored.' The bastard must have been ringside by my corner. Then they all burst out laughing. Did they think I was tired or what? They were still laughing when I punched them all to the ground. That was more like it, more personal without your knuckles covered up.

I spoke to Bobby Warren a week later. I said, 'Bob, I think I took that Roy Shaw a bit for granted last time. Sort out a return with good money and I'll definitely beat him.' So Bobby's gone to see Alex Steen and Joey Pyle, who promote Roy and everybody else, licensed or unlicensed, and got me another fight.

In the meantime, Bob said to me, 'Len, I'll sort the business side, you get yourself nice and fit, and we'll bring your mate, young Frank, in to do all the running about.'

Now Frank is a nice kid, but as I said to Bob, 'What the fuck does he know about the fight game? He's down the market most of the time, or running the book on point-to-point races and that hasn't taught him anything about this business.'

Bobby said, 'To be honest, Len, he knows nothing, but he's a sharp kid and a quick learner.'

So that was Frank Warren's first little step on the ladder. That skinny little blond-haired kid went from helping us out to become a force to be reckoned with in the boxing world. He opened everything up. Until he came along, people like Mickey Duff, Barrett and Jarvis Astair had a stranglehold on all the promotions. Little blokes were frightened to step on their toes. Not Frank. He worked hard on the way up, then when he got his promoter's licence he looked round and said to himself, 'Why should they have all the big venues, all the television bouts, and all the big money with it.' So he grafted well and used his nut all the way until he got the cake, the cherry and loads of cream. He didn't just help himself, though, he helped all the other little promoters. He opened the door for them, so they've got a lot to thank him for.

He has had his fair share of slagging off from a lot of people, but if you get to the top there are always jealous mugs who want to pull you down. Myself, I've got to give him ten out of ten. There was only one thing that gave him a right knock-back and that was the business over him getting shot. It wasn't the shooting that did the damage, it was the way he was attacked in the media afterwards for the way they thought he handled the situation, what with Terry Marsh getting a pull and all that. I don't want to go into detail, after all the man is family, but Terry got a not guilty and, weighing it up, I don't think Frank could've gone any other way.

When I was in Brixton Prison I flared up at a few people who'd been banged up with Terry Marsh when he was on remand for allegedly shooting Frank. They were saying, 'This Warren geezer, he's your mate ain't he?'

I said, 'So what?'

They said, 'Why couldn't he have said it was a black bloke shot him or somebody masked up instead of fingering Terry Marsh?'

I said, 'Hold up, don't you talk a load of bollocks about things you don't know nothing about. That man never said a word. It was witnesses that put Marsh in the frame. Another thing is, I don't think you mugs are having a serious pop at Frank, you're just trying to dig me out, and you've given me the hump.' So I well obliged the three of them.

Anyway, going back to the fight, young Frank got stuck in, had the posters and tickets fixed up, and Bobby got a place organised over Croydon way for the fight. That just left me to do my bit and that was to train.

Frank said to me, 'Tell you what, Len, I'll pick you up in the morning and we'll go over Victoria Park. I'll bring some gear and run with you.'

We got there about eight o'clock in the morning and we're looking round to see where to start. We saw some runners so we shouted over, 'How far right round the three parks?'

They didn't even slow down. 'Four miles.'

'Fuck that,' I said, 'we ain't in that league yet.' Another load of runners, blokes and girls, steamed past, so again I shouted over, 'How far round this one park?' What are they on, these people? They were nearly out of sight before I had finished speaking. 'One mile,' came floating back.

I said, 'That'll do us, Frank, come on.' We were about halfway round when Frank dropped on the grass.

'Lenny, I'm fucked. I'm going to have a heart attack ... you carry on.'

I said, 'Come on, we've only done half a mile.'

He got up, coughing and spitting. 'I shouldn't be doing this,' he said, 'I'm not fighting.' We finished the mile, though — we walked the rest of the way.

'That'll do for today, Len,' he said, 'don't want to overdo it. Let's nip over the pub and have a quick one.' We slipped in the boozer and were both sitting there absolutely knackered. I drank about four lemonades before I could speak. 'Frank, son, this is going to be hard work, but I can handle it. I'll be running up Everest in a fortnight.'

So that was the first day's training. After that I said to Frank, 'You're going to do me more harm than good, you'll hold me back, so the best thing you can do is get on with the promotion and I'll crack away and get myself fit.'

It was a lot more painful than I could have imagined because I was driving myself. I'm proud to think that nothing can beat me, I won't let it, no matter what it is. It paid off and day by day it got easier, so after a few weeks I could run round the three parks and still be ready for some more. I was feeling good.

Frank came back a couple of weeks later and told me he'd had a word with Freddie Hill over Battersea way, a professional trainer who's worked with the very best. I said, 'Frank, old son, I'm a street fighter, I don't need all that shit.' But he wouldn't let it go. 'What harm can it do? I know you're the best, but this fella can give you a few tips, sharpen you up — I dunno, give you a bit of ability.'

So I gave in, went over to Freddie's, and he put me through it for seven or eight weeks solid. He taught me all the moves — taught me everything.

On one occasion I was down the gym having a spar with Kevin Finnegan, who was just the right bloke to get my reflexes sharpened up. We were both sweating cobs so when we finished we slipped out for a drink. He got me a lemonade and Guinness for himself. I gave him a cross-eyed look but I didn't say anything. By the time he was on his fourth pint, I said, 'Should you be putting that stuff away, Kev? You're taking on Marvin Hagler in three weeks.'

'Don't worry, Len,' he said, 'I can handle it.' He swallowed ten pints that night and was well pissed. I don't think it was a one-off, but nobody could stop him. My mate John Huntley went with him to America as the corner boy and he told me that when Kev went to the weigh-in he was dressed in an old T-shirt, jeans and a pair of flip-flops. Then Hagler turned-up in a posh stretch limo, all suited and booted, and his backing mob were all dressed like gangsters. Give Kev his due, even though he was a bit of a piss-artist he stood up to Hagler, who, don't forget, was one of the best middleweight fighters ever, and only got stopped when his eye was too badly cut to carry on. He had a big heart and didn't give a fuck for anyone.

We got ourselves down to Croydon on the night. We were in the dressing room and every five minutes Frank disappeared out of the room. In the end, I said, 'You're making me dizzy going backwards and forwards. What's the matter with you?'

'Lenny, I keep needing a piss, I'm nervous.' It's making me laugh, all this kid's got to do is hold the bottle of water and give the towel a couple of flicks, and he's nervous. Admittedly, he was only young and it was his first fight, even if he was only watching. Outside I'm dead calm, inside I'm boiling to get my hands on Roy Shaw. At that moment I hated him. I wanted to hurt him.

We came out in the first round —- I smashed into him — punched him to the floor. He got up and I smashed him down, stamped on him and kicked him. I put the boot in and they jumped in the ring, got me round the neck and pulled me off him. He was dazed but he's not done.

He got up and bang, they let go of me. I steamed in. One, two, three, four punches to the head and he went head first through the ropes. Everybody's going arse over bollocks as he sprawls over the first and second row.

I've done him. Up went my hand as the winner. He's won one and I've won one. So the promotion's all ours. We've nicked it off Joey Pyle, Alex Steen and all that firm. We've nicked it all.

A nice win that, pulled in £25,000, but I wasn't satisfied. I wanted Shaw again. I want him dead at my feet on the canvas. Well, not literally dead, but you know what I mean. I wanted to smash him to bits and show him and everybody else what it's like to come up against Lenny McLean. Knocking him through the ropes was a technical win. I wanted him in the ring and hurt the next time my hand went up.

It's all about money, this game. In the ring or on the cobbles we hate each other. We want to inflict real damage, break bones, get as close to murder as we can. Yet if I bumped into Roy Shaw in the street I wouldn't bite lumps out of him. I'd give him a nod, nothing else, because we aren't in love with each other. But the punters, they take it all in, so they want to pay good dough to see these two blokes tear each other to pieces. My camp know it. Roy's camp know it. So we get a return sorted. A real grudge match.

A lot of people got the hump over me doing Shaw. I think they could see their nice little pension flying out the window. And we started hearing a few whispers that there was going to be a bit of trouble ringside next time we got together. Remember, we're not dealing with Boy Scouts. The money that can be dug out of the fight game has always attracted some very tasty characters.

We went to see our friend Ritchie, who I've told you was well connected with good people in Glasgow. I said, 'Ritchie, you know about the fight we've organised at the Rainbow, well we've heard there's going to be murders on the night. Can you sort out a bit of help for us?' This man's a gentleman who can be relied on. When he says, 'No problem,' we can rest easy that everything will be taken care of — no need to remind him, it's done.

A few days later, I got a call at home. I picked the phone up and a Scottish voice said, 'Lenny McLean?'

I said, 'Yeah, who wants to know?' A bit aggressive I suppose, but I'm always wary of strangers.

'My name's Arthur Thomson. I'm a businessman up here in Scotland. My good friend Ritchie Anderson tells me you might be having a few problems in the future. I've heard all about you and I know you are a good friend of my friend. Let me just tell you personally that anyone who wants to have a go at people under my wing is having a go at me, and that's not allowed — ever. So I will see you at the fight.'

In the meantime I carried on with my training. Even while I was doing it I was still thinking that it was a waste of time. Sweating my cobs off for days on end ... for what? Thirty seconds ... two minutes? Still, in the very unlikely event of something going wrong in the fight, nobody could point the finger and say I wasn't fit.

Kenny had the bright idea that it would strengthen me up even more if I pulled a car round the park. I had a rope round my waist tied to the bumper of this old Mini, and as I dragged it along I said to Ken, 'Reminds me of that bastard I bought off you that time!' He reddened up a bit and suddenly had to drop back and tie his shoelaces. He knew he was one of the very few to have pulled a stroke on Lenny McLean.

Finsbury Park, Rainbow Theatre, Monday, and I was taking it easy in the dressing room. Everybody else was flapping around, but I, who was going to do the business, couldn't give a bollocks. I just let them all get on with it.

I closed my eyes for a minute, nice and relaxed, then I heard this voice beside me say, 'Hello, son.' I thought I was dreaming, until I opened my eyes and there was Jim Irwin. 'Frank Warren said it would be all right if I popped in and had a word.' I jumped up to get hold of him and he flinched back, then I thought of Mum, sat down again and just looked at the man. I couldn't smash into him, and nothing I could say would ever communicate the contempt and hatred I had for him. 'Don't call me "son", don't even think of me as your son, just fuck off out of my sight.'

He was not the man he was — he had lost weight and was looking old. He just stood there with a funny look on his face. Doesn't the mind work in strange ways? For a tiny second, I felt sorry for him, then it was gone and I screamed at him, 'Get out of here now, you bullying, gutless bastard, and never come near me again!' I turned my head away and when I looked back he'd gone and I haven't seen him since. He might even be dead and, if he is, he'll be a million miles away from Mum and Dad, because a slag like that has got to be burning in hell.

When Frank showed up I bollocked him for letting Irwin into the dressing room, but I didn't strong it. How was he to know how much I hated my stepfather? I was too proud to advertise how I felt.

When I'd cooled down, Frank said, 'Len, I want you to do me a favour. Do what you've got to do to Shaw but don't go too strong if you get him down.'

I said. 'What's up, feeling sorry for 'im?'

'No, you know better than that. What it is, we've got all the television people here and on top of that there's a load of officials from the council. I do my best to make you chaps stick to the rules but it's not easy. If they think the show's out of order I won't get another licence.'

I said, 'The best I can tell you, Frank, is that if he's spark out I won't jump on his head, but if he's still got his eyes open I'm going to give him the full works. Sorry, Frank, but I can't switch on and off like a bloody robot.'

Then Ritchie showed. 'Been ringside yet, Lenny?'

'No, why's that?'

'Arthur Thomson's turned up,' he said. 'He's brought a coachload of his men down from Scotland and every one of them's tooled up.'

'Lovely stuff, Ritchie, we owe you one.'

One of our runners had sneaked into Shawey's dressing room. He was only a kid so no one took any notice. He told us that Roy was walking up and down looking thoughtful. It sounded like he wasn't so confident this time.

Then Gary Glitter started belting out of the speakers, 'Come on, come on', and I knew Shawey was on his way down. I gave him enough time to start wondering whether I'd bottled out, then I gave it the big entrance. It wasn't that far down the gangway to the ring, but I seemed to go down it in slow motion. I could see Roy bobbing up and down in the ring; the crowd was roaring and all eyes were on me. I stopped for a second and looked all round at the punters screaming for blood and I thought, 'You lot have come to see a fight ... well, this one you won't forget,' then I climbed through the ropes.

I looked to my left and a row of hard faces stared back up at me. I gave them thumbs down and glanced to the right. There was Arthur, and all around him his tartan mob were cheering and shouting remarks. I gave them a wave, swivelled round, and fixed my eyes on Roy Shaw. He turned his back on me and shrugged off his robe that had 'Mean Machine' in big letters on the back. He didn't look so cool now and I could see by his eyes that he thought he was going to do this upstart in the first few seconds. Some hope!

We were introduced. The bell went and he tore at me, his arms going like pistons. He was trying to finish me quick.

He got about four good belts in but two of mine sent him backwards and I kept him going with left and rights to the body. A surprised look flickered across his face and he went down. He got back up, but now he was on the defensive. I've got him ... I battered him a full circuit of the ring, then as he gave me two feeble jabs he wasn't quick enough with his guard and I chopped him to the side of his head. For a fraction of a second he seemed to stop dead, then I hit him again and again and again. Solid punches, every one to the head. The ninth one put him down. I've never fought anyone before or since who could've taken half what he did and stayed on their feet.

Frank didn't have to worry. Roy was spark out. He wouldn't need any more to finish him.

His team dragged him to his feet and pulled him into the corner, and as he came to he was trying to carry on. I could hear Joe Carrington shouting, 'It's over, Roy, it's over,' and Roy was shaking his head saying, 'Who done me, who done me?' I laughed inside and thought, 'I done you ... Lenny McLean has fucking well done you.'

I swung round to the crowd — they were going wild. I held my arms high and shouted to them all, 'Who's the Guv'nor?' and a great cheer went round the place. Again, I threw my arms in the air and bellowed out, 'Who's the Guv'nor?' and the roar was deafening. 'Lenny ... Lenny ...Lenny ...' Everybody's on their feet. My mob's going crazy and even Roy's lot are clapping and cheering. I'd done it.

I never really set out to become the Guv'nor, but now I was, and nobody would ever take that away from me.

I was in the dressing room afterwards, sitting there having a cup of coffee and relaxing after my couple of minutes' effort, when I looked up and two blokes walked in. I thought I recognised them but couldn't place their faces. Then the penny dropped and I went, 'Fuck me, it's Superman.' They both laughed at that and introduced themselves — Christopher Reeve and Gene Hackman. Can you believe it, these two superstars wanted me to sign a programme for them? They congratulated me on the win and we had some photos taken. Years after, Christopher Reeve broke his back in a terrible accident and was paralysed. I hear he's slowly on the mend and I just want him to know that Big Lenny says keep fighting and one day, please God, you'll be back up on your feet.

CHAPTER EIGHT

So now I'm the top man. The Guv'nor. I never asked for help or needed it in what I had to do. I didn't go looking for violence in my minding jobs, it came to me. When I went looking for it at the fairs, gypsy camps, or with gloves in Frank's circus, I was doing it for my family — it paid well and gave them a good life. I took on very tough men, a lot of them bigger than me, so I wasn't taking liberties. They knew what they were up against and accepted it. Basically, I hate violence, especially if it's against weak people or the old or the young. I'm not one of those weird people who gets off on hurting others. I do it for defence or money.

Overnight, I'm a bit of a celebrity. I've been on TV and I'm headlines in the papers. I get stopped in the street for my autograph and I'm getting offers for fights from all over the place.

After the Shaw fight I spent a bit of time with Arthur Thomson before he and his men went back to Scotland. The last thing he said to me was, 'Lenny, as soon as you feel like it you and Ritchie come up to Glasgow, stay with me and we'll get a challenge or two thrown out.' I said, 'Lovely, Arthur — we'll do it some time.'

But that went out of my head for a while because I was getting a bit busy, what with the fights and training and, of course, I'm still doing my minding jobs.

I was down the Swan one Saturday night and I saw this bloke setting up a fish stall outside the gaff. I went over to have a word and it turns out to be Alan Dixon. I knew all about Alan and his brother George, but this was the first time I'd met him. I give him a hand to pull his stall up on the pavement and I started thinking, 'This bloke used to be doing really well until the law took liberties and fucked him up. I know he's suffered over the last few years and now he's got to start all over again.'

He must have guessed what I was thinking, because he said, 'You know, I've just come out of a nine stretch. Well, I want to keep my nut down, nick a living, and keep a low profile. So this jellied eel stall keeps me out of the way until I get things sorted and get on the up again.'

I said, 'I know what you mean, Al, but if you get any problems, I'm just behind the door of this gaff so give us a shout.'

He laughed, 'Fuck me, Len, it's only an eel stall, how can I have problems?'

One night a few weeks later I had some aggravation with the Watney Street Mob, young tearaways all in their twenties. This mob's always been about. As one lot get older and move on to bigger things, younger ones move in and take over. Same name, different kids, year after year. Anyway, they're smashing the place up, chucking beer about and threatening the customers. So I do my job and go through the lot of them.

Mob-handed, they think they're the business but they've got no chance. Every time I put one down I got him by the neck and the arse and flung him straight out the door. Over the noise of all this ruck I can hear Alan shouting, 'Ease up, Lenny, you're doing me fucking stall in ... Oh, Jesus Christ, Lenny, don't throw any more out.' What's he on about? I had to keep going. After about 20 minutes I cleared the place and I went outside. Alan was laughing and there were bodies all over the place. As I slung the tearaways through the door they ended up against the eel stall and sent it over, tipping whelks, winkles and eels all over the road.

Alan's got tears in his eyes laughing at all these mugs holding their heads and picking themselves off the deck.

I looked at all this man's spoiled shellfish and said, 'I'm sorry, mate, give us a minute and I'll make it right.' I rounded up all those battered tearaways and gave them a telling off. 'Because of you lot, there's been a fucking liberty taken here ... my friend's had his living kicked all over the road, so what do you say to a bit of compensation for him?' They look at me standing there growling and start digging out a bit of cash. I'm not demanding money, just asking for a little contribution, and those boys were pleased to give it with a good heart. Then I fucked them off.

Al used to be a bit warm on the cobbles himself so he could've nicked his own money back, no problem. But when you've been released from the nick with your bit of remission, you're on parole. You're a 'ticket of leave' man — any bit of aggro you get up to can put you straight back to finish the full term, so you have to be whiter than white. Alan couldn't risk putting himself about.

That was something that never worried him or his brothers, George and Brian, when they were on the streets back in the Fifties and Sixties. To give you some idea of how they grafted in those days, when the law put away the Richardsons, they concentrated on getting a result on the Krays. We all know they got that, then they turned on the Dixon family whom the law reckoned would try and fill the gap.

I've been up against the Old Bill when they're pulling out all the stops to get what they're after. I know how they work. The Dixons were debt collectors. People would ask them to bring in money that was owed because that was their legitimate business. Remember, the people they had to go after were in the rumping game. That's why there was a problem — they were slags who borrowed money and never intended to pay it back. Being slags they go to the law and start squealing that the Dixons are leaning on them with menaces. Lovely, says Old Bill, thanks very much, just what we want. We won't check out the background too much, just get in and get a good nicking.

So that's what they did. They didn't have enough on Brian, but George got a twelve and Alan went down for a nine.

When Alan came out he kicked off with his eel stall, then he moved up into the wine-bar game and opened a club over in Canning Town. He had his fair share of aggro and I think he got stabbed once, but now that's all behind him and he's just a businessman. George came out a couple of years later, took on a hotel and then expanded into the motor trade. He's nicely settled now down on the coast and doesn't get involved in anything. If ever they've got a problem, they know I'm at the end of the phone and I'm always there for them.

Craig Fairbrass, an up and coming actor who's a nephew of the Dixons, told me it's common knowledge that his Uncle George wears a bullet on his watch chain. Apparently, even though he was on good terms with the Krays, he had a bit of a run in with Ron. From what I've told you about myself, you can understand how easy it is to have a flare-up, even with your friends, if you've got the hump and you run on a short fuse. Reg had marked his card that Ron wasn't too happy, but George wasn't frightened of anybody so he turned up in the Green Dragon down Aldgate.

When he went for a piss, Ron followed him, pulled a gun, shoved it in his face, chipping one of his teeth, and pulled the trigger. The gun didn't go off. Ron laughed, took the bullet out, and gave it to George, saying, 'This is your lucky day.' Anybody else would have spent the rest of the night sitting on the toilet, but George took that sort of thing in his stride. And he's got medals to prove it.

He was driving down the road one day when he saw this kid taking shots at everybody. He stopped the car, went back, and took the gun off him.

On another occasion, a bloke started flashing a gun about in the City Arms, Millwall. George grabbed the shooter and downed him. He was awarded a bravery medal both times. They're good people — they've suffered and both paid their dues. Good luck to them.

Now that my reputation has spread all over, Frank Warren was working overtime to cash in on it. He rang me up one day, all excited, and said, 'Seen the papers today, Len?'

I said, 'No, I'll pop out and get one.' So I went round the corner and got myself a *Daily Mirror* and rang him straight back.

'Have you read about the SAS man who tried to snatch Biggsie the train robber from Brazil?'

I said, 'Yeah, he's on the front page — so what?'

'Lenny,' he says, 'I'm going to try and get a match with you and this bloke Miller. Can you see it — McLEAN FIGHTS SAS MAN — we'll rake in fortunes.'

I said, 'Lay it on, Frank. I think anybody who wants to capture a bloke to face 30 years inside deserves to be beaten to death for nothing.'

Frank got through to this Miller but he didn't want to know. He was nicking fortunes out of the papers and touring round universities telling them what a hero he was.

He tried the same with Mr T, the big black guy out of the television series *The A Team*. At that time he was a minder and a fighter like myself, but he'd just been offered the film part, so he didn't want to risk any damage to himself while he had the chance of being a star.

Frankie doesn't give up, though, if he thinks he can make a few quid. A while later he pulled the newspaper stunt again. The phone rang — 'Have you seen the papers? Go and get one.'

'Fuck me, Frank, why can't you just tell me what's on your mind and save me the price of a paper?' He loves a bit of drama.

This time he wanted me to fight John Bindon. Now this wouldn't be such a pleasure as taking on Miller, but John was well in the news and that would bring the punters in.

The word was that John had picked up a contract for ten grand to do away with a bit of a gangster named Darke who was running a little firm on the South side called 'The Wild Bunch'. Who really chopped Darke to bits in a yacht club over in Fulham I don't know, but Bindon got a 'not guilty' and that put him in the public eye. As well as being a bit of a hard man, he'd done a bit of acting, and often used to pop up in *The Sweeney* and stuff like that. So that was his excuse — he was back in the film world and didn't want to meet me. Frank offered him ten large through his girlfriend Vicki Hodge, the model, but he still wouldn't budge.

He was good stuff though. John and I never fell out and I was sorry to hear he'd died. If he's remembered for nothing else, he had one little trick that at parties he'd do at the drop of a hat — or his trousers. He'd balance six half crowns along the length of his 'old man'. He used to knock about with Princess Margaret and her mob, and it would be hard to believe that he could resist opening the royal eyes with his favourite stunt when they were all having a knees up on that Caribbean island they used to frequent.

I've spoken about Alex Steen and Joe Pyle; good men and well respected. As soon as I had stolen the title from Roy Shaw, they started doing a lot of business with me and, why not, they're businessmen, they want to put their money on a winner.

Joe Pyle has had a great deal of respect in South London for years. Back in the Fifties he was arrested on a murder charge and that was when hanging was still around, but he got a 'not guilty' and I think he's lived his life to the full ever since. When Roy Shaw came out of his 15, he and Joe became friends and started doing shows together, Roy fighting and Joe promoting.

Unfortunately, my lovely pal Joe got stuck with a 14-year sentence. For most of his time he was banged up on A Section in a shit-hole of a prison, Whitemoor up Cambridge way. When you're on A Section you're watched all the time and in the cell 23 hours a day, so you suffer double punishment. I've still got a letter he wrote to me one year that reads, 'Len, Christmas was a bastard for all of us here. You probably read about the riots. Well, because of them we spent Christmas day choking on the stink of fires and two inches of water on the cell floor. Wasn't like being at home.'

I won't say anything about Joe's bit of trouble, because after a long struggle he got an appeal heard and his sentence was reduced to a seven, and now he's free and getting on with his life outside. Good luck, Joey, you've been a good friend; enjoy life, you deserve it.

Alex Steen; now there's a character. Friend of the top people in the underworld and the same with them in what he calls the upper world and well respected by both. He has never done a day's bird in his life but he understood what it was like for those who did end up behind the door, and supported them all the way. He's the only person I know who visited Ron Kray from the first day of his 30-year sentence. There's not much he won't do for his own and there's very little he can't do. He's got the ear of everyone and he uses that to help people, stop wars breaking out, and keep things smooth. With his quiet voice and those dark glasses he wears all the time, his friends call him the 'Godfather'. I think he loves it, really. Those glasses are no gimmick though; he has to wear them because he's got an eye problem. He's had business with or managed more famous boxers and entertainment personalities than I'd have room to put down here. He's always there for everybody. Apart from his work, he's a lovely family man and grandfather and I've got lots of time for him.

So these two invite me to Alex's office to discuss taking on a geezer by the name of Paul Sykes, who was under their wing. A very tough man, but no fool. In the dozen or so years he'd spent behind bars, he'd not only got himself a couple of university degrees and a City and Guilds in bricklaying, he built himself up to a professional standard in the ring. In fact, he was fighting Gardner at Wembley about a week later. Alex said, 'If he loses to Gardner I'm getting him to fight you.' I told him I was keen to take on Sykes, but all the ins and outs he could sort out with Frank.

Frank, Bobby and I went to Wembley to see the fight. Before we went in, we saw Alex pull up in his big white Rolls Royce and out stepped Paul Sykes. I don't know about any masters degrees — he looked a right ex-con.

Gardner had done him by the sixth round. Just before it was stopped on a technical knockout, I was watching one of Paul's seconds jumping up and down in the corner and screeching like a girl. 'Do this, do that, box him, throw a left.' It was getting on my tits — I don't know about Sykes. All of a sudden, he turns to the second — dodgy thing to do in the middle of a fight — and bellows, 'Fucking shut up!' Then Jim Brimmel, the ref, grabbed his arm and signalled the fight was over. I found out afterwards that for a second he thought he'd been stopped for swearing because he didn't think he was anywhere near losing.

I said to Frank, 'Go on, shoot round the dressing room and tell him personal that I'll fight him with gloves or without gloves. But I want an "all in" — the whole business, anything goes.'

He came back and said, 'Alex Steen's already blown in his ear and it's all set, but it's got to be with gloves.'

I said, 'Don't matter, I'll do him any way.'

Frank and Bobby were well pleased. They reckoned that if we held it at the Rainbow they'd pull in a hundred grand. They put me down for £15,000, which I thought was a bit skinny, but I didn't say anything. Fifteen was better than a kick in the nuts, though I'd probably get a couple of them before I picked up the wedge. So I went back to training again.

After seeing Sykes perform at Wembley, I reckon he's a pushover, for me anyway. But Mickey said we'd better cover all the angles and one of them was to take a run up to Blackpool and have a word with the bloke who used to train Sykes. I met the trainer and for a little drink he put me wise on the best way to do the business on Paul. Then he sent us along to see a doctor who'd been involved in the training. This Dr McGill said, 'I'll give you an injection that'll make you a very strong man.'

'Fuck off,' I said, 'I don't take drugs. I hate them and I'm well strong enough already.' He gives me some old fanny though, said it wouldn't do any harm, so I let him do it.

Later on, I went for a run. Five miles was usually plenty for me, but this time I couldn't stop. I did 15 and felt like I could do the same again. For two days I was wide awake and raring to go.

I went back to McGill and said, 'What have you put me on? It's driving me crackers.'

'That's a new steroid — very potent.'

I said, 'It's made me like a fucking raging bull. I don't need it, I'm a raging bull anyway.' I have never taken drugs since, unless you count what was forced on me in prison, and that's another story.

A week before the off, Sykes went into a club in Wakefield where he lives, got well pissed and had a ruck with four doormen. He did them all but one of them got lucky and put a cut above his eye that took eight stitches to pull it together. Then he was on the blower to Alex saying the fight's off and we're all bolloxed.

This fight's been hyped all over the place — 'bout of the century' and all that cobblers to sell the tickets. It's been all over the papers and on television. Then Frank gives me a knock back when he says 'Len, it's out the window.'

Anyway, they dug up a geezer from somewhere. Big strong lad, but nutty as a fruitcake. I could've done this kid with no hands, but I didn't. I played around with him. First round I danced all round the ring with him, then just before the bell I knocked him clean out, picked him up, and dropped him in his corner. He had time to come round and we're off again. I whispered in his ear, 'Stay on your feet, go the distance, and I won't hurt you.' He was still a bit groggy from being knocked out but he heard me and gave a nod. I did this for ten rounds, letting him get a few punches in to knock his points up. Final bell, they totalled the points and Donny Adams, who was the ref this night, couldn't believe what he was doing when he had to hold up the other bloke's hand.

I'd been pretty busy with the fight game for a few years but I was still around to help people out or do a few favours. I've said I don't do favours for nothing, but now and then I'll sort something out if I think a liberty's been taken.

I walked into a club one night and I saw a pal of mine, who'll remain nameless. He looked a bit sad and I wasn't surprised because his young brother had been murdered and the slags who'd done it had just got acquitted at the Bailey. I said, 'How you going, mate, holding up?' His eyes filled up and he said, 'No, Len, I'm not. I miss me brother bad and what's gutted me is the c**ts that done him are pissing it up round the Basing House and bragging about their result.' All I could say was, 'Hold it together, son, they'll get theirs when the time's right.'

Now this bloke is well pissed, and has been losing himself in the bottle ever since the trial. He pulled out a handgun and started waving it about.

'I'm going after the lot of them now,' he said. 'Me brother would've done it if it was the other way round.' I took the shooter off him, calmed him down, and talked him into letting me handle it. As I told him, if he went tearing round the pub in his state he was going to get himself killed or end up being lifed off for murder. 'You know you can trust me,' I said. 'I promise you they won't be laughing by the end of the week.'

Now, I'm too well known to put myself up for this one, but I would've loved to have sorted them slags with my bare hands. Got to use the nut, though. No point in saving him from a murder charge and getting one myself. So I got in touch with a firm out of South London and called in a favour of my own.

Within the week, like I promised, the three of them were well sorted and put in hospital — one of them in intensive care. Didn't cost a penny and there was no comeback. Old Bill didn't even interview my pal, so it shows how interested they were in tracking down whoever had done it. It didn't do anything for my pal's brother but it made him feel a lot better knowing they'd got the justice the law couldn't provide. There was no chance of my name coming up in connection with that business, even though it was well known that we were good mates. As it happens, when it went down Ritchie and I were in Scotland, so we were well out of it.

Arthur Thomson had invited us both to stay with him and while we were there he took us to see the Jim Watt fight at Ibrox Park, Glasgow. We got a plane up there and he met us at the airport and took us straight back to his home, where his wife Rita had a big spread laid on. His place wasn't just one house, it was two knocked together and inside it was like a palace. Giving it the once over, you didn't need half an eye to see the whole place was like Fort Knox. Arthur hadn't survived as long as he had without taking a few precautions.

You have to speak as you find. He was a tough man — big barrel chest and a fighter's face — but a complete gentleman who treated me like a son. A lot of people wouldn't have had the same opinion.

The papers called him the most dangerous man in Scotland. Nobody who crossed him ever got away with it, not even the law. In a case during the Sixties, one copper decided he was better off emigrating after being threatened with having his house bombed. On and off in the early years he did about ten years' bird for assault, robbery, safe blowing and housebreaking. Six times the law got him to court for razor slashings, but they never managed to pin anything on him.

If Reg and Ron Kray needed a bit of 'sorting' north of the border, Arthur was the man they called on, and he never let them down. Got himself a nickname as the 'Assassin', that's how well he did his job. Three months after he got an acquittal for killing Jim Goldie and Pat Welch, he was setting off to drive his mother-in-law to the shops, but as he turned the key a bomb went off under the car killing Margaret instantly. Arthur survived but, as far as I know, the bombers didn't.

While I was sitting on a murder charge myself, Arthur wrote to me every week without fail. Then he missed a week and I guessed something was up because he could be relied on. I had to wait until the following week to find out in his letter that his son, Arthur Junior, had been shot dead at the front door while he was on home leave from an 11-year stretch. Arthur was gutted and I don't think he ever got over it. But heartbroken as he was, it didn't stop him from sorting out the bastards responsible. On the day they were burying his boy, the two blokes responsible were found shot dead, in a car, in the East End of Glasgow.

The first thing I set my eyes on when I woke up the next morning was this man that straight people think of as 'that terrible gangster'. He was standing by my bed, a breakfast tray in his hands, and wearing the widest tartan braces I have ever seen in my life — they must have been four inches across.

'Fuck me, Arthur,' I said, 'ain't they invented belts up here yet?' He put the tray down, gave his braces a twang, and growled, 'See these, son? I bought them in Galashiels in 1951 and they're as good as new.' Then he dropped the daily papers on my chest saying, 'I hope you're making an exception for me in your headlines.'

I grabbed the *People* and right across the front page was LENNY MCLEAN SAYS ALL SCOTS ARE PORRIDGE-GUZZLING COWARDS. He was giving me his menacing look. 'I never said that Arthur, honest. What I said was, "They're all porridge-guzzling c**ts."' We had a good laugh at that. 'This is down to Ritchie you know. I told that to him yesterday — I didn't expect him to ring the papers with it, though. What's going on?'

He didn't have to answer. As I read the papers I could see that Ritchie's got me challenging every hard man in Scotland: '*After the Jim Watt fight on Saturday, the "Cockney Guv'nor" will throw out a challenge to any Scotsman willing to take him on. Come on, lads, who will flatten this Sassenach and defend Scotland's honour?*'

Arthur was laughing. I said, 'You and Ritchie set this up between you, didn't you?'

'Aye,' he said, 'couldn't resist making a few shillings out of you while you're here — help pay for your lodgings.'

We saw the Watt fight and with everybody keyed up about the match we sat back and waited for the challenges. On Monday afternoon we got a call from somebody putting up John Curry. 'Leave it out, Arthur,' I said. 'I ain't fighting a poncy ice skater.'

'No, son' — he always called me son — 'this is a very different Curry and a very hard man — well known, and his name will have the side bets pouring in.'

We never even had a chance to have a word with him. Two days later we got a call from the same bloke as before. Curry's got himself nicked doing an armed robbery and he's in custody. So that's blown out.

Straight away we get another challenge, so we grab it with both hands before this bastard chokes on a haggis or something. Five grand side-stake, with six-ounce gloves, as near bare knuckles as the law allows. Not brilliant money, but a good start. Arthur fixed up the fight in one of his clubs, got the tickets and posters sorted, and we're off.

This geezer, Robert Young, looked the business. He was 6ft 7$\frac{1}{2}$in tall, weighed in at 17 stone, and at one time was the heavyweight champion of the First Royal Scots, a right flash Scottish regiment. That's where he'll fall down. I'm a street fighter, he's a boxer — we think different. He's been trained up on all that Queensberry stuff. I don't know what the rules are, and never wanted to know.

I like to get a bit of needle going right from the start; it throws your opposition's concentration. So as we touched gloves, I said, 'Is that right that you guardsmen are all poofters?' Lovely, touched a sore point. We didn't even wait for the bell, he swung a vicious right and I planted one up his derby as it skimmed past my head. I caught him in the ribs with a left and as that brought him down nearer my height I nutted him in the face. He's gone. Both his eyebrows are split and the blood's blinding him. Hit a blind man? Too fucking right. I hit him right on the point of his chin and he was spark out before he hit the deck. One minute twenty-five seconds, not a mark on me and five large in the bin.

That Scottish mob didn't like it one bit. They were booing and shouting and doing their nut. I stamped around the ring like a wild man shouting to the crowd, 'You don't fucking like it, come up here and have some.' They screamed even louder, but it didn't matter where I looked, I couldn't get one of those mugs to catch my eye. I was right, they're all mouth. They didn't have the bottle, though I think that Arthur's boys being all round the ring packing shooters might have had something to do with keeping some of them in their seats. If they hadn't been there, I think I could have had the whole lot climbing through the ropes.

As I moved up the aisle from the ring, somebody tapped me on the arm and said, 'I'll be seeing you, Jimmy,' then he was pushed out of the way by Arthur's team of hard boys. I look back and he's talking to Ritchie — after my autograph I expect.

When we got in the car, Ritchie said, 'I've got you fixed up for Thursday — £16,000 — winner takes all.'

Arthur said to me, 'It's that laddie that spoke to you just now. I know him, he's been running the Bar L for years.'

I said, 'What's that, one of your clubs?'

They both looked at each other and laughed. 'Sort of, Lenny ... it's Scotland's toughest prison.'

I said, 'Make it early, then — I've told my Val I'll be home late Thursday.'

This time Arthur fixes it up in one of his pubs. Well, not inside, in the back yard — bit exclusive. It's going to be all-in, bare knuckles, and as Scottish law is the same as down south we've got to be a bit cagey.

Before we set off for the fight, Ritchie and I packed our gear in our hold-alls. We wouldn't be coming back to Provenhall that night. We'd do the business and get off home. While I was packing, Arthur came in and sat on the bed.

'You're a cocky bastard, Lenny, I like that. Do you never think somebody's going to hammer you?'

'I ain't cocky, Arthur, I'm confident in myself. I'll tell you something. Apart from that git Irwin I told you about, no man has ever knocked me off my feet. Some people have hurt me inside where it don't show, but no man has ever damaged me with his fists or his feet, in the ring or on the cobbles, and they never will.

'I'm not giving you a load of bollocks, Arthur. I don't kid myself I'm Superman, it's just that there's something inside me that won't let me be beaten. I took a lot of shit when I was a kid and couldn't defend myself, and ever since then every fight I have is for that little kid I used to be.'

There was something about Arthur that made you want to confide in him — you knew he wouldn't take the piss. All he said was, 'You're all right, son,' and patted me on the shoulder — good bloke. He knew what life was all about.

We came in the back entrance to the pub — the Barley Mow. The bloke I was fighting, I'll just call him Jock, had a group of men with him straight out of a gangster film. Like Arthur's braces they must have bought their suits and hats back in the Fifties. Jock stripped his shirt off and advertised that he was an ex-con. He was tattooed from arsehole to breakfast time — well, chest, neck and arms, anyway. Prison tattoos aren't like the ones you get outside. They're crude and the colours are all different shades, because they're done with pins, razor blades and whatever colours can be dug out of Biro pens. He had the lot. Dotted line round the throat saying 'Cut here' (might take him up on that), and 'Kill' and 'Death' on his knuckles. What a fucking ape.

As he came at me he had hate oozing out of him and he was growling like a dog. I bet he frightened the shit out of everybody in Barlinnie, but it didn't work with me. I let him hit me about a dozen times just to blow some steam off, and just when he started thinking I don't know how to throw one, I caught him full on the ear. Gloves take the sting out of a punch. Bare knuckles rip, and half his ear flapped down, leaking blood all over him. I don't think he felt it because he came back with a left and a right, very low, one on the hip bone, one on the old chap. I'd be pissing round corners for a week.

I stepped back and kicked him in the kneecap. I could feel my big toe snap, but as he's gone down on his good knee and half swung round I knuckled him in the kidney as hard as I could hit. He's gone all the way down, so I dropped my 19 stone into the middle of his back. He gave a sort of 'whoosh' and tried to roll over but I just punched and punched him until he didn't move. As I stood up his legs twitched so I started kicking him in the ribs and the face. Somebody grabbed my arm and I downed whoever it was with the other one. Then about half-a-dozen people weighed me down, dragging me over to the wall, and Ritchie, I think it was, slung a glass of water in my face.

I came out of it and it was like waking up. My arms and legs think they're still fighting but those blokes had got a tight grip on me. As my breathing slowed down, I was back with them again. I pushed them off and sat down on an empty beer barrel. I watched as Jock was rolled on to his back but he wasn't moving at all.

Arthur came over and said, 'Come on, Len, we'll get you out of here.'

I said, 'Have we got our money, and what's the fucking rush, is he dead or what?'

'Never mind him, Ritchie's got your money and I'm going to get one of my lads to drive you to London. I'll ring you at home tomorrow.' I shook hands with him and realised my hand was broken — apparently, both of them were. The next thing I knew, we were in one of Arthur's Jags and doing 100mph towards the south.

Ritchie said, 'Nice one, Lenny, £21,000 in all.'

I said, 'It's not that funny Scotch money, is it, them notes that look like they're out of a Monopoly set?'

He laughed, knowing I like to wind him up. 'I don't know why it bothers you. They spend just the same ... but in case you're worried they're mostly Sassenach fifties.' He flung me a couple of pills and I swallowed them down. The last thing I remember is him saying, 'Forget this one, he would've killed you if you'd given him the chance.'

I woke up just before we pulled in to Charing Cross Hospital. They did my hands up and we were out in an hour. I never mentioned my toe — I couldn't be bothered wasting any more time; I just wanted to get home, let it mend on its own. I was tucked up with my Val by seven o'clock that morning. Good result, but nice to be home.

Arthur rung me up later that day and the first thing I wanted to know was how that Jock was doing. I don't usually give a second thought about fighters I've done the business on, but this time I had a funny feeling.

'What's up with you, son,' Arthur said, 'did you think you'd killed him?'

I think I laughed a bit too loud when I said, 'Nah, course I didn't. I was just wondering if I've got to come back up to Scotland and do him again.'

'Well, Lenny, considering Jock was unconscious for an hour after you left, you proved a point, but I don't think he'll be looking for a return for a long while yet.'

Fancy me thinking I've done him in — I must be getting soft.

I said to Val, 'I ain't crippling round Hoxton looking like a road accident. Let's treat ourselves and get out of it.' So with plenty of dough in the bin we took a lovely holiday. Set me up a treat.

I wasn't long back and nicely healed up when a relation of mine, Dennis McCarthy, came round with his partner, an ex-copper. They hadn't long taken over the Barbican Club in Smithfield Meat Market and they were having a bit of a struggle because of all the aggro. I knew the club and I knew the bloke they had on the door, Billy Reece. Bill was a nice guy and that was his trouble. He wanted to be friends with everybody. When you have that attitude everybody takes you for a mug and that's when the trouble starts. He was getting it from everywhere and couldn't handle it.

I knew what was coming; they wanted me to take over the minding. I was due for a change of scenery but I didn't tell them that. 'Sorry, Dennis,' I said, 'I'm well fixed up down the Swan. They look after me and give me good dough.'

'Len, we're desperate — how about a £100 a night?'

I said, 'I'll be round tomorrow.' I went down there, straightened all the aggravation, busted a few heads, and everything was lovely ... for a while.

One rule of mine is never to let stag parties into the club. They get pissed up, then boisterous, then nasty. They're a pain in the arse. On one particular night they came in twos and threes; they knew the rule so they were being a bit crafty. They were downstairs — 18 of them. They were all right at first, but now they had passed the first two stages and were just starting on the nasty.

They'd been drinking all night, but all of a sudden they didn't like the prices. When the girl behind the bar asked for £38.00, not bad for 18 drinks, they started telling her to 'Fuck off' and gave her a load of grief until she was in tears. Dennis thought about being the hard man, but having weighed them up he had second thoughts and decided he'd be better off calling me down.

Down I went. 'Right, you mob, pay up and piss off.' Then they're all giving it some; 'fat bastard', 'fucking gorilla' and all that. I said to them, 'OK, you're all drunk, there's 18 of you and you're very brave. You want to fight, we'll go outside,' and I started shoving the ones at the front. As they're on the way out they're picking up glasses, bottles and ashtrays and putting them in their pockets — but I've got them on the move.

Eddie Richardson was sitting at one of the tables with a couple of friends. He used to do a bit of boxing so he's a tasty fella to have beside you. I heard somebody say, 'Are you going to give Lenny a hand, Eddie?'

'No,' he said, 'Len doesn't need any help. He'll square them off on his own in two minutes.'

I was still shoving these mugs out and I thought, 'He's giving me bundles of credit there, but a bit of help wouldn't be out the way.'

As this mob went out of the door, they turned round and started smashing bottles and glasses up the front of the club. I turned to Dennis and said, 'Come on, we've got to hurt this lot.'

He said, 'I'm not going out there ... that's what I'm paying you for.'

I said, 'I know that, but it's your fucking club.' He wouldn't budge though, gutless coward. As I stepped outside, he locked the door behind me — so I was on my own.

The next minute, a good pal of mine is at my elbow; I don't know where he came from. 'Wanna hand, Len?'

I said, 'You are a lovely man, but I think I can handle this one. Mind my back though, and if I get out of breath I'll give you a shout.'

This mob was still hollering and playing up so I shouted, 'Oy! Shut it, all of you. Pack it in and calm down. Now listen ... listen.' As I said that the whole lot were like a load of school kids; they stopped shouting and sort of grouped round me. And I thought, 'Lenny, you've got the bastards.'

All of a sudden, I slipped into them. I pulled a nice little cosh out of my pocket and went through the lot of them. They went down like skittles as I slashed left and right like a maniac. I could hear Old Bill coming. I shouted at my pal to fuck off quick and he gave me a wave and shot down an alley. Nine geezers were on the deck and the rest were on their toes. As the vans pulled up, I slung the cosh right over the roof. Then we were all nicked and shot down to Snow Hill. They rounded up the nine who ran off, brought them into the nick, and banged them up in the big holding cell opposite mine. There were about 13 of these blokes, the rest were in Bart's Hospital. The booze and piss have worn off by now and they aren't half as brave. Me, I don't drink. I'm sober and clean.

The flap on my door was down and so was theirs, and I could see most of them standing about looking sick. I stuck my face up against the flap and I started growling and screaming at them, 'You gutless bastards ... you fucking mugs, you're like little lambs now. Look at me. Go on, look at me. You're not seeing me with drink inside me, I'm like this all the time, a cold sober ravin' lunatic.' None of them wanted to look.

To shut me up, two coppers took me up to the CID room. They said, 'We're going for a section 18 on this one. You've given some of these blokes broken jaws, concussion, and one of them's got five ribs broken.'

I said, 'Don't fucking talk to me, what would you have done?'

They said, 'Len, we wouldn't have gone outside with that lot.'

'I had to, though!' I shouted at them. 'It was my job. I was minding the gaff and, on top of that, it's my pride and reputation.' I think they were on my side, but they still had to go through the DPR.

Three weeks later, I had to answer my bail and I got a result. They said they'd had a note from upstairs saying, 'We do not think it is prudent to use public funds in pursuit of a charge that one man assaulted 18 others.' Of course they wouldn't — it would have looked a bit funny in the papers, wouldn't it?

So that's off my mind and I'm back on the door of the Barbican. On

Monday to Thursday, when it's a bit quiet, I do the door on my own. On Friday and Saturday, when everybody's out on the town, I have a bit of help. It was Saturday so I had Bill Sullivan with me. I was just inside the door, and Bill was chatting to some birds at the top of the stairs.

Suddenly, there was a bang like a bomb going off. The front window of the club was shattered into a million pieces and I was thrown up into the air.

Bill fell straight down the stairs and took the birds with him. I didn't feel anything. I ran out to the front and two geezers on a motorbike were coming along the pavement for another pop. The one on the pillion had a 12-bore, and I took them by surprise. They must have thought I was well shot up and didn't expect me to come flying out. As they went past me I shouted, 'You c**nts,' and I kicked the back wheel. The bike wobbled all over the place, the gunmen let one go up in the air, but his mate straightened up and they were away.

I went back into the club — my arse is on fire and my feet are soaked in the blood that's running down my legs and squelching in my shoes. Everybody's round Bill who's still on the deck — when the bang flung him down the stairs, he knocked himself spark out.

I said, 'Hold up, don't fucking worry about him, I've had my arse shot off.'

Dennis is flapping all over the place. 'I've called an ambulance, Len, it'll be here in five minutes.'

'Five minutes! I'm losing gallons of claret and I can't wait that long. I'm getting a cab.'

I went out, stopped a cab, and told him to get me to the hospital. The cabby said, 'You can't get in my cab, you're smothered in blood.'

'Forget smothered in fucking blood,' I said, 'I'll kneel up in the back. Put the mess on the bill.' He dropped me at Bart's and when I asked what I owe him, he said, 'Leave it out, have it on the firm.'

I walked in the hospital about half-twelve. there was a porter sitting in his cubbyhole reading a comic. I said, ''Scuse me, pal, what can you do for a bloke with two arseholes?'

He let out a screeching laugh. 'Hey, man, you drunk or what?'

I said, 'No, I've been shot,' and I turned round and let him see the bloody mess through the hole ripped in my trousers. I must admit I was feeling a bit dizzy by then. I stayed on my feet, though.

All hell broke loose. I had got myself there under my own steam, and now they wouldn't let me walk to Casualty. I was laid on a stretcher, they stuck a drip in my arm, and I was rushed up to theatre so they can dig the lead out of my bum and stitch me up.

When I came round next morning, Old Bill's sitting by the bed reading the *Daily Mirror*. I said, 'What do you want?'

He said, 'I've been waiting to get a statement off you.'

'You're going to have a long wait, then, pal. I don't talk to you people. I'm saying nothing so you might as well bugger off.'

He said, 'Suit yourself, but I'll be back.' He came back three days later and I had to sign a form saying, 'Mr McLean does not wish any enquiries to be made into the firearms incident at the Barbican Club.'

In the meantime, McCarthy come up to Bart's with his arms full of fruit and stuff like that. 'Sorry you got shot, Len,' he said.

'Don't worry, Den, goes with the job. What I'm going to do is discharge myself at the end of the week and I'll be back on the door Monday. Good news or what?'

He shifted uneasily in his seat, so I guessed something was on his mind. 'Actually, Lenny, we're going to let you go. The police have said that if you stay on the door, they won't renew the club licence when it comes due. They said the reason is nobody's going to settle grudges with you unless they're tooled up. That means a lot of gunplay. Somebody's going to get killed and the law won't have it — so we can't keep you on.'

'Well, Dennis my old pal, that's tough because I ain't fucking going. You come here with a bag of apples and tell me to piss off after what I've done for you. I sorted all your agg, and now the fireworks are going off you can't wait to pull the plug on my pension. Forget it.'

I thought he went off with the hump, but he came back the next day, dropped an envelope on the bed and said, 'Five large there, Len ... shall we call it severance pay?'

I said, 'That'll do me, lovely. Mind how you go, Dennis. Be lucky.'

What a star. He showed his true colours when he locked the door behind me at the first sign of trouble. I was well out of it. I put the word out but never got a whisper about who'd shot me. It could have been any one of 500 people. I'd hurt a lot of blokes with my hands, and had been involved in some heavy stuff, so it was anybody's guess which particular one had got the hump with me.

A pal of mine, Donny Adams, got in touch. He'd done a lot of bird in his time, and was very useful as a bare-knuckle fighter in his younger days. He said, 'How's the bum, Len?'

'Lovely, Don, healed nicely and I'm back in the game.'

'Good stuff,' he said. 'I've got something to put to you. There's this little boy over Canning Town, he's about three years old. If he don't get a brain operation in America very soon he's going to die, so I'm trying to raise some money.'

'Poor little sod, put me down for a monkey.'

'No, Len,' he said, 'it'd be better if you'd have an all-in bare-knuckle fight for him. Nobody else could pull the punters in like you could. What do you think?'

'Smashing idea, as long as the kid gets every penny. I'll fight anybody — go ahead and set it up.'

Donny and a few others did the business. They got a tasty geezer from South London to take me on and tickets were selling really well. It all had to be done on the Q.T. because time was running out for the kid. There wasn't even enough time to have a newspaper campaign — he needed big money, quick.

His mum rang me up and she cried on the telephone while she was thanking me. 'It's a wonderful thing you're doing. I hope you don't get hurt, though.'

I said, 'Listen, I can win, lose, or break my hands. I promise you I ain't going to lose and if I bust something, a couple of weeks and it's mended. But your baby will live the rest of his life, and he'll look back and I hope he will think about us chaps that saved his life.'

A week before the fight some grassing bastard phoned the law and gave them all the details and it had to be cancelled. We pleaded with the police to turn a blind eye but they wouldn't budge. All the money had to go back and the baby died. The bastard who grassed us up might as well have gone round and stuck a knife in that little boy because they murdered him anyway.

That would have been the first fight I'd taken up since I was shot, so what with the word going round that I was back on the cobbles, I got a bid from a fighter by the name of Brian Bradshaw, a scrap dealer. He was a bit handy with his fists and liked to call himself the 'Mad Gypsy'. He'd got himself backed by some well-known 'names' so the purse was well into five figures. Not that I gave a bollocks. Money was nice, but if somebody challenges me I'll knock them down for £20 or £20,000.

I was up Freddie Hill's gym doing a bit of training, nothing too heavy, just toning myself up. There was a kid there doing a bit as well. When we put fights on he'd be on the undercard. I'd be top of the bill, and all the rest made up the numbers to give the punters a warm up. The kid, Billy Quinn, asked me to give him a few rounds sparring because he didn't have a partner. I said, 'No problem. What I'll do, 'cos you're such a weedy little bastard, is I'll put on 18 ounce gloves, then I won't hurt you. I'll just fiddle about.'

So off we go and he stuck a few on me. I got him moving about but I'm holding back because it's only a spar. After a bit I said, 'Billy, look, I'm going to have to slip a few in — let you know I'm here, or you might as well be on the bag.'

He said, 'All right, Len, away you go.'

I let him play around a bit more, and then I've given him two up the derby and he went over like a sack of shit. He jumped up all red in the face and shouted, 'That's out of order, you big c**t.'

I said, 'Hold on a minute ... I'm doing this for your benefit. You're too slow and you ain't fit.'

He was well narked. 'We're supposed to be sparring and you've took a liberty, so fuck off.' Then he climbed out the ring and went into the showers.

I took my gloves off and followed him in. I got him by the throat and pinned him up against the shower, his feet swinging off the floor. 'Listen, you mug, don't you ever swear at me in front of people. I oughta kill you stone dead.'

'All right ... All right ... All right. I'm sorry,' he spluttered. I left it at that, we got dressed, and no more was said.

A week later I was upstairs at home. The kids were out and Val was down the Roman Road market doing a bit of shopping. The front door bell went and I shouted down, 'It ain't locked, come on in.' As I said that I went to the top of the stairs and looked down. The door opened and Billy Quinn stepped in. 'Hello, Bill,' I said, 'how you doing?'

He stuck his hand inside his coat, pulled out a gun and fired straight at me. Bang. Bang. One past my head, one in the stairs. I flung myself to one side and he shouted, 'Think you're tough? Well fuck you!' and he let three more go. He missed me again but murdered the banister. I dived down the stairs, grabbed a short baseball bat I kept behind the door, and went after him, but he was away. Now my nut's ticking over. Has this slag got the hump over a little tap up the derby, or is he working for some firm who want me out of the way? First the Barbican, now this.

At least I know this one. When I find him, he's in dead trouble. I went everywhere looking for him. I put the feelers out but nobody had seen him. He'd done a runner.

One afternoon I was sitting at the traffic lights in my car down

Hackney way, and there was a tap on the window. I looked up and this fat old geezer, Stevie Pearce, was waving his arms about. I leaned over, opened the door, and he said, 'Len, I know who shot you down the Barbican.'

I just said, 'Get in,' then I pulled through the lights and parked up. He gave me a name. I said, 'You sure? I know the name but he's with so and so and they're good people.' I won't talk about who these people are because this firm's still active.

Stevie said, 'Straight up, Lenny, I got a good whisper, it's definitely down to him.' So I bunged him a tenner and tore off.

I cruised round a bit making enquiries eventually ending up in the Feathers. Looking looking through the window, I can see the slag on his own in the corner. I got hold of him and dragged him into the toilets before he knew what was happening. 'Right, you c**t, before I tear your face off I want to know what's behind you digging me out with a shooter?' He was shaking like a leaf

'Gimme a minute ... gimme a minute, please. Who told you it was me?'

I said, 'Fella by the name of Pearce.'

'Jesus Christ, Len, he's pulling a stroke, honest. What's happened, I've lent him three grand with good heart because he was in trouble. Now he wants you to sort me out so he don't have to pay it back. He knows what you're like so he thinks he's got me squared off.'

What could I say? I bought him a drink, we shook hands, and I went to find Stevie. I found him. I hope he's still praying to God every day that Lenny McLean isn't a liberty taker. I told him, 'If you wasn't 64 years old I would break every bone in your body.'

He's whining like a pup. 'Sorry, Len, I was desperate.'

'Sorry ... fucking sorry. You nearly got a bloke seriously hurt, or worse, so you could rump him. I never want to set eyes on you again. Cross the road if you see me coming, or get out the pub when I walk in, because you're the biggest slag I've ever come across. You're worse than that bloke that shot me in the back.' He was white as a ghost and lost two stone in sweat. 'And, oh yeah, while I'm at it, I'll have that tenner back.'

No more came of my enquiries so I put it all out of my head and got ready to take on Bradshaw. By now I'd heard he was a nasty bit of work, but then I think he'd have to go some to get anywhere near as nasty as I could be.

The fight was held in a pub over in Eltham, the Yorkshire Grey. It was a big place, so we squeezed plenty of punters in — about 1,000 of them were there looking for blood. I didn't like being over the south side much, so all I wanted to do was put him away quick, pick up the wedge, and get home — no hanging about.

Reg Parker the promoter had put on a good do — TV cameras, the lot. I was in my corner sizing up this gypsy character and thinking, 'Five seconds and I'm putting this glove right through your ribs.' Nearly ready for the off, we centre ring, touch gloves, and I can't believe it, this arsehole has nutted me. We had agreed on a straightener and immediately he had given me the nut.

I stepped back, shook the steam out of my eyes, and went for him like a fucking raving lunatic. I smashed him twice in the head and he went down. I got him by the hair, lifted his head up, and smashed it again. Punch after punch I drove into him as he was laying there, then in went the boot — in the face, neck, body, head, I drove my foot in as hard as I could and as he sprawled on his back I stamped on his chest and, to finish him, on the head. He took quite a liberty fighting dirty. Now he'd paid the price. From what I heard afterwards, I must have been in front of the telly with my Horlicks before he regained consciousness. Forty-five minutes he lay in the dressing room out cold. I'd broken his ribs, jaw and cheek-bones, and he had concussion. It was a month before he came out of hospital. I didn't sympathise one bit — he knew the score.

Of course, there were ructions in the media. They said I was evil, an animal and a lunatic. Stuff 'em. The police checked out the video to see if they could do me, but they couldn't. The firm who owned the pub gave the manager a load of grief — it all came to nothing though. It was wonderful publicity for me. Good or bad, it doesn't matter — if your name's up there, it's worth money.

Our little scrap was shown on the television programme *Today* showing the horrors of unlicensed boxing. Mugs. Why can't they understand that nobody gets forced into the ring at the point of a gun? All of us know the score. The best of it is that half of those people saying how shocking it all is are the ones who come to watch.

Out of the blue, I got a phonecall and this very polite voice said, 'Lenny McLean?'

I said, 'Yes, speaking, who is that?' I can turn on the old plum when I want to.

The voice said, 'This is Frankie Fraser. I've just watched your fight with the gypsy — great fight, very, very violent. I've got to say you're a bit of a spiteful bastard.'

That made me laugh. Coming from Frankie Fraser that's like the pot calling the kettle black, because there's no one as spiteful as he used to be.

The man has been a legend for many, many years, going all the way back to Spotty and Hill. From when he was about 14, he managed to get himself put behind the door on and off for something like 30 years plus. One occasion was when he got a seven with my uncle Bob Warren for doing Jack Spot. Another was when I was at Borstal when he got a ten with the Richardsons. He never spent one easy day in prison. He hated the system and the system hated him because it couldn't control him. If he wanted to chin a screw he did it, never stopping to think about the consequences. It didn't matter who it was, if they upset Frankie they copped it. Once, back in the Fifties, he planted one on the prison governor for being, as Frank put it, 'bang out of order'. For that he was sentenced to 20 strokes from the cat-o'-nine tails.

We were talking about the old days once and he said, 'Len, you wouldn't believe that flogging lark, it was like something out of the Dark Ages. If you was to treat a dog like that you'd have got locked up. What they done was to strap your wrists and ankles to this big wooden frame that had a big square of leather stretched over it. There was a slit in the leather and one of the screws would shove your head through so you couldn't look behind and see who was striping you. It'd go all quiet for a bit, then the governor would say, "Stroke one," and there'd be this sort of whistling whoosh, then, *bosh*, the bollocks was knocked right out of you as them nine strips of knotted rope cut across your back. If that whip caught you low on the back it drove every drop of air out of you and there was just time to catch a bit of breath before, *bosh*, it started again. By the time they flung you back in the cell, the blood was running out the bottom of your trousers.'

If those bastards thought they'd got a result and were going to quieten Frankie down, they had to think again — and again — and again, because he got the cat or the birch loads of times and never opened his mouth. All they achieved was to make him harder to handle and hate the system more than ever. He was called 'Mad Frankie', but he's one of the sanest, nicest blokes I've ever met. The prison system hated him as much as he hated them, so it didn't matter where they moved him, every nick wanted to get rid of him double quick. The screws would go out of their way to wind him up, he'd do his nut and belt a few people, then they had a good excuse to transfer him. Sometimes they'd give him his dinner, then as he was taking it the screw would spit in it and up he'd go again, smash the place up, and then they had an excuse to beat him unconscious. But they never crushed his spirit.

I heard that when Bobby and Frank started their seven, the first thing Frank did was to dig out the biggest, meanest screw, shove his fist under the screw's nose, and ask him, 'How do you want it with me — the hard way or the easy way?' It didn't do him any good. Bob was shipped somewhere else and did four years, eight months. Frank served every single day of his seven.

I was speaking to his sister, Eva, not long before he came out of the last sentence. She said, 'If only he'd sign the parole papers they'd let him out, but all he says, is, "I'm giving them fuck all, even if they keep me another twenty."' He didn't do himself any favours, but he had his own set of principles. A good strong man.

Now you might be thinking that every time I mention someone in trouble or who has done their time or made a name for themselves, then I say they're good people. Well, they are. It's not just something to say — I mean it. I look around me and I see a lot of straight people going about their business and they're in another world, one that's full of little jealousies and pettiness. They talk about friendship, then they wouldn't piss on their friends if they were on fire. When you live on the other side of the fence, every day can be a threat so we stick together. We haven't got time to mug each other off; we're too busy keeping trouble away from the outside. When my back's against the wall, give me these people who know what life's all about, because too many straight people are only interested in themselves.

I might not mix with many straights, but I won't stand by and see the weak ones taking stick from anybody. I came out of a club one night and I could see a bit of a ruck going on up the road. I walked up to see what was happening and there were these four drunks dancing round a car. They were banging on the roof and trying the door handles. As I got closer, I could see a woman and two little kids in the car and they were terrified. These slags are shouting, 'Show us yer fanny. Come on darling, flash yer tits.' I'm into them ... I don't even think about it. I tore in and smashed them up. As usual, some bastard phoned Old Bill and I was lifted before these mugs had come round. I can't believe it — I'm doing the right thing and all they're worried about is doing me for GBH.

I was in court and getting well pissed off with what the suits were trying to do to me. I jumped up and shouted at the judge, 'What would you have done, you silly old bastard, let them rape that woman?' He had me taken out and I was sentenced while I was sitting in the cell downstairs — £500 fine, two years' suspended. It could have been a lot worse. Perhaps the old prat did have a conscience. You see why I hate the system? It's got no heart. I didn't want medals, but a 'Thanks, Len, you've made the streets a bit safer,' might have been better than the treatment I was given. It wouldn't stop me from doing the same tomorrow, though.

Another incident occurred up the West End. One night I was standing outside the Hippodrome, where I was working, watching people go by, as I often do when things are a bit quiet. Up the road a couple of yobs were messing about. They then thought it was a good idea to start smashing milk bottles from outside one of the shops. Round the corner came a policewoman, she didn't look any older than my daughter, and she tried to sort them out on her own. The slags knocked her notebook out of her hands and started pulling and pushing her about and laughing while they were doing it. I jumped over the barrier, ran up the road, and belted the pair of them. They weren't so brave now and ran off down the road. I checked out the WPC and she wasn't hurt, so I went back to the club.

The next night, this tiny little girl came in and said to me, 'I want to thank you.'

I said, 'Thank me for what? Who are you?' She said, 'I'm the policewoman you helped last night.'

'Fuck me,' I said ''Scuse my French, but you don't look old enough to be out on your own. You mind that road when you go out of here.'

She laughed, thanked me again, and that was that.

A week later, I was outside the club again. Right under my nose there was this old couple in their seventies slowly walking past. Up the other way came a Rastafarian barging his way through the people. He shoved the old lady, and when her husband said something to him he came back and punched the old boy in the face. I couldn't believe what I was seeing. I only had to walk three yards to belt this Rasta to the ground. He was down but it wasn't enough. I got hold of his mop of hair, lifted his head off the ground, and gave him four solid belts in the face.

It's funny, they're never around when people need them but, all of a sudden, I'm surrounded by Old Bill. One of them told me I'd be going down for this and they didn't want to listen to my side of the story. The old couple had disappeared and it looked like I was in the shit again. Then I clocked the policewoman from last week. 'Oy,' I said, 'don't you stand over there saying nothing ... put your mates in the picture.' I see her having a word with a copper with a couple of stripes, then he came over.

'If this man you've hurt wants to make a complaint, I'm afraid there is nothing I can do, but for the time being I'll give you the benefit of the doubt. Between you and me, though, I feel it's going to end here, and while I'm at it, thank you for assisting one of my officers.'

He was right, it didn't come to anything, but it was very close. It makes me wonder sometimes if it's worth getting involved; but I know if the situation arises again, I'll be there, putting my neck on the line.

CHAPTER NINE

There were still rumours flying about that I was marked down for being murdered or badly hurt. I couldn't pin it down, though. When I asked, 'Who told you this? Who told you that?' all I got was, 'Heard a whisper from a mate,' and so on. I thought it was about time they got on with it. I wasn't hiding, so I wasn't hard to find.

Johnny Price came into the Green Man one night. He wasn't a bad fella, but someone who's always on the ear'ole, so when you see him you know he's after something. He bought me a lemonade, and that's a result on its own. Then he said, 'Len, can I borrow your car for an hour? I want to shoot down the Nile and see a bloke.'

'OK, John,' I said, 'don't be too long, and keep your eyes open. Some firm's got the hump with me.'

Off he went down the Nile, and parked up outside his pal's house. He'd been followed. He walked about four yards, a motor pulled up, the door opened, and *bang,* he took two barrels in the back of the legs. Whoever had done it must have thought it was me, because he was tall and big and was in my car.

When I found out about it, I went to St Leonard's Hospital. He was all wired up, tubes everywhere and a big cage over his legs. The first thing he said was, 'Len, I don't want you here. I don't want you round me, you're too dangerous.'

I said, 'John, I warned you.'

'No, you didn't. You said somebody had the hump with you. You didn't tell me there was guns on offer — now I'm fucking crippled.'

He was, and I felt bad about it. I bunged him a nice few quid to help him out so his family wouldn't suffer too much, but what else could I do? I couldn't buy him a new pair of legs.

Then my pal Ritchie came to see me. He said, 'I've found out what this is all about. When you were down the Barbican you sorted a bloke out and broke his jaw and his arm. You'll not remember as it's one of a hundred, but this particular man is family to an East London firm and they want you taught a lesson.'

I said, 'I thought that firm had more bottle than to sneak up behind me, but thanks, mate. Now I'll go and do a few people myself.'

'No, Lenny,' he says, 'that's what I'm trying to avoid for your sake. There's no winners here. You're tearing about ready to kill someone with those fists of yours and the other firm's doing the same with guns. One man's in a wheelchair and somebody's going to get killed or lifed off so I want to call a meet and sort this out.'

I've got a lot of time for Ritchie. He's shrewd, he's tough and he's got bundles of nerve, so if that's what he thinks is best, I've got enough respect for him to go along with it. He arranged a meet and I went along. This firm's got the needle and so have I, so neither of us is going to give it all that 'I'm sorry' bollocks.

Ritchie said, 'Shake hands on the deal.'

The guv'nor of the other mob stuck his hand out, but I said,' I don't want to shake your hand because you're fucking cowards, all of you. I'll call it a day, though.' So it was sorted, though I felt bad that it hadn't stopped sooner — it would have saved Johnny's legs.

A few weeks later, my Val kept saying she was getting funny phonecalls late at night. I was minding a club down at New Cross so I didn't get home until one or two in the morning. Another time, she said there had been a ring at the door at about eleven o'clock. She had looked through the peephole and there was a young kid standing on the step. She didn't open the door, but called out, 'What do you want?' It made her a bit nervy to see that when he didn't know she was watching through the door, he seemed to be talking to somebody hiding round the side by the window. The kid said he was looking for Lenny McLean, but Val just shouted, 'You got the wrong house,' and he took off.

She said to me, 'It's that East London lot, they're still at it.'

'Doll,' I said, 'they ain't kids, if they've said it's over then it's finished. You're getting wound up about nothing.'

The next night, on my way home from work at the club, I got shot in the back.

I had got out of my motor, turned to lock the door, and the bang and the pain came both at the same time. I spun round and fell against the car, and just before I hit the deck, I copped the geezer's mug before he ran off. I know him. I know the slag.

It feels like I've been smashed with a hammer, but I'm not dying. So I get back in the car and drive myself down to the hospital. Am I lucky or what? The kid's used a .22 handgun, which doesn't fire much of a slug. Still, it's put a neat little hole in my back and out the front of the fatty bit just below my ribs. I don't know what's in there but the bullet missed the important bits. I gave the doctors a false name and address. They injected me, packed the wound, and did me up, and I slipped out the side before Old Bill's turned up. Fucking hospitals always grass you up.

I was back indoors by half-two and Val was still waiting up for me. 'You're late,' she said.

'Sorry, babe, got myself shot.'

She screamed and covered her face up. 'God help us, Len, I'm going to get a call one day telling me you're dead. I don't think I can take much more.'

For about three days I could hardly move. One of our neighbours who was in the St John's first-aid mob came in every now and then to change the dressing. One of your own he was; kept his mouth shut. After a week I was fit enough to get a few things sorted — it wouldn't take a lot of effort.

I told Val that I was popping out to see a pal — no need to worry her — and drove over to Hackney. I knew just where to put my hand on this fucker. The bloke must have had an easy conscience or none, because he didn't even have a sly look out of the window to see who was knocking. As I banged on the door he opened up straight away and I grabbed him and pulled him outside. 'Tell me who's behind this and I won't hurt you.' He was shitless, and didn't even try to argue.

'Quinn, it's Quinn, Billy Quinn', he said.

'Right, where can he be got at?'

'I dunno. He phoned me and offered two hundred — I haven't seen him, honest.'

'Good boy,' I said, 'you haven't wasted my time by trying to lie your way out of it.'

The look of relief on his face was comical. I turned to walk away, swung back and hit him full in the face. It split all ways and he just dropped to the ground. I can't say it hurt me more than it hurt him, though it did give me a bit of a twinge in the side. If he didn't have to be wired up and drink soup through a straw for the next month I would have been losing my touch.

When he could move his face enough to talk, he told Old Bill he didn't see who did it, so they were bolloxed. It was a liberty what he tried to do, but I had to give him ten out of ten for that. Believe it or not, we palled up some years later, no hard feelings.

I couldn't lay my hands on that Quinn. He was like that Scarlet what's his name — they seek him here and all that cobblers. I sought that piece of shit everywhere but he'd gone again, so I put it on hold. I didn't forget it, I just got on with other things.

Freddie Starr was a bloke I'd laughed at many times on telly. I'd never met him, but I thought he was the funniest man around.

Fred had a problem so he got in touch with some people. They were pals of Johnny Nash so they rang him, and then John phoned me. See how we all graft for each other? If something needs sorting, we all work together until it's done. So John phoned me and we arranged to meet at the usual place, Highbury roundabout. Fred's got a club down in Windsor and John had already said to Fred that we'd see him about half-ten.

We got down there with a bit of time to spare. Freddie wasn't there. The two of us sat there like a couple of lemons and time rolled on. Eleven, twelve, one o'clock, and I'm getting the right hump. I said, 'John, this bloke ain't making me laugh this time, he's taking the piss. When he walks in that door I'm going to bollock him. Do you make me right?'

John agreed, he wasn't too pleased either. 'Len, you are a hundred per cent right.'

Half-past one. Bang, the door opened and in walked Freddie Starr. He had both hands over his eyes and he said, 'I'm so sorry I'm late.'

I said, 'Sorry? You've taken a fucking liberty with us.'

He's still got his hands over his eyes. 'I ain't had a wink of sleep, I've been up all night with a bird.' As he said that he let his hands go and two big bloodshot eyes came shooting out on the end of springs. Me and John fell about. How can you tell off a geezer like that? This bloke's a star all right, he's the same off stage as he is on.

We settled down and I asked him what the problem was. It turned out it was hardly a problem at all, or I should say, to me it looked like nothing. To be fair to Fred, because I don't want it to sound like he didn't have any bottle, if you're straight, certain things can get all out of proportion in your head and that's what had happened. One phonecall, and two minutes later it was all squared away. When we went down to see him we didn't know what to expect; it might have been World War Three, it didn't matter, we never questioned it, we just put ourselves out for him.

Fred was well chuffed that we'd been able to put his mind at rest and wanted to give us a good bundle of dough apiece, but I wouldn't have it. As we left, he said, 'If ever I can help you, you've only got to call.'

Later, when I was banged up on a murder charge, he phoned up my Val and offered to pay for bail or barristers, anything, money no object. And he wanted to visit me in Brixton Prison. I would have loved that, but he was a big star and it would have turned into a circus. He understood that.

When I got out I took Val to see one of his shows at the Circus Tavern. He heard we were there and invited us backstage before the show, gave me a cuddle, and wished me all the best. At the end of the show that lovely man said, 'I want to dedicate my last song to a big-hearted man in the audience, Lenny McLean and his wife Val. They've had some rough times recently but they've come through it.' Then he sang that song, 'You Always Hurt the One You Love'. I knew what he meant.

We had our photograph taken with him and I had it framed and it sits on top of the telly. Whenever I look at it I think, 'I was there when he had a problem, but when I was in trouble Freddie was there for me at a hundred miles an hour.'

On another occasion, a very well known boxer came to see me. He said he'd got some problems with a certain crowd of people and could I have a word with them. I told him it would cost a few bob and he asked me how much exactly. I had a little think because you've got to weigh up what's involved, gave him a figure, and he pulled a face.

'All right, Len, thanks very much. When I've raked up the dough I'll come back and see you.'

I said, 'Hold up, what do you mean rake up the dough? You must have a fortune tucked away.'

He just put his hands up. 'I haven't got a tanner. Things have gone downhill. The missus buggered off and got everything — house, money, the lot.'

I couldn't believe it. This bloke was at the top not many years ago, a world champion, now he's an odd-job man.

A few months later he came down the club again and said, 'That bit of bother, Len, it's all sorted now, but thanks for being there for me,' and he shook my hand.

I said, 'I was there for the money. I don't have to tell you it's a cruel world and you've got to dig a living where you can.'

He said, 'Never mind, thanks anyway.'

I used to talk some bollocks sometimes. I was never as mercenary as I made myself out to be. But you've got to be careful you don't get taken for a mug.

It's funny how you think that stars have bundles of wedge. They're right up the top of the tree and coining it in. As soon as they stop what they're doing, bang, they take a dive. Unless they've used their nut while the money was good, they end up without a pot to piss in, yet all the punters still think they're up in the clouds. When Danny Macalindon was British and Commonwealth Champion, and a good crowd drawer, Frankie Warren went to see him and tried to arrange a fight with him and me. Like I said, Frank always had an eye on the main chance. Danny turned it down. 'Mr Warren,' he said, 'I've just heard about the fight Lenny had with Roy Shaw. One of them's just come out of Broadmoor, and the other one's on the way in. He's a nutcase, so if you don't mind I'll stick with what I'm doing, boxing proper and earning a nice few quid.'

Since then I had fallen out with Frank, and Macalindon wasn't at the top any longer. At that time I was minding The Camden Palace, a high-class place, well known, and all the stars used to hang out there.

I went to work one night, and as I walked in someone said, 'Danny Macalindon's upstairs at the bar and he says he's come to see you.' I thought, 'Hello, he's taken his time to accept a challenge, but never mind.' I flew up the stairs and went right up to him. 'I ain't in Broadmoor, son, ready to take me on?'

I had put on about three stone since he saw me last, so he went a bit pale. 'No, mate, no, I don't want to fight you, and that was a joke about you being a nutter.'

I knew it was, I was just getting him going.

'I'm a bit down on my luck, Len. I was wondering if you could fix me up with a bit of work.'

I thought, 'Fuck me, another one having a problem making a living.' But if somebody's polite, I don't mind looking out for them, so I got him fixed up with a job on the door.

Everything was lovely for a bit. There wasn't much aggro and the little bit there was he handled nicely. No punch-ups, just diplomatic. Like all the places I look after, on Saturday nights I like to have the door covered two-handed. So on one particular night I had Danny with another doorman called Basil Bell. He's a fella who had been minding for about 15 years and knew the game. I was upstairs and I had just got myself a nice lemonade and a coffee, when I got a call that there was trouble at the door. I had just got down to the door in time to see my two blokes get plunged by this pair of drunken slags. Down they went and these drunks are standing over them waving knives about.

I did one with a right and the other with a left, and they were both spark out. I didn't hurt them any more because I was concerned about Danny and Basil lying there bleeding. I picked the knives up and dropped them in the bin, went over to Danny and pulled his shirt up. He was cut right across the stomach. He said, 'Am I going to die, Len?'

'No, mate,' I said, 'you'll do. Ambulance will be here in a minute.' I went over to Basil. He's holding his stomach and he's crying and there's blood pouring through his fingers. I said, 'Straighten yourself up, you mug ... fucking crying. Macalindon's cut worse than you and he hasn't said a word. Be a man and stop showing yourself up.'

Then Old Bill arrived at the same time as the ambulance, and the four of them were carted off. I told them I didn't see anything. All I knew was that these two slags were causing a disturbance so I knocked them out. I didn't see the stabbing so I didn't know if they had done it or not. They asked me to give evidence but I said, 'No. I've done my job without you, so you fucking well do yours and leave me out of it.'

Bell and Macalindon pulled through all right and spent a bit of time in hospital. The other two were nicked for GBH and I was asked to go to court. Five times they came round my house but I fucked them off every time. In the end, I told them if they didn't pack it in I'd get myself a brief because they were harassing me, and anyway even if I had seen anything I wouldn't go to court — that's not my game.

So they left it out and went to court without me. I don't blame Macalindon for getting up and pointing the finger because he's a straight guy. What choked me was when Basil Bell gave evidence that got the two blokes four years each. What's the difference? I'll tell you. Bell ducks and dives, he knows the score and he's been on the other side long enough to know you don't help Old Bill. It doesn't matter that he got a little stripe across the belly, he's still a grass. He knows we've got ways of dealing with our own who step out of line.

I don't see Macalindon any more, he's better off sticking to the straight world. As for Bell, he knows better than to show his grassing face near me. I don't want him around — he makes me sick.

An old guy I had become friends with through Alex Steen asked me to visit him at his home in Canterbury to discuss a proposition. He didn't have to ask me twice because I had bundles of respect for him, so the next day I jumped into the motor and drove down to see him.

He met me at the door of his great big house. He was wearing a dressing gown and looked like your grandad. But this 70-year-old Italian–American was a semi-retired Mafia Don. Or if you don't want to shout the words out a 'Man of respect'. If you saw him out walking you'd want to help him across the road, and the little slags who are growing up today would probably shove him off the pavement. They wouldn't have a clue who he was or what he could have done to them by snapping his fingers.

We went in, had a bit of lunch, and then he dug out the brandy and cigars. This old geezer knew how to live. 'Lenny, my friend,' he said, 'I was talking to one of the family in New York; he rings me every week to keep me in touch. After business, we spoke of boxing and I told him in this country we have the toughest street fighter I have even seen. No one is a match for this Lenny McLean.'

I said, 'Now that's a lovely gee, but you didn't ask me down here to tell me that, I know.'

He patted my knee. 'Hold on, Lenny, there's more. My friend said that the family have a champion by the name of John McCormack, who is also unbeatable, so we talked some more and now I want you to go to New York and show him he is very wrong, but only if you agree.'

'Agree?' I said. 'Give me the address! I've never turned down a fight in my life.'

'I knew you would say that. Everything is arranged, even your purse, which in sterling will give you about £14,000, plus expenses, of course.'

'Good stuff,' I said, 'and what are you getting out of it?'

He just tapped the side of his nose. 'What I get is what I get,' and he laughed.

On the way out, just as I was getting in the motor, he called over, 'Lenny, should you lose, look for a horse's head in your bed.' He had a sense of humour.

'The horse is safe,' I said, gave him a wave, and drove off thinking about America.

A week later, we were on our way. I took a pal of mine, but I'll leave his name out because he's a high flier in the straight world now, and his clients might get a bit fidgety finding out who he's mixed with in the past. Some geezer with my name printed on a piece of card met us at Kennedy Airport and took us to a motor that I swear was as long as our street at home — it was like three joined together. We were dropped off at the Plaza, and this place even had a carpet outside. Red carpet all the way up the steps and there's an old fella hoovering away for all he's worth. In we went and everything was laid on — posh suite each, everything on the family slate — the business.

The guys we were dealing with picked us up that night and took us out for a meal. Waiters were flapping all over the place, treating us like royalty. I couldn't help wondering what my mates back in the East End would think if they could see me now. We had a nice meal, sorted the business, and arranged for a pick up the next day for the fight.

These guys run most of the business in New York. Forget the Mayor, forget the police. I'm putting away a two-pound steak with four men who are looked up to by everyone in the city. Funny though — no dark glasses, no menace. Just four businessmen. Pretend you don't see the Rolex watches, $5,000 suits and handmade shoes, and these blokes could be your own.

The next morning, my pal and I shot down to Central Park so I could have a little warm up. This was Saturday, which meant that all the gates were shut to traffic and only pedestrians were let in. And they make the most of it. I've only ever been used to Victoria Park in the East End. This place is two miles long and a mile wide, and as far as you can see it's packed with skateboarders, joggers, roller-skaters, groups doing aerobics, all working their bollocks off to get fit. I fell in behind this old girl who had to be 85, wearing a pink leotard and going like the clappers. I couldn't keep up with her. Either she was very fit or I was fucked before I even started.

Come the afternoon, I'd had a bit of a nap and was ready for the Irishman. The same motor picked us up, stretch limos they call them, and we were driven out to a big warehouse on the other side of the Bronx. It was a bit like Notting Hill, but bigger. Same faces going by, though.

The warehouse had a big sign on the front saying Bottles & Rags. I didn't see any rags, but there were millions of bottles on pallets stretching for miles. The doors were locked behind us and the driver led us to an area right in the middle where all the others were waiting.

Who said McCormack was an Irishman? He was as black as the ace of spades. Big bastard, 6ft 8in, 24 stone, give or take a pound. He was stamping up and down and punching one clenched fist into the open palm of the other, over and over again. Our mates with the suits are there and they had some hired help to do the running about. The suits know what they are, so they were quiet, polite, and behave like gentlemen. But the help, because they're fuck all, were dressed up like spivs and gangsters and look like extras from *The Godfather*. There was one light bulb above our heads and most of the help were wearing sunglasses. The one doing the Cagney impersonation checked me over to see if I was clean. It was like being in the nick. I thought, 'Any minute now he's going to feel round my nuts and I'll down him, gun or no gun.' I could see he was carrying from the bulge in his jacket. He didn't though, and the fight was on.

I tucked my head down, flew at McCormack, and drove him back against a concrete pillar with a flurry of tight punches. As he backed up I swung one to his forehead, cracking his head against the post. If he hadn't grabbed hold of me I think he would have gone down, because for a second his eyes rolled up.

I was being crushed by his massive arms and I couldn't move. Down came his head to nut me senseless, but I got mine in first and did his nose. He let go of me and I got four rib-breakers into him, then jumped back and kicked him as hard as I could in the balls. He was wearing a codpiece so it didn't have the effect it should. Rattled him though. The atmosphere was like a fight I had at a fairground over in

Leytonstone, dead quiet — it was all too serious for a bit of cheering.

We broke apart and we weighed each other up.

With a big lump on his forehead and suffering a good bit of pain from his ribs and nuts he looks beaten, but he's not. Whoop — look out, he came at me like a fucking bull. I side-stepped, clenched both fists together and smashed him in the kidneys.

My belt and his own momentum carried him into the hired help and I was right behind him, knocking them all over the place. He fell on to his hands and as he got up I kicked him full in the face, rolled him over, and kicked him again. I won't give him a second, I want to destroy that black face. He's trying to fight back but it's all reflex. I don't think he can even see me.

Six punches to the jaw, cheek and forehead finished him. Blood was pouring from his nose and torn lips and dripping on to the stone floor and making a little pool beside his head. Hard luck, son, but you would've done the same to me, that's the name of the game.

Funny really, I've just smashed the family's best and you'd think there would be a bit of a fuss but there was no reaction at all. The suits handed over a briefcase with the money, wished us all the best, and were gone. They never even looked at their man laying flat on the deck, bleeding and still spark out.

Twenty minutes later, my pal and I are back in the hotel and my hands have come up like balloons — both busted again. I said, 'I think we'd better get out of here. The bosses seem good stuff but some of their boys were looking a bit cross-eyed, and they might just take it into their heads to get the money back.'

We slipped out, grabbed a taxi and took off for Kennedy Airport. Seven hours we hid in the place until our flight was called. I stuck out amongst the punters like a sore dick. My face was bruised and my hands were cut and broken, so I got some funny looks, especially from security. But nobody put themselves out to front me up so there was no trouble, and we got back to London without any problems. I squared my pal with a few grand, got my hands plastered up, and went home.

I gave Val the money and went upstairs to lay on the bed. When she brought me up a cup of tea and counted the money, she was crying. 'Oh, Len, I wish you'd give up fighting, the strain's doing my head in.'

I gave her a kiss and a cuddle and said, 'Doll, it's a hard game but it don't half beat cleaning windows. I'd have to wash and polish Crystal Palace twice to earn the sort of money I've just picked up.'

I was dozing on the bed and I could hear the kids downstairs saying, 'Daddy's been fighting again.' They're just like Val, take it all in their stride.

When I was training down at Freddie Hill's gym a few years before there was a skinny little kid, John Huntley, who used to come in and spar about with us. I suppose he was about 16 then, dark haired, a nice kid. Nothing of him, but game as a bagel. We never used to hit him, just played around, but he took it all dead serious and would steam into a fighter three times his size. It didn't make much of an impression but it shows you what he was made of. I took a liking to him and when he went to fights all over the place, I'd let him walk into the arena with me, or front him up with all the big villains who were about, and he loved it.

Time went on and he grew up into a good-looking bloke. What with his bit of boxing, training and looking after his body, he got into modelling. One thing led to another and he got webbed up with five other lads and they formed a group of posers called Excalibur, in the same game as the American Chippendales. They went down a bomb with the ladies, who couldn't get enough of them. So John was on the way up. Soon afterwards, he was all over the newspapers as page seven fella of the year and flying high mixing with all the right people.

Of course, being page seven he was working with those lovely page three girls and whenever I saw him around with some little darling on his arm, I'd think, 'Lenny, you got yourself into the wrong game.' So he dated bundles of these models until eventually he met Dee Wells and she was special, in a class of her own. She was gorgeous to look at, had a lovely personality, and was like the girl next door. Well, not like any girl that ever lived next door to me, but you know what I mean. She was the sort you could take home to Mum, down to earth, a proper home girl, and on top of all that she idolised him. Don't some blokes have all the luck?

John came down to the club one night, fought his way through all the birds trying to get his autograph, and got himself up to my office. I gave him a cuddle, because I'm always pleased to see him, got some coffee in, and we had a bit of a chat. I could see in his eyes that he was trying to get round to asking me something but was putting it off. In the end I said, 'What's up John? You in a spot of bother, or what?'

He said, 'Len, you know I don't take liberties with our friendship, I never ask for anything, do I?'

I said, 'Hold up, son, before you go on, I know just what you're going to ask me. You can't handle all these girls that's chasing you all over the place so you want me to take a few off your hands.'

That made him laugh. 'No, Len, what it is, a very good friend of mine has got himself into a situation that looks a bit heavy and I wondered if you could step in and see what you can do.'

'Look, son,' I said, 'you don't have to go all round the houses to ask me for a favour. If he's a pal of yours, he's under my wing. What's the problem?' So he put me in the picture.

This friend of John's, a fella in the same game, modelling, page seven and all that, had got himself involved with a page three girl as well. The trouble was, when they met, she was still going out with a guy from East London who came from a good family of money-getters. This fella had a bit of a jealous streak in him and I can't blame him for that because we can all be a bit possessive where our ladies are concerned. Anyway, the girl got a bit tired of not being trusted and fed up with the boyfriend getting the hump every time she had a photo shoot with some of the good-looking blokes who had to work with. So she wanted to park him up. John's pal knew she was involved with someone, so at first he kept her at arm's length. But as time went by and they couldn't help themselves, they got closer and closer. Somebody put the bubble into the boyfriend and next thing there were some heavy threats being put about.

What can I say? I hate bullies, especially when they're hiding behind menacing phonecalls, upsetting straight people and their families. So I said to John, 'Get your mate to call round to my house on Monday morning, then I can get all the details from him and work out the best way to settle the business.' This was Friday night. I said ta-ra to John and put it out of my mind for the moment.

I keep pretty late hours, what with the club and other business, so it was about four o'clock on Sunday morning and I was just getting myself ready for bed when there was a bang on the door. I had a quick look through the spy-hole before opening up just in case some mug was going to have a pop with a shooter and all I could see was a face I didn't recognise, covered in blood.

I pulled the door open and this game little fucker said, 'Hello, Mr McLean, I'm John's friend. Sorry I'm a bit early.' What a state he was in. I'll tell you what, he didn't look anything like the good-looking fella I'd seen in the papers often enough. He looked like he'd been run over by a bus — face swollen up and bleeding, clothes all torn and shivering with shock. I sat him in the kitchen, Val got of bed, and we cleaned up the cuts and bruises as best we could. Once we'd got him a bit comfortable with a big mug of tea in front of him, he told us what had gone down.

He and a mate, a famous pop star who has since died, were just coming out a club up West when a big flash motor pulled up. Out jumped two blokes and they were both carrying guns. One of them stuck a gun into this bloke's chest and forced him into the car, the other one pointed his shooter at the pop singer and told him to fuck off or he'd get it on the pavement.

Don't ever think that because these lads take up modelling for a living that they're pansified or soft. I know John can handle himself, what with his boxing training, and it seemed like his pal was made of the same stuff. He was wedged between two big guys with a gun each side of his head and he tried to fight his way out. He landed one of them a back-hander in the face and the other bloke knocked him unconscious. By the time he came to, he was being dragged out of the car in the middle of Epping Forest — near London, nice and quiet, and no nosy fuckers to poke their nose in.

There was another motor already waiting in the woods, and out got the boyfriend who had been making all the threats, and has he got the raving hump or what? Two of the blokes force this young guy to his knees and hold him while the other brave bastard sticks a gun in his mouth. 'One warning ... keep away from my girlfriend or you are a dead man.' Then he beat him round the face and head with the gun, threw him back in the car, drove to London, and dumped him in the street.

He didn't want to go home and frighten his mother so he got a cab and had himself delivered to my front door. So here he is, and I've got to square things off for his sake and for John's.

I told him, 'There are two things you can do. Walk away and don't have no more agg or fight back.'

He said, 'What do you think?'

I said, 'Never mind what I think, do you love this girl or not?'

'Len,' he said, 'it sounds a bit poetic but I'm willing to die for her.'

That's all I want to hear. 'Good kid. You won't have to fight and you won't have to die because I'm going to have a few words and get this all straightened up. Now I don't want to upset you but I've got to say that, personally, I think you've taken a bit of a liberty with this bloke. How would you feel if somebody nicked your bird? Still, looking at you sitting there, I think he's gone a bit outrageous so that's why I'm going to help you.'

I didn't have to growl or chuck my weight about because the family I had to deal with were reasonable people. I had a quiet talk with the father of the boyfriend, who had no idea his son was playing up, and we shook hands when he said he would get him back in line.

Everything turned out right. The ex-boyfriend must have had respect for his father because, when he was told to behave, he let it go and never gave John's pal any more aggravation. He and his girl carried on seeing each other and had a lovely relationship, though I've heard since that he got himself another problem, but this one was something I couldn't help him with. I don't want to say any more about that, I'll just say life's full of ups and downs; some you can sort, some you can't.

I'm still nicking a few quid out of the fights. Not as much as I used to because with my reputation there aren't too many who fancy having the shit belted out of them and losing their money. Still, there's always the odd mug who fancies his chances. One of these was Man Mountain York, and we'd fixed up a fight down at Woodford. Two things happened on that night. Well, three really, if you count the fact that I smashed the bollocks out of Mr York. He'd got them to put on the poster: I am 24, 6ft 7in and 25 stone. LENNY HAS HAD HIS DAY. What a comedian. I kept doing his ribs until I'd got him down to about 6ft, then a blinding right stretched him across the canvas. And I was giving him a dozen years.

Before that, though, when I was in the dressing room, a pal of mine said, 'Guess who's a late entry on the undercard?'

I said, 'King Kong?'

'Nah, it's your old mate Quinn, the geezer you was looking for.'

'Lovely, where is he?'

'Right next door in the other dressing room. He's in there with York, the bloke you're fighting.'

All these dressing rooms have got connecting doors, so I tried the door and, as you'd expect, it was locked. I've got my wild up thinking about that low-life slag sitting in the next room. Two kicks and I smashed it to pieces and tore inside. They were both shocked enough to look as though they had shit themselves. I growled at the big fella. 'Don't fucking move or I'll hurt you now instead of in the ring.' He never said a word.

I got Quinn by the ears and smashed his head back against the tin lockers. It made more noise than hurt him but it frightened him so much he was shaking, then he started crying. I said, 'Shut up, you mug, you were big enough with a gun in your hand or paying somebody to shoot me. Now look at you.'

'Please let me explain ... please let me explain,' he screamed.

The big fella moved behind me and I shouted at him, 'Keep out of it or you're in trouble.'

Quinn was still crying, 'Len, please, I was on the gear, I was on drugs ... I didn't know what I was doing.'

What am I going to do with this mug? If I'd caught him after the shooting I could have broken every bone in his body and never thought about it. But too much time has gone by and what satisfaction am I going to get out of hurting this cry baby? I flung him down the end of the dressing room and he put his hands up to stop me jumping on him, but I'd finished — he wasn't worth it. 'Please let me apologise ... let me shake your hand.'

Shake my hand? He's trembling from head to foot. 'OK,' I said, 'I'll shake your hand to say it's over but I want you dressed and out of here in two minutes. Forget your fight, just get as far away from me as possible.' We shook hands and I never saw him again.

A year later he was found dead with a bullet in his head. I've got to be a bit careful with this one because a lot of people were pulled in over his killing. I had a problem with him and some reckoned I had him straightened but, on my Val's life, I never did. If I tell somebody a grudge is finished, it's finished. I stand by my word and don't sneak up on anyone. Apart from that, I'm a fist-fighter, I don't need guns to hide behind. He was on drugs — he was taking liberties all round. He got what he asked for.

That was before the fight. After I'd fucked off Quinn, I said to York, 'You can close your mouth now.' He was wondering what he'd let himself in for, and had probably never seen anybody blow up like

I'd just done in his whole life. 'It's too late to change your mind now, old son ... see you in the ring.'

Like I said, the big fella got his about five minutes after. So I'm back in the dressing room and, with no door on, I can see him being carried in, still spark out. The next thing I know, some bloke's on my ear'ole.

'Hello, Mr McLean. My name's Jack Iandoli. Bernie Cole's given me your address but I knew you were fighting here tonight so I thought I'd come and have a word.'

I said, 'What do you want, a challenge? Who you fronting for?'

'No,' he said, 'what I want to put to you is ... have you ever considered having a film made about your life?'

I gave him the old cross-eye. 'If you're taking the piss you'll be the third one to get a bollocking tonight.' Anyway, he assured me he was on the level and would I at least think about it. I was ready for home and my Horlicks so I said, 'Gimme a bell sometime and we'll have a talk.'

When he came out with it, at first I thought he was a nutter. Who'd want to pay tuppence-ha'penny or whatever to see a film about me? Two minutes and the punters would be asleep. After a bit, though, my nut starts to tick over. Perhaps it's not so stupid. I've been pretty busy most of my life.

I'm the toughest minder money can buy, an unbeatable street-fighter, and everybody knows I'm the Guv'nor. Now that would make a blinding title. I can just see it over the local Odeon: Lenny McLean — The Guv'nor.

When the fella gave me a ring a bit later, I was ready for the camera to start rolling. It wasn't as easy as that though. First, a film script. I said to Jack, 'Remember, I'm no writer — fighting's my game, so I don't know what you expect.'

'No, Len, leave all that to me. You give me the facts, I'm a brilliant writer, I'll do the script.'

I thought, 'I don't know about writing but I know you ain't fucking modest.'

So we got together. He stuck a tape-recorder on the table and away I went. I told him all about the fights — this one, that one. How I got started, all about the different people involved — Kenny Mac, Ritchie, Frank Warren, and on and on. When I told him about the American fight he nearly came off the chair. 'Oh yes, great — oh yes, super angle.' I suppose it was — I never gave it a thought at the time.

For the first couple of weeks after he'd gone off to put it together, I couldn't wait to see what he'd made of it. Then a month went by and it started to go out of my head. If I'm doing something, I want it now, otherwise I'll park it up. I gave him a few rings, but he told me he was still cracking away. So I thought, 'Oh bollocks, I'll get back to work.'

Giving you a few clues about my life over the years might give the impression that I get up in the morning and start fighting people until I go to bed. What I'm leaving out is the ordinary parts, the good parts that make life worthwhile: my two smashing kids growing up; their first little steps; taking them to the zoo; watching them in Christmas Nativity plays at school; teaching them to ride a bike. All these things make a happy life. And, of course, there was Val and me. The older we got, the closer we became. Again, it's the little things that make life happy.

Going to shows or out to dinner with good people, or just sitting indoors watching telly and having a cuddle, all that is miles and miles away from how I brought bread into the house. I lived in two worlds — one by choice and the other by necessity, because that's all I knew. So my life wasn't all violence, but sometimes it seemed like it. It's like waiting for a bus. You stand in the pissing rain for two hours, then four turn up nose to tail.

It must have been the silly season down the club because there was no end of aggro. Usually the job's nice and steady. All I've got to do is sit in the back drinking coffee. The word's out that Lenny's minding the place and that keeps everything nice.

I was relaxing with a nice lemonade in the back of the club when one of the other minders came over to tell me I was wanted out front. When I got to the door there was this big black guy fronting a little mob of brothers. He was done up like some African chief — funny hat like Tommy Cooper's stuck on his head, and a full-length afghan, bright enough to knock your eyes out. I can see trouble written right across his mug.

'You McLean, the Guv'nor?' he says.

I know what he means but I keep calm. 'Yeah, I'm Lenny McLean, but I only work here, I'm not the governor.'

He gives his mates a look and a wink. 'I'm Cool Ken from Peckham and I could do with a job on your door.'

'Sorry, pal,' I said, 'we're all fixed up. Leave your name at reception and we'll get back to you if we get any vacancies.' He knows he doesn't want work, I know he doesn't want work, but we're both going through it.

He finished by saying, 'How about if I had your job?'

I said, 'That's it, you black c**t, I reckon you've come here to make a name for yourself in front of your firm of wankers, so let's go to work.'

Crash — right hand, over he went. Quick left and he's spark out. The brothers didn't know whether to join in or run away. I ran at the five of them and gave them a growl, and they all shot out the door. There's loyalty. I returned to Cool Ken. He was still out, but I hadn't finished with him. Anyone comes looking for a reputation, I've got to hurt them. So while he was unconscious I hit him six or seven times in the face. Now just in case you're thinking I'm a bit of vicious bastard, remember, this guy was bigger than me and thought he could take me out. He made a mistake and paid the price. When he woke up he'd think twice about trying the same stunt again.

This fella's mates had disappeared, so I said to one of my blokes, 'Get rid of him ... I'm going to finish my lemonade.' Five minutes later he came back for a word. His tie was all over the place and his shirt was hanging out, so I thought the mob had come back and had a go. I said, 'What's up, pal?'

He said, 'Len, I can't lift him. He's about 19 stone.'

'Use your loaf, roll the c**t and make sure you bang his head on every step.' So he was rolled round the back and parked up. I don't know if he lived or died, and I never heard from that little lot again.

A bit later, I got the hump with another black geezer. Nothing to do with the colour of his skin, because as far as I'm concerned there's only two kinds of people, polite or troublemakers. Black, white or yellow. One lot has an easy ride, the others get a fucking good hiding.

I took on this bloke as a minder down the club. After a bit, I began to wish I hadn't because he was a right surly bastard; no matter how you spoke to him, back would come a bit of lip. I can be as reasonable as the next man but his manners were giving me the hump. Then he caught me on a wrong day, gave me some old backchat, and I downed him. When he came to I gave him the choice: bugger off or work on the back door. That's a right come down; you don't see anybody all night and it's bloody boring. This geezer, called Gwami, needed the work so he swallowed it, but then I started hearing whispers that he was doing a bit of dealing with drugs. Nothing definite, but I couldn't take any chances because one of our jobs was to keep that sort of shit out of the club.

A lot of people think that minders or bouncers are a load of gorillas waiting to bash up anybody who looks at them cross-eyed. Parents should realise that we are hired to look after their kids when they're out having a good time at a club. The people we're belting are the ones who might pull a knife on other customers or cause a ruck and spoil the night out for the other punters. One of our biggest problems is making sure that these youngsters don't get mixed up with druggies. So I only needed that whisper about Gwami and I booted him out the door. Before he went, I told him, 'You're a mug being mixed up in that game and one day somebody's going to cut your throat for what you're doing.'

I'm no fortune teller, but while I was working on this book, I read in the papers that Gwami (though now I think that was a nickname) was shot dead. Unfortunately, at the same time a special constable was also killed and that was bad news. If drugs weren't involved then both those men would still be alive today and their families would have been saved all that grief.

I hate drugs and anybody mixed up with them. So when I got a call from the ex-wife of a cousin of mine I was over there at 100mph. Ian and I had lost touch with each other years ago, in the way I lost touch with most of my pals from the younger days. He went his way and I went mine. As far as I know, he got in with a few people, did a bit of this and that, and ended up being a pretty tasty con man, one of the best. Unlike me and a lot of the others, he never did a day's bird, though he did get a few pulls here and there from other villains, but by sticking my name up, he got out of bother without getting me involved.

He had a few bob stashed away, but he wasn't one of those yuppie prats, though he did like to be a bit flash. The same as a lot of those people, he had a little dabble in small drugs, then bigger and ended up on heroin. That's when he started to come apart. He had a big house in Chelmsford, money in the bank, a nice Porsche to run about in, then bang, it's all gone. He lost the lot — wife, kids, house, every tanner, and he went from twelve stone down to eight.

His ex-wife still cared about him, though, and while she told me all this she was crying and begging me to help him. She said, 'I know who started him on that horrible stuff and the same man is still supplying him. Please stop him, Len, I don't want to see him die.'

I had to explain that Ian was a serious drug addict who couldn't help himself. It didn't matter how many dealers I took out, he'd find another one to supply him, then another one. I just wanted her to understand that no matter what I did, it wouldn't help. But that didn't mean I wasn't going to have a little word with the slag.

I went to his place, and by the time I got there I was steamed right up thinking about the laughs Ian and I used to have. These dealers are no mugs when it comes to looking after themselves, so I knew he'd have about ten locks on his door, and wouldn't open it unless he was sure who's there. So I parked up and waited for somebody to knock for me.

I sat there for about an hour, then I saw this hippie type going up his path. I walked down the road really casually, then as I saw the door open, I made a dive through the gate. I barged the buyer out of the way so hard he went over the wall into the next door garden, and forced my way in. This no-value git made a dive for the stairs, but I got him by the ankle and dragged him down, banging his face on about half-a-dozen steps.

The fully grown man was screaming like a baby and kicking like a donkey. He broke away, ran upstairs and into the bedroom. What he intended to do I have no idea; he might have had a gun or a knife or something, but as I entered the room, he headed for the window. Three steps and I caught him, grabbed his hair, and slammed his face into the glass. Then I got him by the arse and held him over the sill.

There was no point in making a speech; these c**ts don't listen to anything. All I said was, 'If you sell one tiny piece of shit to my cousin Ian, I'm going to come back and throw you out of this fucking window. I've been asked to talk to you and this is how I talk.' His face is running blood and his chest and stomach must be sliced up lying across the broken glass. I'm really wild — this bastard's been dealing his shit gear to kids the same age as my Kelly and Jamie, and they've probably ended up like Ian. If it happened to mine, it would be the end of my life. That man was lucky I didn't throw him down on to the concrete there and then, but I don't want to be lifed off for a slag like that.

As for Ian, I didn't think what I did would help him. And it didn't directly, but ages later I spoke to his ex-wife and she told me he'd got himself into a clinic. It seemed that being there for him had given him the heart to have a go at getting himself together. He wanted to show me that he still had the guts and spirit he had in the old days. He never said as much to me, in fact he's never been in touch. Perhaps he's waiting for the day when he can walk through my door, clean as a whistle and full of his old self.

CHAPTER TEN

About this time, Jack Iandoli came back to me with the film script. I don't know anything about this game, but it looked the business, all bound up and printed out. I said, 'Now what do we do?'

He said, 'We've got to get a few people interested ... get an agent.'

'Crack away then, Jack,' I said, 'sooner the better.'

We both put ourselves about but it was hard work. Time was going by and nothing was getting off the ground. Then I met a woman by the name of Sheena Perkins. She seemed a bit of a go-getter and was in the film business. She looked at the script and said, 'It's a good idea but it's not laid down right.' So away goes Jack, makes the changes she wants, and brings it back. He had been up every night for weeks, bent over his typewriter, and she said, 'No, it's not good enough.'

On the quiet, she said to me, 'I've got to be brutally honest with you, Lenny. While the idea for the script and the facts from your life are a very saleable item, the actual script in its present form is not.' She must have clocked the look on my face. 'But don't worry, if we can raise the necessary finance to pay a professional script-writer, there is no question of the film not being made.'

Jack wasn't happy when I marked his card, but it's a tough world. On the other hand, I had to agree with Sheena, because since Jack and I had first met, I'd found out that he'd never written or published anything before. Still, I had to be fair with the man, he had come up with the idea in the first place, so I calmed him down and told him he was still aboard.

A pal of mine, along with a few others, stuck a few quid in the pot. Well, a bit more than a few quid, because it took the best part of £100,000 for Sheena to hire the top-notch writer Brian Clemens. We didn't have to ask this bloke if he'd ever had anything published; everybody knew he was well connected in the writing business and his name was on loads of really good stuff, like *The Avengers* and *Highlander* films, with another high-profile writer by the name of Stephen Lister, so I reckoned we'd got ourselves a good result.

It might have been a lot of dough, but it turned out to be money well spent. The script was absolutely brilliant. They must have slung Jack's script out of the window, because it wasn't like the same story at all. That old saying about getting what you pay for never seemed more true.

So it looks like we're well on the way now. Sheena didn't hang about; she got stuck into checking out locations, tying up deals all over the place, and even started casting. Once the word leaked out, I discovered that everybody wanted to be an actor, even though casting wasn't down to me.

I wasn't surprised when this young fella come up to me in the gym where we were both training, and said, 'You know I'm an actor, Len?'

I didn't know this young Craig Fairbrass very well, but he was a nephew of George and Alan Dixon, so he had to be good stuff. I said, 'Leave it out, son, the only part you've got is running a take-away bar down the market.'

'No, honestly, Len, I'm working on a film called *Queen and Country* with Denzil Washington at the moment, but I'd love a part in your film.'

So I had a closer look at him and, yeah, he was a strong-looking bloke. I know he'd done a bit of boxing and on top of that he was a good-looking bastard, like I was at his age.

I took him down to Pinewood and stuck him up for an audition with all the other young blokes who were looking for the part. Ray Winstone was there, and he's been in loads of films. Glen Murphy — a bit of a boxer and looked good — was also there, as well as a lot of others who've been in films and on TV. Craig hasn't got a big name, so he was a bit shy about getting himself up front, and all the others were giving him the shoulder. I couldn't blame the other lads, there could only be one Lenny and it's a tough old game. So I shoved him up the front. Sheena clocked him over the heads of all the others, pointed at him and said, 'That's Lenny McLean,' and he got the part. It was nothing to do with me — he got it on his own merit. All I did was give him a push.

Then, instead of steaming ahead, all of a sudden the film went flat because the money was a problem. Loads of people want to have a slice of the cake, but aren't too quick at dipping in the pocket. After a while, it seemed like it had never happened and everybody started to lose heart. I didn't though, because I knew it was a winner.

A bit of aggravation cropped up around that time, putting the film out of my head for a while. There is a load of money in the film game once it's at the box office, but until then you don't get a tanner, so I was still ducking and diving, taking on the minding and working at a little club round the corner.

One evening, we were getting close to shutting up for the night when there was a bunch of lads making a bit of a ruck. They were all well pissed, but not causing any trouble — just making a load of noise singing and larking about, so I left them alone. After a bit it was getting late, so I went over and told them to drink up and be on their way. I was polite and reasonable.

Then I got the usual 'Fuck offs', and the beer started talking. I made a grab at the biggest one, because if you get him down the rest usually bottle out, then one of the others pulled a knife out. I knocked it out of his hand, got him by the throat, and belted and belted him. I didn't notice that one of his mates had picked the knife up until he stuck the bastard five inches into the top of my leg. I went down and the slags have had it away. My pal came down from upstairs, pulled the knife out, and we were both covered in blood. He took me to the hospital, they cleaned me up, gave me some stitches and a couple of injections, and I went home.

My leg was a bit stiff and it hurt like hell, but I could walk so I carried on with some work that had been arranged by Alex Steen. I don't let anybody down, stabbed or not. The financier Ronson had some heavy business going down, so both sides at the boardroom meeting wanted minders along to make sure everyone behaved. So every day for five days I stood at the back of a big posh office, watching a load of suits barking and growling at each other. My leg seemed as though it was on fire, but I stuck out the week, picked up £2,000 in wages, and got home just before an abcess I didn't know was forming burst and sent poison right through me.

I was in a bad way. I was rushed to the Mile End Hospital, and at first they thought I was going to die — not that I was aware of this because I was sky high. I had a box thing stuck on my arm pumping morphine into me 24 hours a day and, to be honest, if that's what dying is about, it's not too bad.

I had fantastic dreams brought on by the drugs that I thought were real. Mum and Dad came to see me while I was lying there. Tony and I went to Scotland to see Arthur Thomson, and I did Roy Shaw all over again. Val and I had some good times as well, going to clubs and dances, though every now and then she was holding my hand, crying and looking older. Then I came back to earth and the surgeons were talking about amputating my leg.

I was looked after by an angel. I've got to give them a gee, all the nurses were angels, but Amanda Page, the sister in charge, fought and fought to save me. The poison was cleared out of my system, but gangrene had started in my leg. I remember saying to her, 'Look, don't let them amputate my leg. I'd sooner die. I'm Lenny McLean, the street fighter. I'm full of pride and if I'm on crutches all the mugs will be queuing up to have a pop, and I couldn't take it.' She called my wife over and they had a chat.

Val said, 'Len, if that's what you want, I'll stand by you.'

Mandy nagged at the doctors, because they'd given up hope. The hospital was on a three-day week and there were cutbacks all over the place, so the white coats had their own problems. But that lovely girl never let go. She got them to have another go at my leg, and there is a God in heaven because, three days later, she came flying down to my bed smiling and all excited. It was funny, really, because she was always so cool and prim — you know, a proper sister.

'Len,' she said, 'I'm so happy for you. The X-ray shows your gangrene has cleared.'

I felt choked up. 'Sweetheart,' I said, 'how can I thank you?'

She said, 'You just did — that look on your face is all the thanks I want.'

I gave her a kiss and hugged my Val, and I think we all had tears in our eyes.

Three weeks later, I was discharged and I sent all the nurses tights and flowers, and Mandy the biggest basket of fruit I could get from Harrods. I even joined the nurses on the picket line outside the hospital. They were trying to get a few bob extra on their wages, and I was right behind them. They deserve £1 million a week, not just for what they did for me, but for what they do for everybody.

I invited Mandy and her husband down to the Camden Palace and drowned them in champagne all night. It was lovely to see her let her hair down. Mandy, wherever you are now, I love you and I'll never forget you — you saved my life.

I'd been out of action for about three months and, to be honest, I hadn't given business much thought. I got in touch with Sheena Perkins and it looked like we were bolloxed for finance. Trying to drum up a bit of publicity to catch the eye of the money people, every now and then Sheena would get a bit of a spread in the newspapers. She'd stick in pictures of me and Craig squaring up, or mention a few names of the actors who were considering the script, like Michael Caine or Phil Collins. Phil had the right haircut to play me, but I think he was up for being Kenny or someone else. None of it did any harm, but it didn't bring in any money.

From all that publicity, I was clocked by television people and invited on to a few programmes. The first one was Derek Jameson's. Derek's one of your own, a good mate of Reg and Ron and a lot of other chaps. He was brought up in the East End so he knows what it's all about. I thought that show went off pretty well because he's not a piss-taker.

Another one was with Nina Myskow, and on my way to the studios I was thinking, 'I've got to watch this one.' Backstage, before we went on, I got her to one side and said, 'I've watched a lot of your shows and half the time I want to smack your arse for the way you mug people off — I'm just warning you, take the piss and I'm going to flare up.'

We go on and first thing she says is, 'Now here is a man you wouldn't like to meet on a dark night.' I gave her a funny look but she didn't start nothing.

The idea of the programme was to discuss the merits or otherwise of boxing. Alan Minter was there, and Mickey Duff the promoter. When the subject of brain-damaged fighters came up, Duff looked over at me and gave a funny smile. I thought, 'I'd like to get up and knock that smile off your face.' He doesn't like me because he knows I opened the door for Frankie Warren who knocked a dent in his pension. And I don't like him — full stop.

Now Ruby Wax ... what a bastard she is. I gave her the same talking to that I'd given Nina Myskow. This was before we went on when she was polite, timid and very pleasant. In front of the cameras, she comes over like a man — big mouth and all aggressive. I was holding my own but she was getting a bit flash. So in the break I said to her, 'Look here, you saucy fucker, pack in with the lip or I'll pull you right over my knee in the middle of the show.' They should stick me in the *Guinness Book of Records* for being the first bloke to get Ruby Wax to shut her mouth for more than two minutes!

There were a few others. Joey Pyle and I went on *Channel X* and the host was Jonathon Ross's brother. I had a spot on Danny Baker's *Londoners* — he's another one of your own — and bundles more I can't remember.

It was all a bit of a laugh at first, but I got fed up with it after a bit. What do half those prats know about life? They're all poncing about like they were God's gift, treating everybody as though they are half-wits because they haven't been to university, and acting like it should be the greatest honour in the world to be on their poxy show. Afterwards, people look at you and think, 'That Lenny's making a fortune, he's always on the telly.' Little did they know all I got were a few glasses of lemonade and a bit of exes. Fuck 'em, I had better things to do.

I did meet a few people, though, and got a bit of work. Jerry O'Dowd approached me and asked if I'd step in between his brother Boy George and some slags who were giving him some grief. I can't say George is my cup of tea, but he was polite and showed me a bit of respect, so I squared his problem.

I also helped out a producer. She said, 'You're just the man I've been looking for.'

I said, 'Steady on, girl, I'm a married man.' I like to give the ladies a gee up.

She said, 'No, I need someone to look after a small party we're having.'

'Sweetheart, I'm all yours,' got another blush and giggle. What she wanted me to do was mind the cast of *EastEnders* when they had a bit of a knees up. This do was in L'Escargot in Berwick Street.

A few days before I had been telling a pal of mine, Oggy, about a party I was going to mind. He said, 'Len, I'd love to get in and meet all the stars.'

'No problem,' I said, 'when the time comes, I'll slip you in.'

So I was just inside the door keeping photographers out and making sure everybody behaved. The stars came in and as they went past me they'd say, 'Cor, you're a big fella. We're well minded tonight.' Dot Cotton, or whatever her real name is, gave my muscles a bit of a squeeze and went, 'Ooo-er.' Lovely woman. I took to her more than any of them. Some were a bit stuck up, but not her. Then up came Peter Dean who acted that silly prat in the market. He don't say hello or kiss my arse, he just gave me his coat. 'Hold up,' I said, 'don't give me your fucking coat, hang it yourself. Cloakroom's over there.' He gave me a look but went and did it.

Everything was sweet and I was chatting to this one and that one, and back he came. 'I thought your job was to keep gatecrashers out.'

I said, 'You're right, what's the problem?'

He didn't look happy at all. 'I've just bumped into Peter, a bloke I used to go to school with. Well, he's not in the business so I don't think he should be here.'

I said, 'Don't you worry about Oggy, he's with me.'

He stormed off and I thought, 'Hello, he's going to complain that the hired help's getting above itself,' but nothing more was said.

It's funny, really. I find that actors and actresses who are well up the ladder are nearly always as good as gold. It's the bit players and hangers on who have their noses in the air. One actor I do have a lot of time for is Chris Ellison who played Burnside in *The Bill*. I met him while I was minding the cast and I couldn't help pointing out that he reminded me of Bob Hoskins. He seemed genuinely pleased. 'I take that as a compliment, Len, but I'd rather have his money.' He's one of your own and though he lives down in Brighton I do meet up with him every now and then.

Reg Kray had asked me to pop down to the movie set where they were making the film *The Krays* just to see how things were going and keep him in the picture. I was sitting there once and up came Billie Whitelaw, who was playing Violet Kray, and she asked me ever so politely if, when she came to do the scene where she climbs into the ring, I would help her up. 'My pleasure,' I said. She came down and, while the camera was running, I helped her up. She did her bit and, still on camera, she went, 'Thank you very much, Lenny.' Beautiful woman, lovely actress, and a proper star.

The next thing I knew, the cameraman's daughter was trying to climb up the other side of the ring. I thought, 'Another lady in trouble — I'll do the same for her.' I put my hand on her arm to steady her and she went, 'No, no, no, no, no, no, ... take your hands off.' I went mad. I called her all the names I could think of. Her old man came over and I threatened to punch his stupid head off. It was bloody chaos. The director said he would shut down filming if I didn't leave the set. He was polite, though — he didn't want to risk getting thumped himself.

Another time I visited the set with a very famous boxer out of the East End, Ted 'Kid' Berg. He was a lovely old fella, well in his seventies, but still as game as a bagel. Alex Steen was there and Charlie Richardson's son, Lee, with his pals. None of us are a bit shy when it comes to earning a few bob, so when the film people want extras for ringside, we're all up the front on wages. The Kemp brothers are in the ring being Reg and Ron, and we're supposed to be cheering them on. I was giving it some, yelling and shouting, 'Come on, Reg ... come on, Ron,' and, beside me, Ted's shouting at me, 'When do we get paid? When do we get paid?' Have a look at the film. You'll see us all there. Sadly, Ted died not long after. He was a legend and will always be remembered.

I had a lot of time for Reg and Ron Kray, and whenever I got the chance I slipped in to see them. Visiting was a bit restricted for them both, so it wasn't too often. If they needed any favours done they knew they only had to ring Lenny. When they were out thirty years ago I knew of them and I saw them in passing, but I didn't really know them personally. It was only since they'd been away that we became friends, after they heard of me and asked me to visit.

The first time I went to Broadmoor with Alex I didn't know what to expect. I mean, you hear stories and don't know what to believe. On the way in, I said to Alex, 'Fucking grim old place this is.' He pointed through a gateway and I looked — it was all gardens with trees, flowers and shrubs, really nice and peaceful. Inside, we got all the business. Security check, photos on computer and all that, then we were taken down miles of corridors to the visiting room. Ron was already there because they bring them through first. He was sitting down, but as we came in he stood up for us — a proper gentleman.

One minute
before I put 'Mad
Gypsy' Bradshaw
in hospital.

Top: Backstage with Ruby Wax.

Bottom: I never went into the ring expecting to lose.

Top: With the family – my Val, Jamie and Kelly.

Bottom: With Martine McCutcheon – Tiffany from *EastEnders*.

Top left: Me and my cousin, John Wall. He died of cancer recently.

Top right: With Vinnie Jones, my co-star in *Lock, Stock and Two Smoking Barrels*.

Bottom: Working out – again!

Let's go to work!

Top: With Freddie Starr and my Val.

Bottom: Roy Shaw took twenty head punches before he went down –
now I'm The Guv'nor.

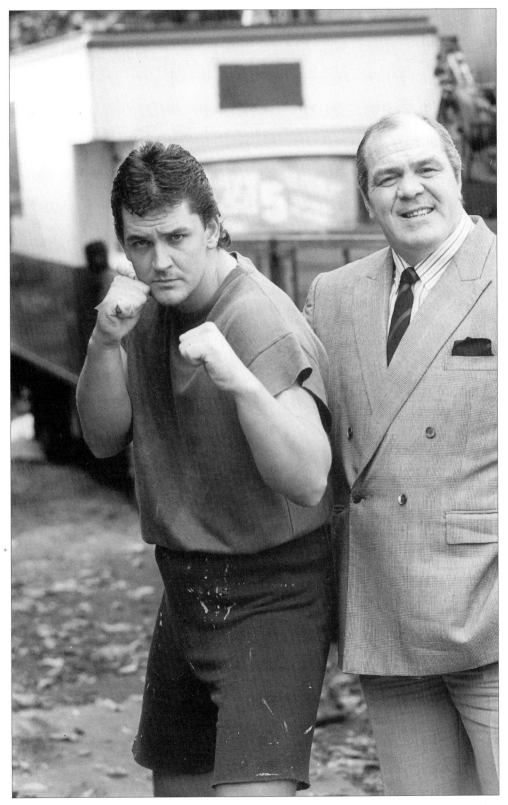

With Craig Fairbrass, star of *London's Burning*, who was to play me in the film of my life.

With Val, my strength and support.

The patients are allowed to wear their own clothes, and this man is immaculate. He didn't have a hair out of place, his suit was nicely pressed, and you could see your face in his shoes.

We sat down. I put a cigarette in my mouth and Ron was there with his lighter. As he lit my fag I couldn't help noticing his cuff links — gold and diamond with two 'R's on them. I've seen doctors and lawyers who were more menacing than this polite and considerate man sitting opposite us. I kept looking at him and wondering how he had had a stranglehold on London in the Sixties. He appeared to me like a man you'd let babysit your kids. All right, he knows what he did. I know what he did. But it was all kept within the underworld. The same as me really; I've never crossed the fence to have a go at some straight guy.

While we were talking, he said, 'Len, do you know Roger Daltrey?'

I said, 'Yeah, everybody does — good singer, good actor. Why, what's the problem?'

'Do you think you could get hold of him and bring him in to see me as soon as possible?'

I said 'Ronnie, consider it done. What do you want me to say? You want a bit of a chat?'

'Say nothing, Len. Just get him here so I can plunge the fucker.' As he said that he stabbed this imaginary figure in front of him. One of the screws — or nurses as they call them — looked over a bit cross-eyed but didn't come near us.

Alex calmed him down and asked him what it was all about, and he said, 'You know he was going to do the Kray film before this other lot took over? Well, he's taken a few liberties and now he's going to get what Cornell got.' I just said, 'Leave it with me,' and changed the subject.

On the way home, Alex said, 'That business with Daltrey ... I think it's all a bit of a misunderstanding, so don't get too involved.'

I said, 'I already thought that myself. I think Ron gets a bit frustrated because he can't deal personal with his own problems. I can't go round tugging big stars so they can be murdered, but if he asks me again I'll have a quiet word with Roger.'

So, Mr Daltrey, thank your lucky stars Big Lenny doesn't always do what he's asked, otherwise you'd have got your wish to die before you got old. Ron never referred to the incident again.

Sadly, Ronnie died not too long after. I wasn't surprised really because he used to smoke 50 fags in a two-and-a-half-hour visit.

Peter and I were invited to his funeral and I've got to say it was a blinding send off. The church service was just like you'd want if you were seeing your dad off, but outside the miles and miles of crowds made it like being in a circus parade.

One thing that lightened the mood a bit was when the driver of our limo got himself lost on the way to the cemetery. One minute we were all in this solemn line of cars, the next we were on our own doing about 80mph out of the East End as the bloke panicked. The roof of the Bentley was covered with wreaths and flowers and we were doing a circuit of Brands Hatch. There was me, Eddie, Peter and a couple of other faces hanging on for dear life. Eddie leaned over, tapped the driver on the shoulder and said, 'What you doing next week pal?' The driver's now red in the face, sweating cobs and shitting himself. He goes, 'Nothing, why?'

Eddie — dead pan — said, 'We're planning a blag and want a driver who knows his way about.'

Of course, we all pissed ourselves as the driver nearly burst into tears, shouting, 'It's all right for you to take the piss. It ain't my bleeding fault, I'm from over the river.'

Having known Ronnie made me realise the difference between old-time villains and the toe-rags about today. I know it's been said many times, but if men like them were still active, the streets would be a lot safer. Charlie Richardson put it in a nutshell. He said all the chaps from the old days, including himself, are like dinosaurs. Today, there are villains out there who would kill women and even babies if it helped them earn a living, and I know that the Twins or any of the others would never have been involved in anything like that.

Now Reg is a different man altogether. Polite, considerate and smart, Reg is a live wire. His mind's going all the time. He doesn't want visitors who sit there talking about the old days, this club, that club, old so and so's died. He wants to talk about what's happening, get involved, do this deal, do that deal. On the ball all the time. Again, there's no menace, and he speaks in that soft voice.

I once took a lovely up-and-coming actress in to see him, Sandi Carter. She's the wife of a pal of mine who runs London's Hippodrome. We laughed about a scene from the Kray movie. When Billie Whitelaw, as Violet, is having the twins, she's screaming and kicking her legs in the air — well, the legs weren't hers, they were Sandi's. Still, it was a couple of parts in a film for her.

When I was talking to Reg on the phone one day, I told him about my book and asked him if I could take his photograph to put in it.

He said, 'You know they won't like it, Len.'

'Don't tell me, Reg, I know what the bastards are like, but if you don't mind I'll have a go.'

Next time I visit I'm kitted out with a camera my book man fixed up. I pick my moment and 'click, click' I've got it. No flash, very fast film.

Over comes this young screw. 'You're taking photographs,' he said.

'Who do you think I am, David Bailey?'

He looked down his nose, so I got up from the table and steered him away. I didn't make a fuss and spoke quietly and politely. I said, 'Look, don't you think that man sitting there has suffered enough without you making a ruck on his one weekly visit? Go and have yourself a coffee and never mind what I'm doing.' To give him his due, he fucked off good as gold. I wouldn't say he was intimidated by me, he only had to blow his whistle and he'd have got us all in trouble — he just saw reason. Good man.

Back home, I got a call from Arthur Thomson. He said, 'I sent one of my men down to London on an errand, and he's got himself picked up by the law. Can you help out?' I'm on to it.

Apparently, Arthur had sent down £20,000 in cash to cover a deal. The bloke carrying the dough arrived in London with the money in a little case, but after he had a few drinks, for his own reasons he'd transferred the money into a plastic carrier bag. By two in the morning he was pissed and nearly legless. Staggering along the road, he bumped into Old Bill and they gave him a tug, checked the bag and whipped him down the nick.

When he sobered up he wouldn't say a word, so they held him. By the time Arthur found out where he was and got in touch with me, he'd been held for three days. I went into the nick, approached the sergeant on the desk, and said, 'Excuse me, I understand you have a friend of mine here who has £20,000 belonging to me.' Arthur didn't want his name brought up with this business, so I made a few phonecalls before I turned up. When the law wanted to know all the ins and outs, I told them that a boxing promoter in Glasgow had sent the money as an investment in my film. They checked my story, which I'd set up already, and they had to let the money go — they were choked.

I went to a room to pick up the money and there were two CID officers waiting for me. As I went in, one said to the other, 'Go and make Mr McLean a cup of tea.'

'Forget the fucking tea,' I said, 'just give me the dough.'

'No, I insist, my friend here will make you a nice cup of tea.' Anyway, he's counting the money out and saying, 'If I want I can make things really difficult. I could have all these numbers on the notes checked for a start.' I know what's coming. 'Am I going to be looked after or what?'

I said to him, 'You greedy c**t, no wonder you was keen for your mate to disappear.'

He just laughed. 'Make your mind up.'

I slung him a grand and he pulled a face. So I said, 'You can fucking well straighten your mug up 'cos you ain't getting no more.' He went cross-eyed then, bomp, it has disappeared into his pocket double quick. I know it wasn't my money, but it hurt to slip some of it to Old Bill.

I delivered the 19 large and phoned Arthur. 'Sorry, mate, I had to let some of it go.'

'No problem, it was a bit hot anyway. And, by the way, tell my messenger not to bother coming back to Scotland.'

I said, 'I don't think he has to be told.'

It's a pity the money wasn't really for the film because we were still scratching around for finance and every little helps. Then my Italian friend rang me from Canterbury to tell me that he'd heard we needed money. 'I've made a few phonecalls to America, and if you can get over there it may do you and your film some good. Go to the Plaza as before, book in, and someone will contact you.'

What could I say but 'Lovely'?

I got in touch with Jack and he got all excited. I had to slow him down a bit. 'Don't forget this trip's coming out of our own pockets, not like before when I went over there.'

'Worth laying out for, Len ... we'll be able to raise £5 million from those Yank film people, that's peanuts to them.'

'Yeah, we'll see.' I was excited myself, but I didn't go overboard.

We got ourselves over to America, although it stung a bit coming out of our own pot. We parked up in Room 44 and waited for our meet. After a few hours, we were picked up and driven to another hotel. Here we go. Same mob as before, different faces.

I passed over the script. It was flicked through and put down. I stuck it in another geezer's hand and down it went again. All they're talking about is Stallone, Stallone. Three-and-a-half hours I listened to this shit, then I got Jackie on one side and said, 'Look, fuck this — they're giving us the run around.'

His eyes popped out like Freddie Starr's when he had the springs on. 'Steady on, Len, we don't want any trouble.'

'Forget trouble, I'm giving them a tug.'

I went back and raised my voice a bit. 'What I'm here for is to raise money for my movie and all you lot want to talk about is other films and Rocky and Stallone.'

'Hey,' one of them said, 'hold it down, big fella, we can get you a starring part in Stallone's next big film.'

'Well, you can stick it up your arse,' I said. 'I'm not interested. I'm tired, I'm fucking worn out, shagged and jet-lagged. Gimme the phone, I want to get in touch with the guy who sent us here.'

It was four in the morning back in England and I got the old guy out of bed and bollocked him. I shouldn't have done it to him, but I was wild. I told him, 'Your people are taking the piss out of me. I've come halfway round the world to listen to a load of shit. All they want to do is talk about making me a film star. They haven't even looked at the script yet, just rabbited on about the film game.'

He talked a bit of sense and calmed me down. 'Lenny, my friend, don't take their attitude personally, remember their culture is different from yours, even though it seems the same.'

One of the Americans took the phone, then he hollered down the line, 'Your big friend is being unreasonable, we can't talk to him. We're trying to help him and he's lost his manners. He's a nice guy but he doesn't appreciate how we work.'

When the phone went down, I said to him, 'Listen, you fucking Yankee mug, don't talk about my manners like I wasn't here. I don't care who you've got behind you, any more of your lip and I'll unload you.' I'm steaming, so I turned on the others. 'You lot are all too long-winded for me. If you ever get round to reading the script and want to come aboard that's fine. Get in touch with our friend in Canterbury, but right now me and my pal are going home.' With that we walked out, leaving them all with their mouths open.

We were both gutted. All that dough on the fares and hotel down the pan for nothing. Before we parted company at Heathrow Airport, Jack said, 'While you were asleep on the plane, Len, I gave all this business a lot of thought. This film's going nowhere so I'm going to write a book about you instead.'

At that moment, I didn't give a bollocks either way. 'You do that, pal,' I said, 'it'll be a bestseller.'

I'm not the sort of bloke who mopes around thinking about what might have been. Like I said at the beginning, I don't look back. Of course I was pissed off with the way things were going, but that didn't mean I was going to give up.

I've got to give young Craig Fairbrass a gee. Everybody else was starting to look the other way, but he was still there for the part. When Sheena Perkins pointed him out at the audition and said, 'You're Lenny McLean,' she was dead right. She couldn't see it, but inside he's made of the same stuff as me; you've got to keep going, keep punching, don't give up.

When we thought everything was going ahead, he'd put his heart and soul into getting fit. I'd said to him, 'Look, son, your weight's about right but you're carrying a bit of puppy fat so I'm going to get you trained up like a fighter.' That made him pull a face.

'Len,' he said, 'I'm an actor, I'll just be pretending when I'm on the screen.'

I said, 'Don't matter, you've got to look the part.'

I got hold of my cousin, Johnny Wall, and he took Craig under his wing. Good stuff, John. He was Lightweight Champion of the South once, but when his dad died it seemed to take something out of him and he gave up the ring. He kept himself up to scratch, though, so he was just the bloke to get Craig in shape.

The three of us would get ourselves over Hampstead Heath and do what they called the boxer's run, seven miles in all. I reckoned I was fit enough so I rode a bike behind the pair of them giving encouragement like, 'Come on, you lazy bastards, step it out.' It was the middle of winter and all I could see were these two clouds of steam puffing along in front of me. When that was out of the way, Craig would break the ice on the reservoir and jump in. Looking back, it's a wonder the shock didn't kill him, but he was a tough boy and he'd get out blue with cold, put on a dressing gown and do press-ups and shadow boxing until he was warmed up.

He used to say, 'You're sure I have to do all this to play you in the film? I'll be knackered by the time we start filming.'

I'd say, 'Yeah, I'm sure and, no, you won't be knackered. You'll be as tough as I was then, and look where it got me.' Good kid, he kept up that punishment for two months, then, like I said, the film sort of ground to a halt. Craig got tied up in film and TV work and had to let it slide. But he never let go of the idea of playing the Guv'nor, he's always lived and breathed it.

In the time since he was first offered the part, some years have passed and he's grown physically and mentally, and has become a well-respected actor. It gives you some idea how much when I say that Sylvester Stallone chose him out of thousands to play alongside him in *Cliffhanger*. Always looking out for our film, when he got the chance he slipped the script in to Stallone who reckoned that Lenny McLean was like a real-life Rocky, and that he'd like to meet me some time. That's a good gee from a big star.

One night, Craig came down the club with an actor mate of his and got an idea what it's like for me being the Guv'nor. I saw them come through the door. Craig introduced me to his mate Dave, we shook hands, and I suggested we went upstairs to the restaurant. As we opened the double doors, two big drunks came barging their way through, shoving us out of the way — no excuse me, nothing. 'Excuse me,' I said, 'do you mind?'

One of these mugs said to his mate, 'Look up, it's McLean — the fucking Guv'nor,' and he made to throw a right hander. Craig stepped back, Dave went as white as a ghost, and I unloaded the pair of them. One left hook, one right, and they're on the deck. In the same breath, I said, 'Carry on, boys, quick, it's a bit quieter upstairs.'

Craig said, 'Len, that was brilliant — like something out of a John Wayne movie.'

I said, 'Never mind that, step over them. They'll be all right in a bit.'

We got up to the restaurant and we had only just sat down when Denzil Washington walked in and he was all excited. 'There's an ambulance downstairs and the police.'

'Oh yeah,' I said, 'someone must have got run over.' Then I gave Craig a wink and he burst out laughing. 'Ain't you glad you're just acting the part? That's what I have to put up with nearly every night.'

At about this time, I moved on to look after another club — the Hippodrome. It was a right fancy gaff, so I reckoned I was on a cushy number, good dough and no aggravation — or so I thought. I was what they call a Reception Manager, or as one comical prat once told me, Door Policy Mediator. What I had to do was tuck myself away in my office upstairs and leave the donkey work to the new breed of doormen, big lads squeezed into dress suits and bow ties, looking like they should be in a circus ring. They handled all the little bits of trouble, but at the first sign of anything heavy, I got a buzz and I'd be downstairs in seconds.

I was in the office having a bit of dinner when John came in to tell me there was a bit of a problem. I looked at my steak and said, 'For fuck's sake,' but I shoved it back and led the way down. On the stairs we met up with Peter, another minder. He was black, and as good as gold and a perfect gentleman — a good man to have on your side. He said to me, 'Len, there's an eight-handed mob of blacks off the Broadwater Estate and they're looking for trouble. Why don't you let me talk to them — might save a bit of damage.'

'Good thinking, Peter,' I said, 'we'll stand back and let you brother them up a bit. See if you can nip it in the bud.'

So he went up to them and did a bit of the old high fives, and it started to smooth down. Then one of them looked past Pete, clocked me, and screamed, 'Who you looking at, honky bastard?'

Now I don't take that sort of shit from anybody. I dived at him and smashed him to the floor. All hell broke loose. I hurt four or five of them and John and Peter sorted the rest. Then we slung them all out of the door on to the pavement and left them in a heap. Nice bit of teamwork. Peter said to me, 'Len, you went at that lot like a maniac. I thought you was going to kill them.'

I said, 'What do you expect? Them slags took a liberty — they ruined my steak.'

The next night, somebody come in and told me that something seemed to be going down outside because there were a couple of blacks on every corner watching the place. I got the others together and another bloke, Brian Gregson, and told them it looked like we would get a comeback from last night. So what we'd do was to slip out the back way, come round from behind, and spring them. So that's what we did. They were spark out before they knew what was coming. They were all carrying guns, so we dumped them down the drain, carried these fellas down an alley, brought them round so they'd know what was coming, then beat them unconscious again. Lovely result.

Another time, I was standing outside the club getting a bit of fresh air, and a motor slowed down and parked up about 50 yards away. It wasn't until the geezer in the car got closer that I recognised my good pal Dave Lee. Nice bloke, Dave, and a top stunt man to all the major stars all over the world — Stallone, Van Damme, Bruce Willis. Think of a star — he's worked with them. He was just shaking my hand and saying, 'Nice to see you, Len,' when there was a scream from down the road. I looked up and there were three blokes with their heads through the windows of Dave's motor, and he had a couple of lady friends sitting waiting for him. I ran down the road and gave them the lot — feet, fists and a couple of head butts. Dave came up and the three of them were lying in the road, crying and moaning. I said, 'Nice to see you mate, but fuck off quick before Old Bill turns up.'

He said, 'I owe you, Len,' and drove off.

I slipped back into the club and went upstairs. The law came and questioned a few minders, but they couldn't pick out anyone, so they had to go off without a nicking. Good stuff, my lads, none of them grassed. I found out later that one of the blokes was a presenter on children's television, a lovely example for little kids who think he's the business.

Over the years, I've minded some of the roughest and toughest clubs and pubs in town. I've worked with hundreds of doormen and, to be honest, I don't give any of them much room. Whenever there was trouble I was always the front man, though, to be fair, I suppose I stuck myself at the sharp end — I never was one to follow anybody else.

If I'm giving gees out it would be for one man, and that's John, one of the craftiest, most cunning minders I've ever worked with. We've been together at different clubs for years, and whenever there was a problem he'd take the long way round. I used to say, 'Hold up, John, come this way, it's quicker.' He'd just say, 'Quicker or slower, we're still getting the same money and won't get thought of no better.' It wasn't my way, but perhaps he was right because a while later he went round the houses while I rushed at a bit of bother and got nicked for murder. I'll come to that in a bit.

A lot of people think that minders are suited-up thugs, and when something goes down it's them who have started it. Well, that's all bollocks. The bottom line is that we get our wages from the place we're minding. The idea is that we make sure everyone behaves so the property isn't damaged and ordinary blokes don't get hurt. After all, it's their money that keeps the place going. None of us would have a job very long if we smashed up the customers every time we got annoyed. We try and avoid trouble, not cause it. The problem is the booze.

Let me tell you about Albert, a good pal of mine. He's a very big black guy, well over 20 stone and about 6ft 8in. He's very powerful and menacing, but when you talk to him he's as placid as a teddy bear. A nice person, and very intelligent as well.

At the time I'm referring to, he was at university studying for a master's degree. He was in a club one night having a quiet drink when he got a tug from some loud-mouthed, white Afrikaan bloke, who probably had the hump because of Albert's colour. Another three geezers joined in, taking the piss and digging him out, so he did them with a champagne bottle. Fucking carnage. Anyway, he was nicked, went to court and got a seven for GBH. He sat behind the door for 15 months, then the system saw sense and let him out on appeal. So he's happy; he carried on with his studies and put it all behind him. Don't forget, though, he's a 'ticket of leave' man. One slip and he finishes his seven.

So he came down to see me at Cairo Jacks in Soho. I said, 'Good to see you, Albert. Tell you what, nip over and get a drink for yourself and a coffee for me and we'll sit over in the cubbyhole away from all these mugs.' So off he went. While he was waiting to be served, there were five muggy office workers standing round him. They'd been in the club since five, now it's half-nine and they're drunk as sacks. One of them gave him a pinch on the chest and said, 'Cor, you're a big lump, show us your muscles.' Albert stepped back, said, ''Scuse me,' and walked away, leaving these mugs laughing like drains. When you've got a seven hanging over your head you've got to be very careful.

When he brought the drinks back, I could see the look on his face, so I said, 'What's up, mate?'

He said, 'Don't matter, it's nothing.'

'Forget nothing, has somebody given you a pull?'

'Sort of. One of them geezers pinched me chest and said, "Show us your tit," and I can't do nothing.'

'No, but I can,' I said. 'What is he, a fucking poof?'

I went out to this lot and shouted at them, 'Who's pinched the big fella's tit?' Full of piss, they all think it's funny. I said, 'Tell you what I can do. I can smash the lot of you to pieces and put you in hospital. Then tomorrow when Old Bill wants a statement you'll all put your hands up and say, "We took a diabolical liberty and Lenny belted us, but he was in order." Like fuck you would. No, you worthless cunts would say you was having a quiet drink when this animal started knocking you around for nothing. Then I'm up in court and the judge is going to say, "McLean, you are a very dangerous man, you must do five years in prison."

'That's why I hate you straight mugs because I have to live my life round people like you. You lot start trouble with your pissed-up mouths and then people like me get fives, sevens and tens for doing our job. You're of no value, any of you, so leave the drinks and fuck off — you're barred.'

That's what we're up against all the time. Any other time they wouldn't have got the lecture, they'd have got hurt, but I didn't want any trouble with Albert being there. They don't know how lucky they were.

Wherever you are now, Albert mate, take it away. With that degree you'll never look back.

A lot of work I get offered is evicting squatters from properties, and it's the one area of my business where I've had the least aggravation. Give myself a gee, I do look a bit menacing so nobody argues, especially as the people I'm up against are usually straights taking advantage of an empty place. I'm not talking about chucking women and kids out of little terraces, that's not my game. I leave all that to the bullies.

What I got involved in was clearing out office blocks or big stores where a lot of money was at stake. I'll give you some idea. A businessman pal of mine, from Chislehurst, came to see me with a problem. Jim's not one of those who's always on your ear'ole for favours, but he knows I'm there if he ever has a bit of trouble and he insists on paying well for any help. He's grafted well over the years and good luck to him, he's now got loads of money and all the best gear. But Jim's not one of them yuppie gits, he's one of your own.

It seemed that he'd just sunk a quarter of a million into buying a big store over in Woodford. When he sent his people down to sort the place out, ready for him to open a big travel agency, they couldn't do anything because there was already a firm in the place and they were selling swag gear, making fortunes and paying no rent or rates.

Now, Jimmy's a businessman. He's got his credibility and a reputation to think of, so he couldn't go all outrageous and cause a ruck, he had to be diplomatic. He spoke to the people squatting in his gaff, and they told him to fuck off and come back with a court order. Everybody knows the scam. That's where I came in.

Lots of people think we go in mob-handed, smashing the place up and belting the squatters, but we don't. It breaks my heart sometimes, but we have to go a bit steady. I got hold of Graham, a carpenter who does a bit of work with me, and we went down to Woodford. Graham's a very big man but doesn't have a lot to say for himself. All you get out of him are two words, 'safe' and 'sweet', and that suits me because it lets me get on with things without listening to a load of rabbit.

We went in and I told Graham to start changing the locks. Half a minute and the prat who was running the show was on our ear'ole screaming and doing his nut. 'What's going on, what do you think you're doing?'

'Doing, pal?' I said. 'We're doing a bit of maintenance for the leaseholder.'

He went red in the face. 'He can't do that, I'm a legal squatter, he's got to go through the courts.'

Cheeky git, legal squatter, what does that mean? I've marked his card. 'You can be locked in or locked out, make up your mind, but these locks are being changed.'

He disappeared, then ten minutes later he was back with Old Bill. This mug wants it both ways. He wants to break the law on one hand by thieving somebody else's property, then he wants the law to back him up. He came unstuck though, like they all do. I showed the coppers all the papers saying my pal owns the place and told them we were just changing the locks. They asked the squatter, 'Has this man assaulted or threatened you in any way?' What can he say?

'Well, no, not exactly, but look at the size of the two of them, they're very menacing.'

'Sorry, sir, how people look is not our concern, this is a civil action and nothing to do with us.' So they took off.

I can verbal this twat now. 'Up yours, you c**t,' I said. 'Now when you turn up in the morning, all your gear is going to be lying out in the road. How does that grab you?' Nine times out of ten they pack up there and then and leave. The odd few try to stick it out but in the end it comes to the same thing. I've done hundreds of these evictions and never had to belt anybody. That particular job pulled in ten large because we were dealing with a very valuable property, but normally it can be done for £5,000.

I got a call from some bloke who'd heard I was good at this game — bit of a toff by the sound of his voice. 'I have a problem with some gypsies parked on my land and I'll pay you well to take some heavies and get rid of them.'

He picked the wrong bloke. 'Oh yeah, are they pinching your chickens and burning your fences?'

'No, not exactly, but they look a bit untidy.'

'Bit untidy! Look, pal, I don't know who put my name up, but if I find out he's likely to get a good belting because everybody knows I don't take liberties with people trying to get a living the best they can.' I must have frightened him because down went the phone and I never heard anymore.

It's true what I said — I've got nothing against gypsies. I know I've fought a lot of them over the years but that was business. I've got a lot of respect for most of them, and they've got the same for me.

In fact, a very good friend of mine is a well-known gypsy, and he gets bundles of respect from everybody in the community. He knows if he wants anything done, he's only got to pick the phone up. Once, his nephew, Dave, was getting a lot of aggravation from a gang of tearaways out in the country where he lived. He asked me to step in, so I got Big Graham and a fella called Mick and followed him down to this pub where the trouble was.

We were outside and I said, 'Right, how do you want to play it?'

He pulled a bayonet out of his belt and said, 'I know you don't use a tool, Len, but I'm going to be right beside you with this.'

I had to give him ten out of ten — is he game or what? He was 65 years old and ready to go to work. Now that's what I call fucking game because we're not up against schoolkids here. I said, 'Put that away, you won't need it. You've had your day ... put your feet up and let us handle it — that's what you're paying us for.' He wouldn't let it go, though, so I said, 'You've got my respect for joining in but don't get under my feet when it goes off.'

We were all sitting in the pub, and after about an hour a crowd of these tearaways came in. Nothing was said. They were looking at us from one end and we were scowling at them from ours. I was thinking, 'Somebody's going to move in a minute.' I went to the bar to get some drinks in for my people and a lemonade for myself, and the landlord said, 'This one's paid for, mate,' and he nodded towards this group down the bar. I didn't even look at them, I just went back to our table, told the others, and sat and waited. The clock ticked round but we could sit there all day.

Eventually, the landlord came over to the gypsy, whispered in his ear, and went back behind the bar. My mate had a menacing look on his face, he looked down at the tearaways and all he does is raise his hand. That's all. Then he said to us, 'Nice result, they want to shake hands with Dave, so we can fuck off now.' He was a good money-getter, so three large to him is like three bob to a lot of people. Good wages for a Sunday drink.

I worked a bit harder the next time he called me, but not that much. He does a lot of buying and selling quality cars, so he did a deal with a guy in Hertfordshire to send a parcel of Mercs, Rolls and Bentleys abroad. He did his end and then got rumped for the lot. How the guy thought he was going to get away with a stroke like that I don't know. All I can think is that he didn't know the gypsy very well. I was pulled in as usual, so I picked up Graham on the way and arrived at this big farm. It was a lovely place, horses everywhere, so we knew he wasn't short of a few quid. I asked a farmworker where I could find his governor and he told me he was down in a big caravan he used as an office. We found him. Initially, we were both polite. It probably wouldn't last, though, but there was no need for unpleasantness until we found out the lie of the land.

He gave us nothing but promises and a load of bollocks. I was still polite, though. I put it to him. 'If you don't come up with the money, we're going to work our way right through your farm, and just so you know we're not fucking about, your office will do for starters.' He thought I was pulling his pisser until Graham grabbed hold of him and I set fire to his office. It went up in flames. A couple of his workers came running, but they must have known their governor better than we did because they looked at us, saw Graham holding the boss, and buggered off without saying a word.

Graham wasn't holding him back, he was holding him up, because his legs turned to jelly. He was puffing and panting like he was going to have a heart attack, but he managed to say, 'That's enough. I'll sort it. No more.' I patted him on the back, said, 'Have a nice day,' and we were away. My pal's end was worth about half a million and it was delivered with apologies two days later.

I said to Val, 'Sweetheart, how's the old bank balance doing?'

She stuck her head in her little notebook and said, 'Could be better, why, do you need some cash?' I spread the £20,000 on the table and said, 'See this ... I've just had a nice little earner, so bung ten in the bank and me and you are going to have a lovely holiday with this other bundle. The kids are well big enough to look after themselves, so it's just you and me. Give us a kiss and I'll take you on a second honeymoon.' And I chased her all round the kitchen.

It was a lovely holiday, too. No aggravation — all that was hundreds of miles away. Sun, sea, sand. Lovely. It doesn't half go quick when you're enjoying yourself, though. The first week you make your mind up that you want to buy a little villa and stay for ever, but after that it goes downhill a little bit every day.

I'm not knocking it, though; at least I wasn't getting any mugs trying to take me on. We went into a restaurant one night for a bit of dinner and while we were waiting to order, I had a look round. I clocked a face that looked sort of familiar and I said to Val, 'See that old geezer over there? It's Lonnie Donnegan. I'm going over to shake his hand.'

I went over and introduced myself and he asked us to join him and his wife. What a lovely evening we had. He spoke about the skiffle days and I made him laugh when I told him that he'd been our idol and how we sang all his songs in our group. He'd given all that up and just lives quietly in Spain writing songs and music. Smashing bloke, who gave us a lot of pleasure back in the old days.

Anyway, come the last day I've had enough of the blazing sun and I'm not sorry to be going home. Val and I took a last walk down the market before packing up when a voice behind me said, 'Wanna fight?'

I shot round and there was Ronnie Knight laughing all over his face.

We slipped into a bar for a coffee and he said, 'How do you like Fuengerola, Len?'

I said, 'It's beautiful, a wonderful place, but two weeks is enough. I can't wait to get home.'

'Imagine how I feel, then. I've been stuck out here for years, and I'd give a million pounds to get on the plane with you.' I felt so sorry for him. He looked the business. Handsome, smartly dressed, and as brown as a berry, but inside all he wanted to do was go home, and I don't suppose he ever could.

Before we left him, he said to me, 'Do you remember the first time we met? I forget who you was fighting but me, like a mug, put all my money on the other fella. Cost me bundles.'

I've got to give Ronnie a lot of respect, because he's a man who's had a lot of shit thrown at him. He was always a good friend to loads of the chaps. If they were in trouble he'd try and help them out. But because of his club, he mixed with a lot of tasty people and I think that gave Old Bill the hump.

His last words to me were, 'Anyway, mate, look after yourself and don't be surprised if I'm knocking on your door soon for a cup of tea.' I thought he was having a laugh, but I think even then he had it in his head to come home, give himself up to the law and prove his innocence. It turns out he was wrongly advised. He came back looking for an acquittal on handling money for the Security Express robbery, and walked straight into a seven. Seven at 60 — what a fucking knock back. But he swallowed it like the good man he is and just got on with it. Four years went by before he turned up for that cup of tea. It was one Saturday when he was out for the day on home leave. And did we have a good laugh. I was sorry to see him leave knowing he was going back to Send Prison, but, God willing, by the time this book is on the shelves it'll be all behind him. He'll be a free man and we can get together again.

CHAPTER ELEVEN

Was I glad to get home to the East End and have a nice cup of tea! I had a bit of a sleep in the chair, woke up at about nine, had some dinner, then I was back in the armchair in front of the TV. Nothing worth watching. Val had the washing machine going already — she can't sit down for five minutes, but you know what women are like. 'Val, babe,' I shouted through, 'I'm going to shoot round the club and pick up my wages. Might as well be in my bin as theirs.' So I was off.

On the way to the Hippodrome, I called in on a few people to catch up on a bit of business, so by the time I got to the club it was about one o'clock. The place was swinging, as usual, so I ducked out of the way and slipped up to have a chat with the boys. I told them all about my holiday, picked up my bit of scratch from the office, and I decided to call it a night.

John was walking down the stairs with me when up came Robert Lopez and one of the lighting blokes, Nathan, to tell us there was a bit of aggro. 'Fucking hell, nothing changes and I'm not even back at work yet.'

Nathan said, 'We've got a streaker on the dance floor.'

John said, 'You go the front way, Len, I'll come round by the back.'

'Go on then, John,' I said, 'Let's get this over quick, I want to get home.'

Me and Robert get down to the dance floor sharpish, and there was this geezer stark bollock naked, pissing and wanking in front of all the young girls. Dirty slag. We went to get hold of him and he did a little dance and ran up the stairs. That's all I need. I was tired, it had been a long day, and I was ready for bed. Still, better tidy this up. By the time we caught up with him he was by the main entrance, still flashing his dick about and embarrassing a group of young girls sitting on the sofa.

He was standing by a store cupboard, so I nipped in quick and shoved him inside and Robert followed me in. This geezer was full of drugs or beer, and was acting like a lunatic. His eyes were staring and he started banging all round the cupboard and throwing himself at me. I put my hands up, caught him by both arms, and held him to calm him down. He went hysterical, screaming a load of nonsense and fighting against me. So I let one of his arms go and backhanded him across the jaw. He stopped struggling and looked at me like he'd just woken up.

'Now you dirty c**t,' I said, 'are you going to behave yourself or do you want some more?' He gave a bit of a nod so I let go of him slowly in case he was ready for the off again, but the slap in the face had knocked the fight out of him and he just stood there. What a fucking state to get in.

'Robert, for Christ's sake, get his strides and cover him up, he's not a pretty sight.' Somebody flung in a T-shirt and a pair of trousers and we dressed him. That's all we had, so it would have to do. It was June so he wouldn't freeze to death. I took him to the side door, opened up, and told him to fuck off and not to show up here again.

I said to Robert, 'Look at me, that mug spat blood on my shirt and he's ripped my jacket. I'm going to collar Mick about this and get a bit of exes. I'll talk to him tomorrow. I'm knackered, I'm off home.'

I fell into bed at about four o'clock. I cuddled up to my Val and said, 'Sweetheart, it's hard to believe we were in Spain this morning ... what a day,' but she was asleep.

At eight o'clock the next morning, the phone went. It was Mick Theo, a pal of mine. Good stuff. This bloke was Mr Universe one year. He said, 'Len, you know that nutcase you straightened up last night down the club ... well, he's dead.'

He should have been a diplomat, that Mick, he knows how to break news gently.

'Bit early to get me out of bed, mate, and too late for April fool — what's the game?' I joked.

'No, I'm serious, he's stone dead.'

I couldn't believe it; nobody dies from a back-hander. My nut was racing. I put the phone down and went up to Val. I woke her up and said, 'Doll, we've got trouble.'

She sat up. 'What do you mean?' She could see it was serious.

'Looks like I've killed somebody. I slapped a drugged-up lunatic last night and Mick's just told me he's heard the bloke's dead.'

Val just covered her face and cried and cried.

I gave her a cuddle. 'Listen, I'll have to face it. I'm too old to go flying round the country calling in favours. If I done it I'll stand up for it, but me and you will face it together.'

I made a few quiet enquiries and found that nobody had died near the club, but some bloke had died further west. No problem. Mick's got it all wrong. Had me going for a bit, though. I don't know why, because I've belted hundreds of blokes over the years, and I mean really belted, and as far as I know none of them died, let alone with a bit of a slap. I was so relieved I think I burst into song.

I went back to work and I felt great. The holiday had done me good and the little scare made me appreciate life — bit like when you find a lump on your body and the doctor says it's not cancer, it's a boil. Then Old Bill turned up at the club some days later and things started to unwind. They were back-tracking on the guy who had died, trying to find out where he'd been all Saturday evening. One of the coppers asked me if there had been a naked man in the club the other night. Well, it was no good saying no, so I said, 'Yeah, I've still got his shoes and bits and pieces of clothes.' That's all right.

Then they spoke to Conrad, one of the managers. Talk about silly as arseholes. Instead of telling them that the guy was here, but there was no trouble or anything, he gave them the full SP about his being restrained and all that.

Coppers aren't always stupid so they put two and two together and started quizzing the other people who worked there. It was no good me looking for support from most of that lot, because they were straights and wanted to look after their own arses. All the law had was Lenny this, Lenny that. I could see myself getting deeper and deeper in the shit. Once my name is mentioned down the nick, some bright spark's going to be squealing Lenny McLean, King of the Bouncers, Guv'nor, Hardest Man in London, fucking animal — we've got ourselves a result here.

Anyway, days passed and nothing happened, so perhaps they found out that the fella died of a heart attack or something. Val was in bed and I was sitting in the kitchen talking to Ronnie Joyce. He came round early to see if I wanted to go to visit our pal Ritchie Anderson, who was being held in Brixton on a section 18 and attempted murder. It seems that Ritchie had just started to cross the road when a carload of drunks had come speeding round the corner and knocked him down. He wasn't hurt, but he was fucking mad. If they had known what was good for them they would've kept going, but they stopped and he slipped into them with a knife and got himself nicked.

So Ronnie and I were talking about Ritchie and working out the best time to go and visit him. Then I heard a bit of a noise out front. I shot through to the front room, looked out the window, and I saw the law all over the place. The whole street was blocked off and the place was crawling with coppers. Ron came through from the kitchen, had a look and said, 'What you been up to, Len, no tax on your motor?'

I said, 'No, mate, this is serious. I think I've killed a guy and so does Old Bill — too late to go over the wall.'

Then the bell rang. Here I go. I opened up and two plainclothes officers pushed in. I blocked their way. 'Hold up, what's your fucking game?' Then they flashed warrant cards.

'DI Cater and DI Prunty,' Cater says, 'Leonard McLean, I'm charging you with the murder of Gary Humphries. You have the right to remain silent ...' and all that stuff you've seen on the telly.

I said, 'Who's he? Never heard of him.'

'No,' Prunty said, 'I don't expect you asked his name while you were beating him up. Now get the clothes you were wearing Saturday.'

He called up a uniform and told him to follow me upstairs. 'No you don't,' I said. 'Nobody goes into my bedroom when my wife's in bed except me, so make your mind up. Any of you try it and I'll unload the three of you before you can call up your mob out there.' They saw reason.

I went up, dug out the clothes, and told Val I'd been lifted. She was crying but I told her to be strong. 'We've got plenty of dough in the bank so you'll be all right, but first off get hold of Ralph Haeems, our brief, and get him to work.'

Soon after, I was in Vine Street and banged up waiting for the interviews to start. After a couple of hours, I was told my brief had turned up so they'd be seeing me in five minutes. I thought, 'Good-oh. Ralph's here and he'll sort this lot out double quick.'

I was taken to the interview room and there were a couple of uniforms, Prunty, Cater and a fella I didn't know. It turned out Ralph was too busy, so he sent this South African solicitor instead.

DI Cater read the charge out. 'Unlawful killing of Gary Humphries.'

I said, 'Hold up, I never killed him.'

Prunty said, 'If you didn't kill him, why is he down the mortuary right now?'

'All I did was give him a back-hander and he deserved that for pissing and wanking over young girls, but I never meant to kill him.'

Cater chipped in, 'Whatever he deserved, McLean, it certainly wasn't one of your right-handers.'

'Piss off,' I said. 'I don't want to talk to you, you've got me hung already. It must be in the blood because you're the same as your old man.' His father had been involved in getting the Krays put away.

He had me flung back in the cell. He doesn't like it unless he's got you pissing yourself. I was lying on the wooden bench and I felt like my guts had been ripped out. Murder. That means I'm looking at life. The judge is going to look at me, hear all about my past and decide that I'm too dangerous to be left on the streets. 'This man makes his living with his fists, he's a street-fighter, a minder and an animal, so I'd better give him a rec. of twenty-five years — keep him away from decent people.'

The police cell didn't worry me at all. It was summer, hot and the place was stinking of piss and vomit because of the drunks held the night before. If I'd been banged up for anything else but murder I wouldn't give a bollocks, but a charge like that drains the life out of you. I was 40 years old. I might be drawing my pension the next time I'm on the outside.

I couldn't think about it so I got up and did sit-ups and press-ups on that filthy floor, then I did a bit of shadow boxing until the adrenalin flowed through me and I felt like I was on a high. 'Come on, Cater, try me now.'

He does. As soon as I was back upstairs, some other CID bloke said, 'I know you from some business about 20 years ago. Wasn't it you that smashed and belted the life out of some man and nearly killed him? What are you, a psychopath? Is that what you do every time somebody upsets you?'

On the outside, I would have knocked him down for talking to me like that. He knew it and was trying to goad me into flaring up, but I kept calm.

'Yeah, all right, I did do him, but we're pals now, that's all in the past.' They all looked at each other, then the penny dropped. I'd forgotten all about the tape recorder.

'Oh yeah, I bet you lot think you're the dog's bollocks now I've dropped myself in it. Fuck you, I'm not saying no more.'

Three hours later they gave up. Every time they asked a question I did an impersonation of John Wayne or Michael Caine. They were doing their nut, but that's all they got out of me.

I was doing press-ups again back in the cell. A cozzer opened up and said, 'Come on, your wife's here.' I walked out and I could see Val at the bottom of the corridor. As we walked towards each other I could see tears running down her face. As I got hold of her in my arms she started crying loudly, so I kissed and cuddled her to try and calm her down. I said, 'Listen, Val, listen to me. You and me are one, don't matter what happens. I love you and they can't take that away from us. Be strong for the kids and be strong for me. I know it's hard but don't give these slags in here any satisfaction.'

Then she was taken out. I was shattered, I'd never seen her so upset. I can take anything for myself, but it tore at my insides to see my lovely Val all broken up.

Cater had a beauty waiting for me the next time he pulled me upstairs. 'You going to stop fucking about and come across for this one, Lenny?' I just growled at him and said nothing. 'OK then, try this. What would you say if I tell you we've got Robert Lopez pulled in?'

'No,' I said. 'You've got to be joking — that kid's got nothing to do with this and you fucking well know it.'

He just gave me a cold look. 'I'm going to get a result here one way or another, so if you don't open up I'm going to pick up that phone and have him charged with murder, because one of you killed Humphries.'

He'd got my nuts in the grinder. Robert is a nice quiet bloke. I know he's a minder but he's not a bit aggressive and when I was straightening up the streaker he never laid a finger on him. He'd never been in trouble before so I could imagine what he was feeling like, being banged up for the first time. 'OK. If you drop everything against Robert I'll put my hand up. I chinned the bloke, it's down to me.'

I just signed my life away, but at least I'd done it like a man. Now I've got to look after my own neck.

The next time Val came in, I told her about the cozzer who had remembered the fight 20 years before, and that I'd dropped a ricket on tape. 'Go and see John Nash, Babe, and ask him to have a quiet word with the fella.'

On her next visit, she told me that John had squared it off. He'd gone to Jimmy and he'd told John, 'I ain't got no grievance with Len. It's all in the past. If they want me at the Bailey I'll go up and deny we ever had a fight and say that me and Len are pals who go back years.' Ten out of ten, mate. I didn't need you in the end, but you were there for me. Good luck wherever you are.

Then I found out all the details of that Saturday night that changed my life. Remember, I was sitting there convinced I'd killed a man. But when Martin Lee put me in the picture it started to look a bit different. Martin was the brief who worked under Ralph Haeems. He was really on the ball and what he'd done was to dig out all the facts about the movements of Gary Humphries that night.

It turned out he wasn't on drugs as I'd thought, but he should have been. He'd not long been released from a mental hospital and, being a bit spaced out, he'd not been taking his medication. After a couple of weeks he'd had a breakdown. Who knows what was in his head? He went to the Hippodrome and had a fight with one of the DJs, who had punched him in the face and chucked him off the stage, then his gear came off, and that's when I got involved.

Even if I'd know his state of mind, I don't think I could have handled it any differently. I've already explained what went on. I didn't beat him up, I just gave him a backhander, dressed him and put him out. Then I found out what happened afterwards.

He left the club and, within a few yards, bumped straight into a special constable. Because he didn't have any shoes on he was stopped and questioned. He said some big bloke in the club had beaten him up, but the only damage the copper could see was a slightly cut lip. He was talking normally and wasn't injured, so he let him walk away. If he wanted to go barefoot that was up to him.

All these incidents were like bits of a jigsaw that night. Nobody got the real picture until afterwards, when they were all put together.

From the club he went into a café and tried to get himself something to eat, but because of the way he looked and the fact that he didn't have any money, he was fucked off. Again, he was able to speak coherently, but perhaps the knock back over the grub did his head in, because he then took his gear off again, and he ran in and out of the traffic, naked, and making a right nuisance of himself.

Eventually, he ran in front of a fire engine, which stopped and took him to Soho Fire Station, where they called an ambulance. While he was being helped aboard he decided he didn't want to go, had a scuffle, broke away, and ran off. At this point, Old Bill was looking for him. When they found him he was in Tottenham Court Road, dodging the traffic and banging on cars. After a very violent struggle with a number of coppers, he was overpowered. The law had to put a bit of effort into holding him down because he was like a maniac. So much effort, in fact, that passers-by told them to leave off before they killed him. They got him to hospital and a few hours later he died. Dead, according to Old Bill, from a broken jaw that Lenny McLean gave him in the club four hours before.

Don't think for one minute that I'm giving you a load of flannel to cover myself. What I've told you is fact from hundreds of statements taken by the police.

What do you think? Did I kill him? Did I beat him to death? Four hours doing a marathon round London, fighting all the way. Is that a dying man? The law seemed to think so, or were they covering themselves? At worst, I should have been threatened with a section 18 and bailed.

But no. Somebody thought it was about time I was taken off the streets and two weeks later I was nicked and in front of the magistrate.

While I was waiting for the prison bus in the cell downstairs, my brief tried to cheer me up.

'If things start to look a bit iffy, Len,' Martin said, 'you might have to put your hand up to manslaughter. In your case, that could mean ten years, but at least it would save you getting double on a recommendation.'

I gave him the old cross-eye and said, 'I thought you was supposed to be fucking well cheering me up.'

When he looked a bit hurt at that, I give a laugh and slapped him on the back. 'Only kidding, son,' then I did my John Wayne, 'a man's gotta do what a man's gotta do.' I gave him a hug, the cell door shut with a bang, and I was on my own.

Lying on my bunk, I thought about having to put myself forward for a ten stretch. British justice is the finest in the world, unless you get caught up on the wrong side of it. Here's me innocent, but to save getting lifed off I've got say I'm guilty. Funny thing is, I'd go along with it. Get ten years, do six or seven, yeah, I could handle that. Then I thought about Martin's last words. 'I can't promise you anything, so don't get your hopes up ... I think someone's got it in for you.'

Brixton. Going into prison didn't worry me a bit. I'm a strong man and a very proud man, and wherever I go people give me a wide berth. Even the screws, because they know if I start I'm a ten-man job. Most blokes are more worried about the other cons and screws than they are of being shut away. Same as the kids I mentioned, going into approved school for the first time. They hear all about queers and poofters when they're outside, and that frightens them more than anything. But let me just say not so much of that goes on. If it does, it is by consent — none of all that rape in the showers bollocks they like to put in films. None of that worried me — don't forget, I'm 6ft 3in and 20 stone plus, and I'm like a time bomb waiting to go off.

Normally, murderers or alleged murderers go into the hospital wing first, so they can check out if you're a lunatic or not. My reputation said I was, so I was put in A Section straight away. This is a prison inside a prison specially built for holding killers, drug-dealers, IRA and the very violent. You go through about four thick iron doors to your cell, and there are cameras everywhere watching you. Unlike cells in the nicks outside, you do get a bit of privacy on the toilet because there's a sort of half-shutter and the camera can only see your feet or head. They unlock the doors for meals and a half-hour walk round, but the rest of the time is spent behind your door. Ordinary prisoners can't speak to you if you come into contact with them in case your influence makes them worse than they already are. You can only speak to other A Section inmates, and that's all right because you're all in the same boat looking at long sentences. The only thing I can say in favour of A Section is that it's cleaner than the main wings and there's only one to a cell.

While I was out on my half-hour walk I used to fuck about with the screws, picking them up and dancing around and giving them what they thought was friendly aggravation. But it wasn't and they hated it.

'McLean, you'll get us the sack, this is all on camera you know.'

I said, 'All right, if you unlock me for an hour a day so's I can visit Frankie in the next cell, I'll leave you alone.'

So that's what they did — not bad as screws go really. Sometimes they'd do it the other way round and Frankie Simms would come in to me. I remember one afternoon when the two of us went through all my legal papers for about three hours. When we were finished, Frankie said 'How about going through mine, now?' I just lay on his bed, closed my eyes and said, 'Sorry mate, too fucking tired.' He went a bit cross-eyed until he saw me laughing.

One afternoon I was lying on the bed and the heat was killing me. It was the beginning of July and I was sweating cobs. There was a bang on the door. I looked up and Frank was eyeballing me through my spy-hole.

'Len,' he said, 'I'm just making a bit of stew on the quiet. How many dumplings do you want?'

'Dumplings! Are you joking? I don't want no fucking dumplings. I'm lying here thinking about the next 25 years that I've got to spend in prison, it's a hundred degrees, and you're talking about dumplings.'

'Go on, Len, keep your strength up.'

'Fuck's sake, Frank! All right then, make me six.' An hour later the screws let him in and he had a paint tin filled with stew. I just said, 'Hope you washed that tin out first,' when the door slammed shut and the lever came along.

'What's going on, mate? Why we banged up?' I asked.

Frank said, 'Look through the spy-hole.' I had a butchers and there were four Nazi-looking screws going past and in the middle of them was this pasty kid of about 21.

'See that cunt?' Frank said. 'He's the slag that ripped all the insides out of a nine-month-old baby. He's banged up 24 hours a day, gets his tea and meals in his cell, and only gets out for a visit. Screws can't risk us getting hold of him.'

'Frank,' I said, 'we got to hurt this nonce. Why don't we get hold of the cleaners and get them to do him with boiling water?'

'Len, we tried that, they don't want to know — that's why they're cleaners, screws trust them.' I never did get the chance to rip that bastard's throat out, but one of the others got to him and that horrible little beast was well obliged.

Funnily enough, Frank was still inside when Ronnie Knight was put away. They palled up together and, unless Frankie had changed, which I doubt, he would have kept Ronnie laughing all day long. He's a comedian, a live wire and a good man to serve your time with. I bet Ronnie was sorry to be left behind when Frank completed his term a few months ago.

Talking about that scum, that baby killer, reminds me of the time a lovely lady came down the club to see me one night early in 1993. She was really upset because her seven-year-old nephew had just been murdered by some low-life pervert, stuck in a sack and dumped in a lift. I was choked for her and the boy's parents, but what can you say to take away the pain? I got her a brandy, gave her a cuddle, and told her the law would have the slag in five minutes. Give Old Bill their due, they did.

A year later, while I was working on this book, Geraldine Walpole came to see me again. She'd just come from the court after seeing a piece of filth by the name of Colin Hatch getting lifed off for killing the boy. She said, 'Lenny, as he stood in the dock he was grinning all over his face.'

I said to her, 'Let me make a phonecall and we'll get him sorted, get the smile knocked off his face.'

Her eyes filled up when she said, 'Thanks for the offer, Lenny, you're a good friend, but after the trial the family were taken into a back room and warned about taking reprisals. The police said that, if anything happens to that man, we would be the first ones they would question. So, as much as we'd all like to see him suffer for what he did, we can't go against the law. And I wouldn't want you to get into trouble either.'

'All right, Geraldine,' I said, 'I won't get involved, but let me put your mind at rest. I've been inside, I know what goes on, and you can be sure that there is nowhere in the system that he can be safe. Every day of his sentence he'll have to look over his shoulder. He won't get what's due to him once, he won't get it twice, he'll get it every time a screw turns his back. His life will be hell on earth and, after a bit, he's going to start thinking about doing what the law couldn't — topping himself.'

With that thought on her mind she told me she felt a lot better. Some people might think that it's wicked to think like that. All I can say to them is, don't judge anybody unless you've walked in their shoes.

After a month, the Home Office decided I could come off A Section. By this time, I was well settled and I was palled up with

Frankie, so I asked them to leave me where I was. No, can't do that, you've got to go where you're told. I said, 'Well I want to see the Governor.' Can't do that either — see the PO. After being given the run-around, I got to the chief PO and I told him, 'Look, I've got a bit of a name. You put me on A Wing and all the likely lads are going to try and have a pop so they can make a name for themselves. Let me mark your card. Any of them try it on I'm going to paralyse them, throw them right off the tops. On the other hand, you look after me and you'll save your blokes a lot of aggravation.'

He looked at me and said, 'You go where I decide you'll go. Threats do not sway my decision. But you behave yourself, keep that temper under control and I'll put you on the ones.' Lovely — I've got a nice easy job.

While I was in A Section I got chatting to an Irish fella. I asked him what he was in for and he told me he had been involved with bombs and that sort of caper. Now unless a con's a child killer or molester, you have to leave everything outside. You don't judge them and they don't judge you, otherwise you'd be belting every fucker behind the door.

I asked him what bird he was expecting and he said, 'Len, at least 30 years, but I can't do it. My people are working on it.'

I said, 'Good luck whatever happens.'

At about one o'clock on the Sunday afternoon, I was just getting myself some tea — 'Bang up ... Bang up ... Bang up!' Screws were running wild and everybody was slung in the cells. Then we heard what sounded like a car backfiring, then the same again, and I heard somebody shouting, 'They've got guns.'

That was at one o'clock. Then it was three o'clock ... then six o'clock. We were still locked in and we were getting the hump. By eight o'clock everybody was going mad, banging on the doors, screaming and shouting.

We'd had no dinner, it was hot, and we'd all got the hump. I shouted through the door to one of the screws, 'What's going on, governor?'

'We've got a break-out, so you're all staying locked in until it's sorted.'

No supper, no tea, what a fucking turn out.

The next morning I got the story. The IRA bloke from A Section and another con were being brought back from church when he pulled a gun, took a hostage, and both of them have got to the main gate. On the way through B Wing, he let a couple of shots go and afterwards we could see these two big holes in the wall. Once they were let out of the gate, two screws got shot, a car was hijacked and they got away. One of the screws told me the gun had been brought in by a visitor and the reason he wasn't spotted was that the gun was hidden in a built-up shoe. When he came to the metal detector he just walked round it instead of through it. After that, it was like Christmas for all us cons. We were all happy and joking because one of us was out of this piss-hole and pulled a stroke on the system.

Most of the time, days slipped by without any agg, but what made me flare up most were the screws who bullied weaker prisoners. It's bad enough being inside without being shoved around, insulted and given a hard time by no-account mugs who wouldn't have an ounce of bottle if you got them outside.

The bravest little fucker I came across in Brixton was a young kid by the name of Mark Thomburrow. When I first saw him I thought, 'What they doing putting little kids in Brixton?' He was about eight stone, skinny, and looked 12 years old. It turned out he was 18, but to me he was still a baby. They brought him in from another young offenders' prison because he was due for his trial at the Bailey. When I asked him what he was up for he told me that he and a few mates were walking along the road one night when they got into an argument with a couple of black kids. One thing led to another and Mark pulled a knife, went to stick it in this boy's arm, he swung too hard, missed the arm and plunged him in the neck. The black kid died right there on the pavement.

'Len,' he said, 'I didn't mean to do it, I swear I never. It was an accident.'

I said, 'Look, I can't make you right for what you've done. You was carrying a knife and then you was prepared to use it.'

He had tears in his eyes and he was frightened because he was facing No.1 Court first thing. He told me he was being defended by Mansfield, the top QC, and he was going for a manslaughter with mitigation.

'Now, Mark, when you come up at the Bailey and all your family's watching how you shape yourself, be very strong. Whatever they give you, don't waste your time screaming and shouting because it won't change nothing. Don't let them see you cry. Your family can't be proud of what you've done, but they can be proud if you take your punishment like a man.'

'Len, I'm going into court on my own. It's going to be packed with coloureds all full of hate and abuse, and I told my mum and dad to stay away because I can't bear to see them get a load of stick.'

I thought, 'How about that. This little kid's took a liberty but he's still thinking about other people.'

As they took him out in the morning, I shouted, 'Don't forget, be brave. I'll be here for you when you come back.'

I hung about all day waiting for him to be brought back. Don't forget, I'm on the ones, so I can move about without being locked up. At half-three I was down by the glass partition watching the reception area and in he came, covered by two muggy screws. They were going over the top the way they bawled at him, 'Give us your tie, give us your laces.' The kid was ash-white and he was trembling all over, and those fucking screws didn't know what to do next to stop that boy coming through. In the end, I couldn't take it any more. I smashed on the glass and screamed at them, 'You pair of bastards, stop fucking about and let that baby through — look at the state he's in.' They looked at each other, shrugged, and unlocked the door.

As he came through, his eyes were glassy and he was saying, 'I got life, Len. They give me life for murder.'

'Fucking hell, son. Don't cry ... don't let them mugs see you cry.' I took him in the ablutions, gave him a cuddle and said, 'Go on, son, you can cry now.'

He was breaking his heart but at the same time he said, 'I didn't cry until I saw you, Len, I didn't cry in court.'

I cuddled him and said, 'You was a man about it, now you can let it out.'

I sat up with him all night and eventually he fell asleep with his head on my lap, still sobbing. Before they took him away to Aylesbury the next morning, I gave him Reg Kray's book *Born Fighter*. I signed it and said, 'You know I'm mentioned in that book, don't you? Well, every time you look at the book you'll know Lenny's thinking of you, and if I don't get lifed off myself, I'll visit you and keep in touch — don't matter where they send you.' He went off as happy as anybody could be when they're looking at ten to fifteen.

I'm still in touch with Mark today, because if I make a promise I never break it. He has turned 20 now, so he's in the adult prison system, Wormwood Scrubs, and he's been given his release date — 2006.

In case you think my sympathy's misplaced, let me tell you that my heart bleeds for the young kid who died and for his family, because I know how I would feel if it was my son. I didn't take Mark under my wing because he killed somebody, but because of the way he handled himself afterwards. He was sorry for what he had done and took his punishment like a man.

I bumped into my pal Ritchie Anderson who was doing a six. We had a cuddle and I said, 'Fuck me, Ritchie, I was just talking about visiting you when I got lifted. I never expected to be banged up with you permanent.'

As we chatted, this screw shouted over, 'Oy, Jock, get a move on, get back to work.'

Now Ritchie's a lovely placid man until he gets wild, as those drunks found out when he plunged them. He said, 'If that screw calls me Jock again, I'm going to throw him off the landing.' He meant it, too.

The screw came over so I put my arm across Ritchie's chest to hold him back. He had a nice little job and if he started a ruck he'd lose that and some of his remission. Before the screw could open his mouth, I got him under the arms and lifted him clean off the floor — his head was about nine foot off the deck. He struggled, but I wasn't hurting him.

'Now listen, listen, don't complain. I've told your mates and now I'm telling you. If I get out of here, I'm going to buy one of those flats opposite the prison. Then, every morning when you're coming to work, I'll be sitting on the wall with the raving hump. Now you wouldn't want that, would you? So behave yourself.' I've put him down and planted a big kiss on his forehead. What Ritchie and I didn't know at the time was that one of the other screws was a very tasty cartoonist. He'd seen what had happened, quickly did a drawing, and then had it photocopied about a hundred times. Everybody had one. Even the Governor had a copy pinned up in his office. The screw never lived it down.

That little incident was comical, but I wasn't always so good humoured and neither were the screws. I had the hump one day. I hadn't slept all night thinking about how I was going to get through the next 25 years. Val had been in the day before and she'd got a bit upset, so all in all, my nut was going round in circles.

A screw shouted over to me, 'McLain. Cup of tea ... now.' I looked at him and said, 'My name's McLean, like in the toothpaste, not McLain, you ignorant mug. And just because I'm in this hole, don't talk to me like you think I'm some sort of c**t.' He came towards me and put his hand out, and I said, 'Go on, then, lay hands on me and I'll belt shit out of you.' He stepped back quickly.

'OK, McLEAN, you want to play that game, I'll see you later.'

At five o'clock the next morning, they came for me mob-handed with shields, sticks and wearing crash helmets, all the riot gear, the whole nine yards. Ten of the bastards just for me. I fought like a maniac. I was nearly bollock naked because I was asleep when they came in, but I gave it to them, sticks or no sticks. As quick as I put them down, somebody was shoving another lot in the cell. Eventually, with sheer weight of numbers I was pinned in the corner. With a riot shield holding me down, one of the doctors slipped in and everything went black. He'd done me with a drug in a hypodermic.

I came to in the hospital and I felt like a zombie. I didn't question how I felt, it didn't occur to me that I was doped up, I just felt heavy and mellow, and very tired. The crafty bastards must have eased up on the strength when they knew I was to have visitors, so my Val or some of my other pals who came in didn't realise what state I was in.

This went on for something like three weeks, and the screws must have thought it was their birthday because I was like a little kitten. When I kept falling asleep on Val's visits she sussed out that I was on something. She knew I wouldn't take anything like that by choice so she got in touch with Martin, my brief, and he had a word with the Governor of the nick. They argued about prisoners' rights and all that cobblers, but the Governor had the last word because he said that I kept flaring up. Apparently, I was a danger to the screws and had to be kept under control, so I had to stay on medication.

Once Martin had marked my card it made all the difference. Instead of thinking I was just a bit tired, I now knew that I was drugged, so when they gave me my pills I stuck them under my tongue, and then got rid of them. Now I had to control myself. If I flared up, the doctor would know what I was doing, and then I'd get the drug by injection.

God's up there looking after me. I was taken to a different doctor and he immediately told the screws to leave us alone. Now that's a bit unusual. He'd checked that there was no one outside the door and then he slipped me a note: *'Dear Len, this doctor's OK and he's got some trouble. Help him out if you can.'* The note was signed *'Old Connie'*. Good stuff — he'd been inside for 20 years,

The quack was watching for my reaction as I read it. The letter was good enough for me, so I asked him what the problem was. He told me that a young relative of his was being sexually rumped by a big television star. He was well known and respected by millions, and at the same time he was a nonce case.

I said, 'The dirty bastard, have him smashed to pieces.' But he didn't want to do that because it could be all over the papers and the boy's name might come out. 'So what do you want me to do? Don't forget, I'm in here on a murder charge.'

'Lenny, you know people. Can you get your friends to plant heroin in his house then inform the police?'

'Sorry, Doc. Fitting people up's not my game. I can get him belted and warned off, but I can hardly write to my pals giving them the work, can I?' What he really wants is this actor nicked on drugs, then when he's pulled into A Section, which is guaranteed, the doc can do what he likes — castrate him if he wants. Still, he accepts my offer of getting the slag a seeing to and lets me use the phone.

I did the business right there and then from his office, and he said, 'I don't know how to thank you.'

So I said, 'Well, I can think of a couple of favours straight away. First get me off these poxy drugs. You've got the pull — just tell the PO that I'm not medically fit to have any more. Second, I want a phone in my cell.'

He went white. 'Out of the question. I couldn't do it ... more than my job's worth.'

'Suit yourself then. Gimme the phone again and we'll forget your problem.'

That did the trick and he agreed double quick. I got him to meet Val in a burger bar in Bethnal Green. She handed over a tiny little mobile phone that a pal of mine got hold of, and the doctor smuggled it in easily and slipped it to me when I went for an examination he'd dreamed up. Lovely. Suddenly, I'm a yuppie con. That night, I phoned Val up and we had a talk for a couple of hours. If I get lifed off, somebody's going to have a phone bill like the national debt.

What a difference that phone made. If I got depressed, I just had to dial home and I was cheered up. I could do plenty of business as well. I'd ring up John Nash, Alex Steen, Kenny Mac, even Arthur Thomson in Scotland, and they couldn't believe it because I was ringing late at night when they knew I should have been locked in.

A guy came up to me in the kitchens and introduced himself as Danny O'Malley, the brother-in-law of a family out of the Angel. Nice people, business people. He said, 'I'm a bit worried. This is my first time in prison and I've heard stories. You know what I mean?'

I said, 'Your family are 100 per cent so I'm going to look after you. Anybody digs you out, put my name up or come and see me.' So on the strength of his relations, I looked after him. That first day I kitted him out with a parcel of food, chocolate, crisps, biscuits and a few other bits to help him settle in. We became good pals and I put him right about the little fiddles we had going.

A couple of months later, he came to see me and he had tears in his eyes. He said he'd had a row with his wife, said some terrible things, and couldn't wait until the next day to sort it out and apologise. I said, 'Danny, I can do you a bit of good. I'll go and make a cup of tea then I've a surprise for you.'

It was getting a bit late, and while I was brewing up a cup of tea, a new Scottish screw on the wing poked his head in the door and wanted to know what I was doing. 'Making a cup of tea, governor, any problem?'

'Yes, get back to your cell on the double. I don't want you making tea at this time of night.'

I flare up. 'You Scotch c**t, don't talk to me like that or I'll get myself on a double murder charge and it'll be over you.' He threatened to put me on a charge and this and that, so I went back to my cell.

Danny was still sitting there so I said, 'Dan, go and chat up that Scotch bastard and find out where he comes from and where his family's living. I'll get in touch with a friend of mine and when that mug finds out that his family have had a visit from a few likely lads, he'll change his tune about giving me grief.'

Off he went. Ten minutes later he was back and he had the details. 'Right, Dan, good boy. Now I've got something for you,' and I dug the phone out and let him ring his wife. His eyes opened up like saucers

—he couldn't believe what he was seeing. I went to the toilet to give him a bit of privacy and when I came back, he thanked me with tears in his eyes again.

It was early morning again. Crash. In they came, the riot mob. I was beaten up with those fucking sticks and my cell was torn apart. The mobile phone was dug out and I was locked in another cell to wait. Then I was ordered to get ready to be shipped to Belmarsh Prison at Woolwich.

I was just thinking I'd had a bit of bad luck when one of the better screws came in and marked my card. 'Keep this to yourself, Len, or my job's on the line, but your mate O'Malley has been a police plant since day one. That's all I can say, but good luck, mate.'

I wanted to smash down the cell door like Roy Shaw did, but I'd never get to that slag O'Malley before I was stopped so, through one of the cleaners, I managed to get a message to John on C wing, for him to make sure the grass got what was due. Minutes before I was loaded on to the wagon, I got a whisper that it would be taken care of. Knowing that kept me calm on the journey and I didn't cause a ruck.

If I hadn't before, I would have soon found out the rest of the story, because it ended up all over the papers. The doctor was suspended and was waiting to be charged for smuggling in the telephone, but he died of a heart attack before charges could be brought. The poor bastard was effectively killed by that low-life O'Malley. They found out about the threat on the screw and he was transferred. They also heard that O'Malley was going to get it but not by who, so he was moved out sharpish. A fortnight later, he found out that there's nowhere to hide in the system.

Belmarsh was a new prison, about six months old when I moved in. Most of the screws were young kids and I don't know if it was 'new prison, new policy', but prisoners were allowed to wear their own clothes. One visiting day, I watched as one of the cons slipped in amongst the friends and families when they were leaving and walked out with them, cool as a cucumber. They brought him back after a few days, but he had made a mug of the system.

I met a black guy called Gilbert while I was in there. He was brought into my cell, carried by a couple of big Nazi screws, and they dumped him on the bed. He'd had the shit kicked out of him. His hair was matted, he was covered in bruises, bleeding, and he couldn't move his legs. I said 'Who are you, who's done this?'

'I'm Gilbert. I've had a bit of agg with the police and they kicked me to bits and, while I was on the floor, smashed me in the spine with the truncheons.'

I thought, 'Fuck me, this is the same system that gives guys like me ten years for GBH.'

He told me that he's friendly with a good family out of North London, so he's got to be sound. I said, 'Gilbert, mate, this won't happen again. I'm taking you under my wing. I'll mind you, you'll be all right.' He was left in that state for hours and hours, even though I kicked up fuck with the screws. In the end, I said I'd ring somebody outside if they didn't patch him up, and about ten minutes later he was taken to the hospital wing. When he eventually came back, he was in a wheelchair but still game. If a screw said something out of order he'd be there trying to lash out at them from his chair. I've got to hand it to him, they don't come with a bigger heart.

We got to be good pals and we'd sit late at night having salmon sandwiches and Cola, talking about our cases and how we thought they'd go. He was in for being caught with a gun but there was a lot of doubt about whose it was or whether he was being fitted up.

When he went to court, still in a wheelchair, he got a 'not guilty', and I was happy for him. Before he went out he introduced me to a friend of his doing a nine stretch, and by a strange coincidence this pal turned out to be the actual brother-in-law of the North London family — the guy Danny O'Malley had pretended to be. I said to him, 'Pity you didn't turn up in Brixton a few months ago and mark my card. Would've saved bundles of agg.'

Gilbert and I still meet up today and he's still in that wheelchair. I've got to give him ten out of ten for the way he fights back.

While I was behind the door waiting and waiting for my trial to come up at the Bailey, I couldn't think about anything else. By now, I know I didn't kill Humphries. I was being fitted up because Old Bill were a bit heavy-handed when restraining him. It doesn't help my nut, though, because I wouldn't be the first who had got lifed off for something he didn't do. That was brought home to me by one of the screws in Wandsworth.

They must have thought Belmarsh was too clean and comfortable for me because I was just getting myself settled in when they moved me out to Wandsworth. It was better, really, because though it was a piss-hole, I felt like I was back with my own.

This old screw in Wandsworth was about retiring age. He'd been in the job all his life so he'd seen a few come and go. He dug me out one day and got me on the work party, but as he wasn't a bad sort of bloke, he got the young cons to do the graft and he and I were having a bit of a walk. On the way back from the stores, he said, 'Leave the young blokes pulling the barrows, we'll go another way round because I want to show you something.'

Off we went — up here, down there, and we ended up in a brick-built building. 'Look up on the ceiling, Len.'

I looked up and there was a sort of trapdoor in the roof. I said, 'So what?'

He was grinning and watching to see how I took it. 'That's the hangman's trapdoor.'

Fuck me, talk about giving me the creeps. I was on a murder charge and he was letting me see where I might have been dropping through 25 years ago. Like most people, I always thought that the hole would be square or round, but it was shaped like a rugby ball. I don't know why, and neither did the screw

Then he took me upstairs to the screws' tearoom and asked me if I knew where I was.

'Now how the fuck would I know?' I said, and he loved it because he waited a minute before he told me it was the old condemned cell. Was he a comedian or what? If I thought he was taking the piss, I really would have got the hump, but he was an old geezer and I think he just loved giving these little tours now that hanging's a thing of the past. Though it's a big room now, in the old days it used to be three cells, and if you look closely you can see where the walls used to be.

'Stand there and let your mind wander and you can see all those poor sods that sat there waiting.'

I asked him if he'd ever hanged anybody, and he thought I meant with his own hands. 'No, no, 'course not. That was down to Pierpoint, the public hangman, but I sat in on more than I like to remember.'

Then he told me a story that I thought must have been very hard to take. Back in 1962, he had been on the watch before last with Hanratty before he was hanged. Like I said, too many innocent people have been lifed off or topped, and Hanratty's case was a classic. He'd been pulled in for killing Michael Gregson and shooting and raping his girlfriend, Valerie Storie, in what the papers called 'the A6 murder'. You can read about this case in loads of books, but what was terrible was that Jim didn't do it. Everything pointed away from him, but he was convicted at the Bailey and given a death sentence.

So this screw's on the 12.00am–4.00am shift, and Hanratty's due for hanging at 8.00am. He told me that they'd sat and played cards, talked and listened to the radio. Hanratty was so brave, he knew he was innocent and so did all the screws, but he never kicked up in those last hours. In fact, he showed a lot of concern for those looking after him because they were all so upset.

I said to the screw, 'How could you sit there knowing that bloke didn't murder anyone and not do anything about it?'

He said, 'Len, when I left him that morning I had tears in my eyes as we shook hands for the last time, but we was just doing our job. Didn't have no other choice.' Then he told me about Ruth Ellis, the last woman to be sent to the gallows. Guilty, but brave as fuck. I had to pull the plug on him there. His stories were sad and interesting, but in my situation I didn't really want to think about all that.

The next morning I got a parcel. The screw who chucked it on my bed was grinning so I flared up. 'What you laughing at, you fucking mug?' but he slipped out quickly in case I flew at him. The parcel was already open, like everything you got in there was, and when I looked it was from Jack Iandoli and it was the manuscript of the book. Oh yeah, I bet it had been well read by every muggy screw in the place.

I'm not the fastest reader in the world so it took me a fair while to plough my way through all the pages. At the bottom he wrote, '*Ring me as soon as you can, Len — love to have your comments.*' Yes, Jack, and I'm going to love giving them to you.

The queue for the phone was a mile long but I kept calm and got there in the end.

'Hello, Jack.'

'Lenny, mate, lovely to hear from you. Enjoy the book?'

'Enjoy the book? What's it all about? What's any of that shit got to do with me?'

He sounded a bit shocked. 'Lenny, it's what we call fiction. You know, I've stretched it a bit here and there.'

'Well, Jack, I'd like to stretch you for what you've put down here. You've taken a diabolical liberty. You've got my lovely mum, God rest her, down as a fucking alcoholic; my great-uncle Jimmy Spinks as a gutless little old man; and you show me as a bully nicking chips off other kids and mugging pensioners. You publish this, me and you will seriously fall out.' I chucked the phone down before I really did my nut.

Fucking hell, my film's down the pan, the book's absolute bollocks, and I'm getting closer to the Bailey every day.

There were three of us on the landing on a murder charge. Me, Paul Morris and Tommy. The other two were good stuff, particularly Tommy, because he had done for his pal what I had done for mine; he put his hand up for murder to save Paul. A Scottish slag had been giving his live-in girlfriend a really hard time. If he wasn't beating her black and blue, he was messing her about with perverted sex. One night, he stuck a broom handle up her, gave her a haemorrhage, and she had to be taken to hospital. When she came out weeks later, she went to Paul and Tommy because she was frightened that she was going to be killed one day.

These two chaps got a sawn-off shotgun and went round to put the frighteners in. They went to the front door of the flat and when the Scottish bastard opened the door, Paul stuck the gun in his chest. The Scotsman grabbed the gun, it went off and blew him in half.

Paul had a wife and two kids, and he was doing his nut panicking because he knew he was facing life. Tommy lived with his old nan so he said, 'Keep your mouth shut and I'll say I did it.' When they came up in No.1 at the Bailey, that's what he did. Paul got a 'not guilty', but a four for handling the gun. Tommy got a 'guilty' on manslaughter and picked up ten years. Go on, sit and think how many of your mates would do that for you. Hundred out of ten, Tom.

Still, that result was yet to come and in the meantime we became quite close. Then we were joined by a black fella, transferred from the Scrubs, and he was on a murder as well. So we were all sitting there talking about out cases and he said, 'I didn't do it, you know. I didn't kill those two women.'

We knew the story because it had been all over the papers. They'd said that he'd murdered two women over Hornsea way, rolled them up in carpets and got rid of them.

So he was sitting there all polite and talking posh and saying, 'I didn't do it.' I gave the other two a look and said, 'Well, that's a fucking coincidence. I never done mine either, nor did Paul, nor did Tommy. In fact we're all innocent in this nick.' He thought I was digging him out, but I wasn't. I was just having a bit of a joke because he was so posh and serious.

Months later, he had about a week to go before appearing at the Bailey, and he asked me, 'Len, did you kill that man in the club?'

I said, 'I honestly don't think I did. I did at first, but according to my brief it looks like Old Bill done it. What about you?'

He jumped up, looked outside the cell, shut the door and sat on the bed making a roll-up. He went sort of grey.

'Len, you're a pal, you've looked after me. Yeah, I done it. I killed the two women, but I don't think they can prove it.' A week later he came back from the Bailey and was smiling. 'It's looking very good,' he said. The next night, he wasn't so happy, things had turned and I could hear him crying in his cell.

He didn't come back the next day and one of the screws told me he'd got life. He was still denying it right up to the end, but he and I know different. I didn't judge him, that's not my place, I leave all that to Him above. I'll tell you what, though — it kept me awake for nights afterwards thinking that I might be following him soon.

Talking about lifing off, an old boy came back from the Bailey and he'd got the full stretch for killing his wife. He was about 70 years old and he looked like he was going to die right there on the spot. I said, 'I ain't being horrible, but you've had a good life up until now and you probably won't live long enough to finish your time.' OK, looking back I wasn't being very diplomatic, but I was trying to say he was better off than somebody a lot younger.

Another bloke, Dave Matches I called him, came back from court and he was breaking his heart crying like a baby. I put my arm round him and said, 'What's up, pal?'

He said, 'Len, I got six years.'

'Six years? You should be singing and dancing because what you've done should have cost you 20 years.'

It turned out that he'd got well pissed up one night, and when he wasn't thinking straight he'd gone after somebody who owed him money. It didn't occur to him to knock on the door and ask for his money —no, he got a bottle of petrol and threw it through the window. The house burned down and the bloke he was after died. He was nicked because this posh house had external security cameras, and he was caught on video. Lucky for him, what caught him also saved him in a way. Seeing the flames shooting up cleared his nut, so instead of running away, he tried to kick the door down to get the bloke out. Because of that, they slung the murder out and he got a manslaughter. Lucky bastard, really, but right at that moment he didn't see it that way. He would, though, once he'd thought about it.

Months and months were ticking away and, remember, I hadn't been found guilty yet. It makes me laugh when I hear that bollocks about innocent until proven guilty. Tough shit if you do a year on remand, and then they turn round and say, 'Sorry, you're completely innocent.' Still, while I'm away I'm not forgotten, and this is when I find out how many lovely pals I've got. Val was worn out answering the phone and the door to all the wellwishers. If I single out a few for a mention that doesn't mean I think less of the others. It's just that I would need to fill another book if I thanked everyone.

I've already told you Freddie Starr was there double quick. So was John Nash. He came round to see Val and stuck £5,000 in her hand in case she ran short. She told him she was well covered but he wouldn't take it back. John's from the old school, so whenever he called he turned up with his wife, because what you never do when a man is away is visit his missus and give people the chance to gossip. Respectful, that is. She got calls from America from people like Gene Hackman and Mickey Rourke, and I even got a message from Sly Stallone saying, 'We're rooting for the real Rocky,' I thought that was a lovely gee for me.

Charlie Kray showed up with his wife, because he knew what I was going through. I have bundles of respect for him because he's suffered. He lost everything when he got a ten just for trying to look after his brothers, but after that he climbed his way back up and became a successful businessman. Now he's gone all the way back down after being lifted for being involved in some drugs deal. The man's nearly 70 for Christ sake. He should be in his slippers by the fire, not banged up in some piss-hole prison. Just remember, don't believe all you read in the papers and a guilty verdict doesn't always mean that the man isn't innocent. Charlie is 100 percent a gentleman. He was there for me and he knows I'm there for him, any time he needs me.

So, all that support from outside was a comfort, but it didn't get me out. I still had to go on day by day towards whatever was on the cards.

There's good and bad everywhere. Some of the other cons were so bad they should have been put down, but then many of them were diamonds whom I'm still friends with today. The same went for the screws. One of them who was always fair was a bloke by the name of Gary Taylor. On one occasion, I couldn't believe I was actually cheering on a screw when I watched him on the telly winning *The World's Strongest Man* competition.

I saw him in Wandsworth and I gave him a tug.

'Oi, Gary, has my pal outside had a word with you about slipping me in a few ounces of tobacco?' I knew they were mates because my pal's in the bodybuilding game as well. In fact, he was 'Mr Universe' at one time.

'Yes, Len,' he said. 'He's asked me to do you a favour, but I'll tell you what I told him. Can't be done. When I took on this job I promised myself I'd keep straight, then everybody knows where they stand. You lot do your time and I'll do my job — no hard feelings.'

How could I knock that? I respect anybody who's got principles. It didn't mean I wouldn't try to bend one of the bastards who didn't have any.

The next one I tried was a right arrogant git. The first time I saw him he was just giving this skinny kid a belt round the head for not moving sharply enough. He clocked me watching him and went, 'Fucking nuisances, these kids. I want to get home.'

On another occasion I might have belted him for taking liberties, but I thought, 'No, I'll get my hooks into him.' I said, 'You're a big fella, do you use the weights?'

He breathed in and pumped up like a fucking turkey. 'Yeah, I do, and I'm benching 295 pounds at the moment.' Cocky twat.

'Not bad,' I said. 'I'm doing 500 pounds ... how does that grab you?' He didn't say anything, just walked off like he was sucking Tunes up his arse.

When I saw him the next day, I told him I was only kidding. I wasn't, but I wanted to sweeten him up. After a bit, he was moaning about the piss-poor wages, and I thought, 'Hello, you're trying to hook me first. So I said, 'Why don't you get yourself a bit of extras? What I'm saying is between you and me, and if you go to the Governor I'll deny every word.'

He said, 'Go on, I'm listening.'

'What I'll do is get you £100 a week. You get me a load of tobacco and cream off thirty for yourself'.

He agreed, so I set up a meet between him and Val in the same burger bar where she passed over the mobile phone to the doctor.

She met him on the Friday and on the Saturday he slipped me a package with the smokes. I said, 'Lovely, ta very much,' then when I opened up there was only about 30 quid's worth of tobacco in all. When he come back down the landing, I shot out and collared him. 'Oy, you greedy cunt, where's the rest of my tobacco?'

He said, 'I can't risk my job for anything less. If you can find anybody else to do it for you, the best of luck. Otherwise, that's my cut.'

Robbing bastard! I didn't have any choice, so I wiped my mouth and Val carried on dipping out 100 notes every Friday until my trial.

The authorities think that Wandsworth is their flagship, the best and toughest nick all round. What are they going to think about their screws being as bent as arseholes? I won't name that screw because he's still working there. I wouldn't like to get him into trouble!

A lot of the younger kids used to be in and out of my cell all the time. This was because they liked being around 'Big Lenny'; it made them feel that some of my reputation would rub off. I took a shine to one particular kid because he was a live wire and always laughing or up to something.

This Shibberton and a black pal of his were in my cell and they were sitting on my bed having a smoke. I never touched drugs, not even grass, which I don't think does a lot of harm anyway. In fact, from what I've seen it keeps those that smoke it nice and calm and placid. I thought these kids were on Old Holborn but it turned out they were puffing at the waccy baccy. All of a sudden, security walked in and they slung their half-smoked fags under my bed and disappeared double quick. Security was straight on those dog-ends, gave me a look, then they were out the door. Back came Shibberton, looking a bit wary.

'Did they find our smokes, Len?'

I said, 'Too right they did, and right under my bed. Now they're off to the PO and down to you I'm going to lose some time, and I've not even been sentenced yet.'

He said, 'Sorry. I'm really sorry. I wasn't thinking, but I'll tell them it was mine.'

I said, 'You say nothing and I'll say nothing, but afterwards I'm going to belt your ear'oles. What a stupid thing to do.'

Right enough, two hours later I was pulled into the PO's office. He had these fags on his desk and he was flicking them with a pen.

'Guv'nor,' I said, 'before you say anything, let me mark your card. I'm a fighter and I look after my body. I don't need that sort of shit inside me, and if I did I wouldn't be smoking it two at a time. But don't ask me whose they are, because I'm not a grass, even if you charge me.'

While I told him this, his po-face became a grin, then he said, 'Quite a speech, McLean. I'm already aware that this material is not yours, so there won't be a charge. And as we can't be sure who actually was smoking this drug, I'm prepared to let it go this time. But pass on the message that I will crack down in future.' Fucking hell, that was a result. I saw the funny side of it afterwards, so Shibberton didn't get a belt, but he came very close.

Life wasn't all bad news, though, and after I did a little favour for a screw I got a favour myself that's never been equalled by anyone in Wandsworth. This screw had been in the game for about 20 years, and all the cons reckoned he was a very fair man. So when he started speaking to me, I didn't mug him off like I might have.

'You're a fighter, aren't you, McLean?'

'Yes,' I said. 'If I have to, I'll fight every screw in this place.'

He said, 'No, what I want to say is I'm going to Crystal Palace tonight to see a boxing exhibition. If you like I'll bring you back a programme. You might find it interesting to see who is on the bill.'

I said, 'You've been fair, so I'm told, so what I'll do is give you a phone number. Ring it now and you'll get through to Alex Steen. It's his show you're going to tonight, so tell him who you are, mention Lenny McLean, and he'll treat you right.'

Next morning this screw's bubbling over. Alex had got him seats ringside, laid on drinks for him and his wife, and given them a lovely meal afterwards. He was over the moon. I told you he was fair, so he wanted to return the compliment. I didn't know anything about this, but he'd got his head together with Alex and they'd cooked something up.

I was downstairs in the kitchens one afternoon when a screw came down and said, 'Back to your cell, McLean,' and before I could tell him to fuck off he winked at me. Up I went, opened the door, and there was Alex Steen and Bruce Wells — ex-boxer, twice Golden Gloves Champion — sitting on my bed laughing their heads off. I was knocked out, absolutely gob-smacked.

I gave them both a kiss and a hug and just sat there looking at them. Alex got out a bottle of wine and Bruce slipped six ounces of Holborn and 40 Bensons behind my cupboard. What a pair. Every now and then a different screw would stick his head round the door, look in, and go off shaking his head without saying a word. My screw's got them all under his wing, so they don't go running to the PO.

For an hour they sat in my cell and it was great. We talked and talked and it was just like old times. At five o'clock this screw came up, made sure the coast was clear, then slipped them both out the side door, and none of the bosses had a fucking clue.

Alex, being the man he is, offered to bring in some boxers to entertain the cons. He went through the channels and the Governor jumped at the idea. So that's what he did, and it was a brilliant exhibition. Afterwards, the boxers answered questions and signed autographs and it went down a bomb. Alex got a nice letter from the Governor thanking him and his team for their efforts, and even today you can see it hanging on the wall among the photographs of friends of his, such as Muhammad Ali, Henry Cooper, Bruno, Diana Dors, and hundreds of others. I see it every time I pop into Alex's office and it takes me right back to that day in my cell.

On one of Val's visits, I said to her, 'You heard anything from Ray Perry lately?'

She said, 'I told you, Len, I haven't had a penny from him since the day you were nicked. He called round the day after and when I said that you'd been arrested he put the money he had in his hand back in his pocket.'

'Lovely, fucking lovely.'

This bloke came to see me in desperate trouble looking for ten grand. I used to do a bit of money lending if I was sure of the person, and, as I knew him — no problem. He cleared up his trouble and he was giving me good dough every week, on the nail. Then he got nicked on a fraud and got 18 months. OK, Lenny's not one of those fellas who breaks legs when a payment's a week late. In fact, Val says I'm too fucking soft, but I think fair is a better way of looking at it.

I bent over backwards to help him. When he said he was worried about paying me back, I told him to forget it until he was out. On top of that, I gave his missus mortgage money and put my hand in my pocket to square up her bills. If I was in the same boat, I'd like to think my pals were looking out for me. That was before my own nicking, when I was to find out that my pals would stand by me. Apart from money, I helped get him an early move to Ford Open Prison. Usually, there's a three-month waiting list, but as I had some people straightened at the nick he was in, they managed to cut that time in half. So all he had to worry about was doing his time.

He came home and I gave him a few quid to get him on his feet and in no time he was back in business and starting to square me up again. He got his debt to me down to about five grand, then I was lifted on the murder. Everybody knew about it because it was all over the papers. Did he phone up or call round to offer a bit of help? No, he fucking didn't. That slag took it on his toes praying for me to get lifed off and, as Val said, never paid another penny. If you read this, Mr Perry, call round and see Lenny.

So I had already got the hump when I was told to report to the PO's office. I wasn't brooding over the money. I'd give it to the bloke if he was in the shit, but I was gutted that he felt obliged to stitch me up after what I'd done for him.

The PO was smiling like he had my release papers on his desk. Some hope. 'Good news, McLean, they've set your trial date. Two weeks from today. Get your things together for a move to Brixton in the morning.'

Twelve months I've rotted inside, and now the time has come to face the possibility of another 24 years. My stomach turned over and I walked out without saying a word.

As I went back to my cell to get my head together, I bumped into a con and he was reading the paper and laughing. 'Seen this, Len? So much for big gangsters. That Ronnie Knight's just had the bollocks beaten out of him in Fuengerola.'

I nearly belted this mug there and then. 'So you think it's funny that a bloke in his fifties gets a belting, do you, you c**t?'

'Well,' he said, 'these blokes think they're so tough.'

Right at that moment the PO was doing his rounds so I walked off, but I hadn't finished with him. Instead of going into my own cell, I slipped into his before he got back. I hid behind the door and as he walked in I belted him straight in the chin and caught him before he hit the deck. He was spark out, so I laid him on the bed and pulled the covers over him. His cellmate came in and I said, 'Open your mouth and you're next. Your muggy mate's taken the piss out of a pal of mine, and he's lucky he only got the one belt.'

The next morning I saw the con slopping out and his face was like a balloon. He walked past but he kept his eyes on the floor — he wouldn't look at me, and his mate was laughing. As he got closer, he said to me, 'Len, he didn't wake up until four this morning.' To give him his due, he never screamed, but I think he was well pleased to see me shipped off to Brixton later on.

It seems a lifetime since I first came through the gates of Brixton, and in many ways it was. In the last 12 months I've thought and thought more than I have ever done in my whole life. Can you imagine being on a murder charge, and I mean charge, not sentence, and you know you haven't committed the crime? You live and breathe it every second of the day. As you wake up in the morning, for one tiny second it's not there, but count to two and your head's filled. Murder-life-murder-life, and that goes on and on until you fall asleep, and even then it doesn't stop. It's terrible.

It's not the prison, it's the fucking charge. Three hours' sleep every night because your brain won't switch off and when it does, the dreams come. And then it's like being smothered or drowned. Everything presses down on you until you wake up. You can't breathe and one second later, murder-life-murder-life.

Can you, in your wildest dreams, imagine what Reg Kray has been through? He went through a year just like me, but then he had the nightmare of facing 30 years behind the door. Thirty years — try and imagine it. It's the difference between a newborn baby and a settled married man. The difference between a Jack-the-lad at 35 and an old-age pensioner. You can't grasp it, can you? Nor can I.

Now think about Reg again. Could you be so strong? The media treat him like some exhibit in a cage. Whenever they're stuck for copy they stick another bit of shit in the papers. Do they say, 'Look at this man ... 30 years in prison and he's strong, fit and his mind's as sharp as it ever was.' Of course they don't, because those in power want him crucified. Why do I feel so strongly? Because I've known a tiny bit of what he's gone through, so I understand.

I'm using him as an example, and he's the best example. But now I understand people like Charlie Richardson, Tony Lambrianou, Joe Pyle, Charlie Kray, and many, many others, who've suffered and stayed strong.

And all this is going through my head hour after hour as they tick towards my trial. Then one morning I wake up, I've got one second's clear head, then bang, this is the day. I'm suited up, loaded into the wagon, and we're off to the Bailey. Court 12.

As I walked in the court, all I wanted to do was to turn round, not face that fucking judge. I wanted to look round and see my Val's lovely face and that's what I did. I told you I fell out with Bobby Warren over that fight years ago, well the day I got lifted he was round my house offering my Val everything he could give. That hump with each other was stupid, because as soon as I was in trouble, it was all forgotten, so we could have made up years ago. Now he was sitting in court with Val and he said, 'Lenny, turn round, show a bit of respect.' Respect nothing. I don't feel it, so I'm not going to pretend. Why should I? I'm innocent, I shouldn't even be here.

It was summer all over again. I only saw the other seasons through the bars and it was hot in the court. I was sweating and wiping my head with Kleenex tissues and, as they got soggy, I rolled them up in balls and flicked them at Prunty and DI Cater. They were fuming but what were they going to do? Stick an assault by tissue balls on top of the murder? Bobby was getting a bit wound up, for my sake, so he said, 'Pack it up, mate, you're not doing yourself any favours.' So, out of respect for Bob, I packed it in.

I was looking round the court and it was packed. I had a lot of supporters but the rest were punters off the streets looking for a bit of entertainment. I bet that if they lived in Roman times the same people would be right up the front sticking their thumbs down for the gladiators to get the chop. They should try standing where I am; they wouldn't find it so fascinating then. Gary Humphries' family were sitting over to my left and I didn't want to look at them. I wasn't ashamed, because I know I didn't kill their son or husband, but they had suffered and I didn't want them to think I was an arrogant bastard with no feelings who might be trying to stare them out. I just hoped they would hear some truth in the days to come.

If I could remember what was going on or all that was said, I think it would put you to sleep. It was making me nod off and my freedom depended on it. That first day, all the briefs and barristers were just warming up for the off so it didn't seem like much was happening.

It's funny really — I slept better that night than I had done for months and months. It was a bit like going to the dentist — once you're there it's not half as bad as you had imagined.

The next morning I was in reception at Brixton and in walked this very smart man — more than smart, he was immaculate and very relaxed. He said, 'I've heard all about you ... you're Lenny McLean, the street-fighter. I've been banged up with a friend of yours in the Scrubs, Ritchie the Scotsman.'

'Oh yeah, he was in here for a while with me, then they shipped him out. I can't place you though ... who are you?' He introduced himself as John Perry, pulled in on the Brink's Mat robbery, and he was due at the Bailey later on.

We carried on talking on the way to the court, and I asked him how long he'd been on remand. When he told me three-and-a-half years I couldn't believe it. I thought one year was a bit outrageous. Then he laughed at the look on my face. 'I know the system's a bit slow, but not that fucking slow. What happened was, I got arrested in Spain and I've had to sit there all that time while they were arguing about extradition.'

John was one of the coolest guys I had ever met. Nothing upset him, he never got flustered, and always seemed to be on the one level. I think getting pally with him while the trial was going on kept me quiet as well, because I didn't have any flare-ups.

As we travelled into the Bailey every morning in the wagon, John would look round and tell me where the photographers were. Because they're so desperate for a picture for the papers, they jump up and stick the camera right against the windows and snap away. So he'd go, 'On your right, Len, duck. On your left, look out.' It was a bit of a laugh, though it didn't work because I've got some copies of ones they took and used in the papers, and what with the flash in the van and my surprise, I look a right prat in most of them.

So one day was very much like the next and I was backwards and forwards. Nothing was missed at the Bailey, nothing. Every tiny detail came out. Nothing can be hidden because these barristers are shit-hot and what they don't get one way they sneak round and return to from a different angle, and if you've been spraucing, they're on you like a dog on a bone.

Half of what they discussed I didn't understand. In fact, most of the time they were being so technical and clever with words, that only the top few knew what the hell was going on. Even Cater looked like he was falling asleep half the time. I did gather, though, that I was being mugged and my chances were going downhill bloody fast. I understood quickly enough when I heard Judge Lowry saying, 'What I would like to do is take the prosecution, defence and jurors down to the Hippodrome Night Club.'

I thought, 'Fucking hell, they're going to have a knees-up before getting down to lifing me off.' But no, what he wanted was to let them all listen to a mock-up of the scuffle Humphries and I had in the cupboard.

I slipped a note to Val telling her to ring Mick Parker, who was regional director of the club, and mark his card about what's happening. She did that and he said, 'Don't worry, Val, when that lot turn up we'll have the music twice as loud as normal. I know Lenny's innocent, but we won't take any chances.'

Judge Lowry took them all to the club for his little experiment, stuck three jurors in the cupboard, and told them to 'make as much noise as possible'. After ten minutes they opened the doors. These jurors were sweating cobs and their ties and shirt tails were all over the place. Back in the court, all those out in the reception area said they couldn't hear a sound, so that bollocked all those muggy witnesses who said they heard a terrible ruck that Saturday night. I've got to give Mick ten out of ten because he did what he said he would and blasted the music out. But if you allow for the fact that there were a few thousand customers missing that morning, I suppose it all balanced out, so we weren't really pulling a stroke.

One up to me, but the way things were going, the prosecution had about a hundred up on me. Every time Cater looked at me I wanted to smash his head off. The minute that judge gives me a rec. of 25, I'd be over the rail and flatten him.

Then the prosecution brought in their star witness. They'd already had half of London giving me some stick, but this one was an expert. I won't pretend I took it all in, but what she was saying was that I had killed Gary Humphries by breaking his jaw. I think I'm more of an expert on jaws than she is, because I've broken more than she's had hot dinners, and nobody has ever died.

According to Dr Paula Lannas, she's seen six deaths caused by busted jaws. She rabbited on for an hour with all the medical jargon, but at the end of the day it still amounted to her evidence putting me away, and I felt it was nearly all over.

I had a word with Martin and Kenny the barrister. 'She's getting me put away, you know that, don't you? Can't you fucking well give her a tug, because I think she's got it all wrong. And another thing, when she came out of the box she whispered to Cater, "How did I do?"'

Kenny said, 'Calm down, Lenny. Did you notice the old man sitting at the back, glasses, greying hair?'

I said, 'Yeah I saw him. I thought he was a punter come in out of the sun for a sit down.'

'No, Len, no punter. That's Professor Gresham, world's number one pathologist. He worked on the Australian dingo case, and many other high-profile cases. In fact, for a time, he taught Dr Lannas.'

I said, 'Well, get him in the box and ask him what he thinks.'

It was the end of the day, and I was feeling gutted.

Now I was becoming tired. This had been dragging on for eight days and the strain was doing my head in. I couldn't sleep. I was still awake in the middle of the night and singing quietly to myself to stop my head exploding.

I looked like death in the morning and while John and I were downstairs in the court, I was falling asleep. John said, 'Heard you singing last night. I enjoyed it. Do me a favour, give us a couple of verses now to cheer us both up.'

I said, 'Nah,' then I thought, 'Oh, bollocks, why not?' So I got up and broke into 'Carolina Moon' with all the actions. John tapped his feet and clapped his hands, and when I finished I couldn't believe what I'd been doing. I was in the Old Bailey, hours away from a possible life sentence, and I was singing like I was at a party. Why not? At least you won't find me crying about what goes down.

'Call Professor Gresham.'

Lovely — go on, my son, you tell them. He was well spoken and dead calm, but very quietly he ripped into every bit of Lannas' evidence.

This man had had 35 years' experience in anatomy, and you could tell he was an expert every time he opened his mouth. In the same way as the legal arguments, the medical evidence was just as complicated and technical, so I won't even try to explain it. The bits I could understand were that while Gresham didn't deny Humphries had a broken jaw, in his very learned opinion that was not the cause of death. In fact, in 35 years he'd never come across a single death he could put down to just a broken jaw. On top of that, he stuck one on the police, which had Cater looking down in the mouth.

'Again, in my opinion,' he said, 'one cannot seriously discount the possibility that, due to forceful restraint, Gary Humphries died when his neck arteries were compressed in a strangle-hold by police officers.'

I wanted to run over and kiss him, but it wasn't over yet. The judge's summation can be the difference between a win or a loss when he's talking to the jury.

That night, I never even tried to close my eyes, and I'm not ashamed to say that in the middle of the night I got on my knees and prayed. I prayed for my own sake, but more than that, I prayed for Val and the kids. They'd suffered as much as I had, but in a different way, yet they never blamed me once for bringing all that aggravation to our home.

John and I had a cuddle downstairs, then we shook hands and I climbed the stairs surrounded by cozzers. They weren't taking any chances on a bad result.

I mouthed a kiss towards Val as I stepped into the dock and she blew one back.

You could have heard a pin drop. I looked around the courtroom, then I studied the faces of the jurors one by one.

You — what do you know about my life? You look like you should be behind the counter of a bank. And the old girl with the glasses on, are you working out what to get your old man for his tea? The boy with the pimples, the girl who doesn't look older than my Kelly; who are you all? What are you thinking? Not one of them would let me catch their eye.

Reading through a bit of law bumph in my cell, I'd noticed that 'the defendant shall be judged by 12 of his peers'. Ray said that means equals, but don't make me fucking laugh. Look at them. Look at me. These little people, these straights whose only brush with the law was when they parked on a double yellow — they don't know anything about real life and they're getting ready to take mine away. They're going to bury me under concrete until I'm 69 years old

I looked away from them and glanced over to my Val but I couldn't stand the pain in her eyes, so I looked upwards to a little patch of blue-grey sky I could see through the rooflight.

I must have gone off somewhere in my head, because one minute

I was thinking if that was how I would be seeing the sky for years to come, through glass, when all of a sudden I heard Judge Lowry say, 'What is your verdict?'

I just had time to say to myself, 'Please, God, help me for my family's sake,' and the foreman said, 'NOT GUILTY'.

I seemed to stand paralysed for ages staring ahead — then it sank in — 'NOT GUILTY'.

Those twelve ordinary people have suddenly gone from mugs to saints. They were on my side. They'd seen the truth and I loved every one of them.

I gripped the rail as a relief swept over me that I couldn't describe again if I tried. Then I couldn't help myself. I looked straight at Judge Lowry and burst into song.

'Always look on the bright side of life ... Da Da ... Da Da...'

He looked stern, then he smiled and said, 'Take that man down.'

As I walked down the stairs out of sight of the courtroom, I said to the two screws escorting me, 'Come on, boys, let's go down in style.' I pulled each of their caps round so the peaks were over their ears, linked arms with them, and as we reached the bottom of the stairs I started singing again. John was down one end of the passage and he was cheering and clapping; the three of us danced towards him, and I sang 'Always look on the bright side of life', then all the screws were clapping and patting me on the back. I thought of my Val, Jamie and Kelly and shouted as loud as I could, 'I'M GOING HOME!' — then I punched the air.

YES! THE GUV'NOR'S GOING HOME!

EPILOGUE

After my 'not guilty', I was sent to Wandsworth to finish what remained of an 18-month sentence for grievous bodily harm. I could take prison once that terrible charge was lifted and after that I could relax, do my time and plan my future.

My pal John Perry, who helped me face the ordeal of the Bailey, got a sentence of six years a few days after me, but what with his three-and-a-half years on remand taken into consideration, he didn't have to face too much time.

After a bit of a holiday to let my nerves settle down, I was ready to go back to work. All the time I'd been away that lovely man Mick Parker, director of the Hippodrome, had made sure my wages were there for Val every week without fail. He got a buzz from up top saying, 'Knock Lenny's money on the head,' but good stuff that he is he wouldn't have any of it. He stuck by me when I came out as well.

I got loads of bad write-ups in the papers saying I was a lunatic, a crank and a nutcase, so the owners didn't want me back in the club. Mick couldn't get round that one, but he didn't kick me out; instead, he got me fixed up in one of his other clubs round the corner. I can't speak highly enough of him. He's not only straightforward, he's one of the few people in that game who are honest with themselves and others. He doesn't lift a tanner for himself — everything the club takes, he declares. What a diamond.

A few months after I was sitting in the nick, I found myself parked up in a comfy armchair in the House of Lords. Isn't life strange?

Alex Steen had said he wanted me to meet someone. The next thing I knew, we were being escorted through the posh halls and corridors of one of the most famous buildings in London. It was a beautiful place — oil paintings on the walls of top people from the past. Eventually we were shown into a sort of reading room and asked to sit down while we were announced to our host. I still didn't know who I was going to see, and any minute I expected Margaret Thatcher to come through the door. After a bit, Alex gave me a nudge, pointed towards the door, and through it came Lord Longford.

Now this man was not one of my favourite people, but I was polite and we shook hands. He ordered tea and cucumber sandwiches and we sat there chatting about my case and other things. After a bit, lord or no lord, I had to say what I was thinking.

'Tell me,' I said, 'why is it you spend all your time trying to get nonces and perverts out of the nick — you know, people like the Moors murderers — instead of making an effort to get people out who've been fitted up. And there's more than one of them in the system.'

A typical politician, he wouldn't give me a straight answer. He just rabbited on about Ian Brady not wanting to come out and Myra Hindley being a changed person who's completely rehabilitated. I'm not an idiot when it comes to social graces, so I know you don't start telling a lord that he's talking cobblers, no matter how strange his ideas are, so I let it go. But I'll never understand the way he thinks. I've got to say the day was an experience, though.

Jack Iandoli never showed his face again after I bollocked him, so as far as I was concerned, all that book stuff was down the pan. For a bit, I thought the same about the film, because after all these years even I was getting a bit disheartened. Then I got a message from Stallone through my pal, the stuntman Dave Lea, saying, 'Tell Lenny that the script for *Rocky* was kicked about for ten years before it was taken up.' So I thought, right, let's get it sorted.

One of my pals, who'd put money up for the script, and I went down to Pinewood studios, dug out Sheena Perkins, and parked her up. She was still saying, 'Don't give up, I'm getting it together,' but I told her to forget it and just give us our script back. We went into the canteen for a coffee before setting off home and while we were sitting there, two fellas came over.

'Lenny McLean? Nice to meet you. Just want to say we've heard all about you and want to shake your hand.'

I asked them to sit down and we chatted for a bit. It turned out these guys were directors. Now I'm not slow when I see an opening, so I pushed over the script we had just nicked back from Sheena Perkins. They scanned through it, sat back and said, 'This is brilliant, we'd love to get this off the ground.'

Who would argue with that? Remember, this script has been here, there, and even been taken to America, and we were still no further forward. Within a couple of months of striking a deal, these two geezers told me they'd got the wheels turning and, as far as I was concerned, everything was under way. Was I wrong, or what?

I should have sussed something was going on when these two bastards were into my ribs every five minutes for a bit of cash.

What had happened to my third eye that can spot trouble before it happened? Was my judgement put on hold because I was too keen to get the film off the ground? Don't forget, I had to look out for a lot of pals who'd put up hard earned dough because they trusted me and had faith in my movie. I'm telling you this in hindsight and, looking back, all the signs of a scam should have been obvious. But being a bit naïve in those days, I thought that if people were working out of Pinewood studios, they had to be the business. Now I know that if you've got two bob for a bit of rent — bosh, you're in the film game.

So time went on. Whenever I got in touch with them, I'd hear, 'Everything is on line, Lenny. We should be in production next month. Oh yes, before you go, could you find £10,000 so we can start ordering props.' I put up with that bollocks for two years and all that was happening was that my hair was getting thinner and those two bastards were getting fatter.

With no film and out of pocket by £200,000, I made up my mind to pull the plug. By then, I was well aware that the first guy was nothing but an errand boy with a plausible front and a good line in old fanny. The other bloke on the other hand, for all his fancy talk and royal connections, in my mind was a professional con man and a dirty slag. If they weren't straightgoers I'd have hurt them both badly. But as I have said before, what's the point of doing time over no-value dogs? I rang one of them and told him I wanted every penny back. What did he do? He threatened to call the police if I showed my face near the big house he lived in — the house that my pals and I had paid for.

It's funny how life is. I hadn't seen any of the Hayes family since we moved away from Godwin House nearly 40 years ago. Then a few weeks ago, I was walking down Roman Road and there was Alfie and Timmy. I couldn't believe it — they hadn't changed a bit. I took them home for a cup of tea and we talked about the old days for hours. We were little kids in those days so there were lots of things we never knew. One of the things they'd found out since was that their grandad used to train and organise fights with my uncle Jimmy Spinks. Small world.

A few weeks after that meet, Billy Hayes turned up on my doorstep, that smashing fella who had taken me under his wing when I was a little kid. I haven't been able to remember every detail of my past, and he reminded me about how he introduced me to boxing down Repton Boys' Club. He also reminded me that while I could handle myself in the ring, even at eight years old, I was a bit too strong-willed to take the discipline. He added that he'd married Pat, that beautiful girlfriend of his we had such lovely days out with all those years ago.

Talking to Alfie, Timmy and Billy made me think about what might have happened if we hadn't moved away from Bethnal Green and the Hayes family. If we'd stayed, I know I would have gone to work with them down the market. I'm not stupid and I'm a good grafter, so I think I would have followed the same path as those other boys, instead of the one I did.

And what a stony path it's been. I was battered senseless over and over again as a child. I've had between 2,000 and 3,000 fights, some in the ring, many on the cobbles, and many more in the pubs and clubs I've minded over 20 years. I never lost one of them. I've been shot, stabbed, and I've suffered the psychological damage of being charged with murder. And I think it was that threat of being lifed that changed my life and made me think twice about where I was going.

It's funny how things happen. I was thinking about a different move when I bumped into Mike Reid when we were both visiting Reggie Kray in Maidstone prison. On the way out, Mike said to me, 'Lenny, you're a bit of a character, why don't you get yourself into the acting game, it's money for old rope. I only act myself and I'm doing alright.'

It made me laugh at the time, but after I'd thought about it, it wasn't such a stupid idea. I've been performing all my life one way or another, so look at it this way — belt somebody outside and they give you two years; do it on screen, and they give you two grand. So I went for it.

I got myself an Equity card easily enough, because over the past few years I'd appeared in quite a number of adverts, though I got a knock back on one I did for BT when the wife of Gary Humphries complained about a murderer making money from phonecalls. For Christ's sake! I was innocent. BT still cut me off, though. I did wonder if she'd try the same stunt again if I put myself forward for a part, then I thought, 'Oh bollocks, if Leslie Grantham can make a good living after a "guilty" for murder, I'm sure I can after a "not guilty".'

I got webbed up with a decent agency and in two minutes they stuck me up for a part in the television series *The Knock*. Was it a schoolteacher or a priest? No — it was to play a villain called Eddie Davies. I got the part only because the producer, Paul Knight, argued against a lot of others who thought I was a bit too real.

'This man's a bare-knuckle fighter and a bit of a lunatic — we want a real actor.'

But that diamond Paul stuck out his neck and gave me a chance. I've got to give him bundles of respect for that. He allowed me to move out of a dirty and dangerous world into a world where I could make a decent living amongst decent people. I know I justified his faith in me, because I was invited to do a second series, even though that meant rewriting scripts. Eddie Davies was put away for years in the first series, but, in order for them to put me back in, the writers turned his sentence into a suspended.

After that, I never looked back. Talk about turnaround. My next big part was playing a police Chief Inspector in the Bruce Willis film, *Fifth Element*. My latest film has been playing Barry the Baptist — yeah, it always gets a laugh. No, this bloke doesn't follow Jesus, he drowns people — a real nasty bastard. *Lock, Stock and Two Smoking Barrels* — blinding film — look out for the hardest man in Britain acting alongside the hardest man in football, Vinnie Jones.

I'm on my way up. St Johns Wood today, who knows, Hollywood tomorrow.

*   *   *

There were loads of times when I was working on this book that I thought one day, perhaps when I'm in my seventies, I would have to put together a sequel. I'd told of my life up until now, but once that was out of the way it didn't mean I was ready for the pipe and slippers by the fire. No, my intention was to carry on living life to the full like I've always done. And my way, being a bit out of the ordinary though not intentionally, would have made interesting reading for those people that look up to the Guv'nor.

Well it's a thought that I'll never have to think about because the day the doctor told me I had lung and brain cancer was the day the final full stop was put on my life.

I've lived a dangerous life and could have died a hundred times over. But even when I faced guns and knives, or the blood was pouring out of me, I never considered the possibility that my days might be numbered. Though I've got to admit that over the last few years, what with the deaths of pals like Ronnie Kray, Ritchie Anderson, Alex Steen and others, it was brought home to me that nobody goes on forever. OK, most of them were twenty years older than me, but when you're my age and you go to funeral after funeral it makes you realise our time in this world is limited. It didn't worry me too much, just firmed up my conviction that you have to live every day to the full — do what you have to do and never have regrets because, believe me, you never know just what's around the corner.

What has been devastating has been the speed of this illness that's overtaken me. One minute I'm looking years ahead, planning a comfortable retirement with my Val and a steady stream of decent roles in the film game — then bosh, it's all over. And really it all just crept up on me without even giving me a clue that anything was happening.

I told you about the film *Lock Stock & Two Smoking Barrels*. Well, when I was on location some of the scenes were shot in a big warehouse and, to get on set, you had to climb about four flights of stairs. I'd go up one flight then have to stop to catch my breath. Three flights and I was absolutely shagged out. By the time I got to the top I felt like I'd climbed a mountain. I can remember thinking, bastard flu — once you get it, it hangs on forever. Only way to deal with it was cut back on the fags and step up the training.

I've always kept fit but if I was puffing and gasping just going upstairs, then it meant I had to stretch myself even further. So I'd get up about six o'clock, be over Danson Park by half-past and go straight into a five mile boxer's run. Usually three was enough to get the heart pounding, but I thought no, an extra two would sweat that flu right out of my system. But that wasn't all, something else was happening to me that was throwing me right off balance. I'd be sitting talking to people and I'd be there, but at the same time I wasn't, and bells would be going off in my head. I don't think it was too obvious, but for a man who's always been one step ahead in the thinking game, it was getting me down. In the end I worked out this bug has knocked me right down and on top of that I stressed myself out trying to get some business deals moving. Trouble is everybody's so long winded — next week; next month; next year — I want to bang their heads together and shout 'For fuck's sake, do it now,' but it wouldn't have made a blind bit of difference. Perhaps their way is right, I dunno, but it's frustrating for a man like me who likes to make himself busy.

In the end I came to the conclusion that a nice break away from all the pressures would set me up so I could come back raring to go. I said to my Val, 'Go on, babe, book us in somewhere warm and we'll forget all about it for two weeks.' So off we went to Spain and instead of being just the break we needed it turned out a disaster and we both wished we'd stayed at home. One little incident brought home to me more than anything else just how out of shape I was. I was having a bit of trouble getting our suitcases from the taxi into the hotel when some old fella said 'Don't struggle with that mate, let me do it,' and he did. Big Lenny, who at one time was bench pressing 500lb or ripping the door off a car, couldn't lift a poxy suitcase.

Back home I said to Val, 'Sweetheart, I'm tired. There's bells going off in my head and I'm bollocking you and my pals over nothing and that's not like me, so let's get down to that doctors and sort this out.'

The doctor checked me over and told me I had a persistent chest infection, but that he'd make me an appointment for the hospital. No problem, be sorted in no time.

I won't go into all the details but I got myself down to the hospital and was told that they wanted to do a load of X-rays and tests. I said, 'Lively then, I've got things to do.' And away they went. A few hours after they tell me I've got a shadow on my lung. No wonder I couldn't breathe. Seemed like I'd got a touch of pleurisy, which if you aren't too careful can be a killer, so it gave me a bit of a knock back.

Still, no fags for a bit and a suitcase full of antibiotics and I'd be on the mend. Thank you very much. Where's the door? 'No,' they said, 'you'll have to stay in for a couple of days while we do a few more tests, then you can go home'. OK. I'm surrounded by pretty nurses, I'll suffer that for a bit.

Some days get imprinted on your mind more than others. Meeting my Val that night in the Standard. The births of my Jamie and Kelly. Beating Roy Shaw. A 'Not Guilty' at the Bailey — fresh in my mind as though they were yesterday. So the Monday after my tests was set to be one of them. I'd had one of those scan things and I was sitting in my room flicking through the *Sun*, when in came the doctor looking after my case. I shook her hand and she sat down beside me. 'Mr McLean — Lenny, there's no easy way to put this. We have found cancer in your lungs and secondaries in your brain.'

Two thoughts came one on top of the other. I want Val beside me now and how will she and the kids accept something like this. I never really thought about myself — never considered that having just written the final chapter on my life so far, now I was living it as well.

If they couldn't have given me any worse news, it came a bit later. Six to twelve months was all the time I had left. This is the one thing everybody dreads and never wants to hear. Yet strangely enough it made me calmer, understanding that there has been a reason for why I felt so bad.

I can't and won't describe the tears and fears of our private grief, but I can say how I feel. Of course I don't want to die, but I've accepted that that's the hand I've been dealt and I'll deal with it in the same way as I've faced every challenge in my life — head on. At the moment I feel physically on top of the world, and the only pain I've got is when I look at my Val. She's carrying everything and it tears my heart out. I've always been strong for her and my family — now she's being strong for all of us.

I'm not afraid of dying. I don't remember coming into this world and I'll go out of it in the same way. I won't give up and I'll fight this thing inside me right up to the end. But unlike all the other fights in my life, this is the one and only that I know I can't win — I'll give it my best though.

Lenny McLean died on Tuesday 28 July 1998